THE LIFE OF
CHARLES JAMES FOX

CHARLES JAMES FOX, *circa* 1783–4

From an engraving by JOHN JONES *after the portrait by* SIR JOSHUA
REYNOLDS

THE LIFE OF
CHARLES JAMES FOX

BY

EDWARD LASCELLES

*' I love idleness so much and so dearly,
that I have hardly the heart to say a word
against it; but something is due to one's
station in life, something to friendship,
something to the country.'*

C. J. FOX.

1970
OCTAGON BOOKS
New York

First published in 1936

Reprinted 1970
by special arrangement with Oxford University Press

OCTAGON BOOKS
A DIVISION OF FARRAR, STRAUS & GIROUX, INC.
19 Union Square West
New York, N. Y. 10003

This work is a reprint. The author might have wished
to revise it but this was not possible since he died in 1956.

LIBRARY OF CONGRESS CATALOG CARD NUMBER: 78-96183

Printed in U.S.A. by
TAYLOR PUBLISHING COMPANY
DALLAS, TEXAS

TO
LEILA

PREFACE

An attempt at a biography of Fox needs explanation, if not apology; for the subject is not a new one, and eminent historians have chosen it for their most distinguished works.

It is true that much has been written about Fox, but it is also true that until recently biographers have been attracted by the first rather than the second half of his life. This is perhaps due to the fact that the first half contains the early days of adventure and folly leading to the glorious years of opposition during the American War when he led his party to triumph and 'divided the Kingdom with Caesar', while the Fox of the later period is a much less spectacular figure. That period includes the twenty years of opposition and defeat, the long agony of Revolution and War leading to Fox's secession from Parliament, when hope was lost and further efforts seemed useless.

But to-day those twenty years of opposition have a new interest. The life of a statesman hopelessly calling for peace when the country was at war, and the career of a reformer at a time when revolution abroad had spread fear and suspicion at home, have to-day an interest which is something more than academic. As reluctant students of the effects of European war and the repercussions of European revolution, we may now find reality in historical events which may have seemed a generation ago almost as remote as the burning of heretics.

And there is another and more attractive reason for an interest in Fox's later years. In our own time letters and diaries have been published which have the double value of throwing light on some of the obscurities of the later eighteenth century, and of providing some of the most pleasant reading to be found in all that century of letter-writers and wits. The publication, for instance, of John Robinson's notes and estimates on the constituencies has made the defeat of the Coalition—why the King acted when he did, why Pitt took office, why he postponed the dissolution—more intelligible; the diary of Colonel Fulke Greville has revealed Fox's justification for challenging the doctor's bulletins during the King's illness; the researches of Mr. Meikle, Professor Trevelyan, and Mr. Veitch have shown whether Fox or Pitt was right in his estimate of the revolutionary movement in this country; and Lady Bessborough's letters tell us what really happened in the negotiations for a united government in 1803 and 1804. And publications of the last thirty years have contributed something more than evidence on matters which were obscure. The story of Fox's early life is illuminated by the current gossip of writers of such quality as Horace Walpole, Storer, and Selwyn. The letters of Lady Bessborough and Creevey supply an extension of that commentary on the same level of excellence for Fox's later days, when Walpole and his contemporaries were no more.

I wish to record my sincere thanks to Professor G. M. Trevelyan, O.M., for allowing me to read the original Fox letters in his possession and to quote from letters in *Lord Grey of the Reform Bill*; to the Hon. Cyril Asquith, Messrs. Coutts & Co., Mr. J. L. Hammond, and the Earl of Ilchester for information and advice; to Castalia, Countess Granville, and Sir John Murray for permission to quote from the *Private Correspondence of Lord Granville Leveson Gower*; to the Earl of Ilchester and Sir John Murray for permission to quote from *Henry Fox, First Lord Holland*; to the Countess of Ilchester, Lord Stavordale, and Sir John Murray for permission to quote from the *Life and Letters of Lady Sarah Lennox*; to Sir John Murray for permission to quote from the *Creevey Papers*; to the Earl of Minto and Messrs. Longmans, Green & Co. for permission to quote from the *Life and Letters of Sir Gilbert Elliot*; and to Mrs. Henry Lascelles for six of the illustrations.

CONTENTS

LIST OF ILLUSTRATIONS

*The device on the cover is taken from the
label which Fox stuck to the backs of some
of his books.*

CHAPTER I

1749–1757

Henry Fox, the first Lord Holland, undoubtedly had his faults. They were indeed so conspicuous as to attract, even in the tolerant eighteenth century, such adverse criticism that he is now remembered mainly as a corrupt and shady adventurer, a 'public defaulter of unaccounted millions'. His contemporaries, when he died, had little to say in his favour; and in 1803 his former friend and later enemy, Lord Shelburne, wrote an analysis of his character, which reveals the nature of the writer as clearly as it attempts to define the imperfections of Lord Holland. 'Mr. Fox', wrote Lord Shelburne, 'was infinitely able in business, clear, penetrating, confident, and decisive in all his dealings with mankind, and of most extraordinary activity. His first connexion was among the Torys. His ambition was quite of the modern kind, narrow, interested, in short, the ambition of office, which had the Court for its object, and looked on corruption as the only means to attain it. I give you so much and you shall give me in return, and so we'll defy the world, and sing Tol de rol, &c. His abilities and conversation taking this tune, habit had so confirmed it that, when I knew him, he looked upon every other reasoning as mere loss of time, or as a sure mark of folly or the greatest knavery, "for every set of men are honest, it is only necessary to define their sense of it, to know where to look for it; every man is honest and dishonest, according to the sentiments of the man who speaks of him; every man is artful too, to the extent of his abilities, God made man so, and he's given it to him in lieu of force". Mr. Fox was thus extremely honest in all his dealings with individuals. His good sense made him so if his nature did not. He was extremely artful too, and for this purpose was really to the greatest degree open, except in cases of the greatest necessity. Possessed by this means of the short road to power, he despised, as it were, knowledge, or at least put men of that stamp in a second class, and looked on all public spirit as the spirit of faction. This was his political creed in which he believed himself, and recommended to others.' It is fair to add that Lord Shelburne was not without provocation, for Mr. Fox had described him more tersely as an 'infamous and perfidious liar'.

But Fox's reputation earlier in his career had been very different. In 1748, for example, Horace Walpole was able to write of him without any suspicion of irony that 'he is equally incapable of mystery in pretending to know what he does not, or in concealing what he does', and 'to the great detriment of the Ministry has turned one of the best sinecures under the Government into one of the most laborious employments, at the same time imagining that the ease with which he executed it will prevent the discovery of his innovation', and, finally, that the writer could 'say nothing of his integrity, because I know nothing of it but that it has never been breathed upon even by suspicion'.

Fifteen years later such a testimonial would have been read as an ironical paradox, and we must look to the events of those years for the causes of that immense loss of reputation. When Horace Walpole wrote his appreciation, Henry Fox was everywhere known as a rising politician of unusual ability and unusual aptitude for hard work. He had been a junior Lord of the Treasury, promoted to be Secretary at War, and he would, it was believed, rise higher. As prudent in private as in public life, he was at that time saving half his official salary and offering to hand it over to his elder brother Stephen to help him maintain the dignity of the new barony of Ilchester. But Lord Ilchester refused the offer, advising his brother, with a prevision, which time was to prove only too accurate, that 'whatever you do save, for God's sake, save it for your children; they may or may not want it, 'tis more than you or I can tell; but your only opportunity of saving for them is while they are young'.

It was not only as a rising politician that Fox's name was known. He had made himself a character of romance by his runaway marriage in 1744 with Lady Georgina Carolina Lennox, the eldest daughter of the second Duke of Richmond. It is difficult to-day to appreciate the intense excitement aroused in the polite world by the news that the Duke's daughter, only a few weeks after her twenty-first birthday, had secretly left her father's house, and had been married to a junior Lord of the Treasury, as Henry Fox then was, by a clergyman who did not even know the names of the couple before him. London was delightedly horrified, the Duke was furious, the Court was appalled, and the Prime Minister lamented about 'this most unfortunate affair' until Lord Carteret 'thought that our fleet was beaten, or that Mons had been betrayed to the French. At last it came out that Henry Fox was married, which I knew before.' The Duke's anger was such that for four years Lady Caroline was not forgiven. But in each year his son-in-law showed increasing promise of a political career. Every year he carried the Army Estimates against the clamour of the Opposition for reduction, and every year saw some improvement of his position in the Government. In 1746 his future seemed so secure that he took on lease the much neglected and dilapidated Holland House with its quiet, gently sloping garden among the meadows of Kensington. It had belonged to a Lord Holland who had been the lover of Queen Henrietta Maria, and Henry Fox began to spend his savings on putting it into a condition worthy of a rising statesman. Their eldest son, Stephen, was born in February 1745, a delicate child, alarmingly affected with 'a distemper they call Sanvitoss dance'. Fox was beside himself with anxiety at Stephen's bad health, and he was nearly heart-broken when his second son Henry Charles, who was born in October 1746, died after a few weeks. When the third child arrived, Holland House was in the hands of decorators, and Lady Caroline was living in Conduit Street, where, on the 24th of January 1749, Charles James was born. The name of Charles, given to the second and third child, has been borne by every Duke of Richmond since Charles II conferred that title on his son by Louise de Keroualle, Duchess of Portsmouth. Illegitimate descent on his mother's side was not the only association of Charles James with Charles II, for his father's family had risen to distinction from comparative obscurity through the services of successive members to King Charles in exile and at home. The new bearer of the name was a delicate child, but stronger than Stephen, and his father, with a candour unusual among parents, wrote to Lord Ilchester that 'it's incredible how like a monkey he looked before he was dressed'.

This unfortunate first impression was soon dispelled, for Charles became almost at once a remarkably attractive child. Within a year his father was writing ecstatically of 'the éclat of his beauty', and his enthusiasm became even greater when the child began to speak. For from his earliest days Charles showed signs of astonishing intelligence and character. It was not merely the precocity which might, perhaps, have been expected from that rather Semitic cast of features, derived, it has been suggested, from the Medicis and not from Jewish ancestry in the family of Louise de Keroualle. It was something more than precocity, and it was already accompanied by signs of that compelling charm which remained one of his chief assets in life.

The youngest child, Henry, was born six years later.

Fox could spare plenty of time for his children. The Army was undergoing its not uncommon experience of reduction and reform, but the process was not arduous, and the Secretary at War could turn his attention from military to domestic economy. Some attention to his own affairs was necessary, for, in spite of past savings from his official salary, and a prize of £10,000 from a lottery in 1748, for which the bells of the village church were set ringing in pious recognition, it was not easy to find money for Holland House and his growing family; and he began to reflect enviously on other and more lucrative offices in the Government. There was the office of Paymaster, for example, in which his rival, Mr. Pitt, was securely entrenched, and envy was perhaps increased by the knowledge that Mr. Pitt, with self-denial unusual in those days, refused to take the customary profits from his post.

In 1750 the Duke of Richmond died suddenly, and the Duchess died in the following year. Their deaths had an unexpected influence on the upbringing of the Fox children, for Henry Fox, completely forgiven for his marriage, was appointed one of the guardians of the Lennox children, who thenceforward were constantly in and out of Holland House. Lady Caroline inherited a legacy of £5,000 from each of her parents, which, with another unexpected legacy of £5,000 in 1751, helped to tide over those years. It is, indeed, possible that this series of windfalls may have had a decisive influence on Fox's life, and may even provide a clue to that remarkable change in his character and reputation during the years which followed. With increasing expenses he may well have treated as income the series of accretions from the lottery and the three legacies, which for five successive years amounted to an addition of £5,000 to his resources; and, when the five fat years were over, he was faced with the alternatives of either uncomfortably reducing his expenditure or shaping his political course more urgently and openly in the direction which would lead to money.

Meanwhile life at Holland House was blissfully happy. The earthquake of 1750, which drove a stream of Londoners past its gates to escape from the imminent destruction of London, seems to have produced no repercussion in Kensington; and in the riots of the following year for the eleven days lost from the Calendar Kensington was equally undisturbed. Mr. Fox was much occupied with the planting of his elm avenues, and Charles was interested in 'getting on the steps at the hall door, playing with the dirt that is scraped off people's shoes'.

In 1753, when the last of his windfalls had been gathered,

Fox showed that he could still disregard his financial interest in politics. The Government, in an unusual mood of social-reform, introduced a Clandestine Marriages Bill to put a stop to the scandal of secret marriages. It was not easy to find any honest or logical defence of the Fleet parsons, but all, and more than all, that could with any reason be urged in their favour was said by Henry Fox, who regarded it as an affront to his family that Parliament should seek to amend those simple formalities, which had made his own wedding so easy. He fought aggressively, and found himself with new enemies, among whom was the formidable Lord Chancellor.

It was a bad moment for making enemies, for in the following year the Prime Minister died and every place-hunter in England was alert for promotion. 'The Chancellor', wrote Horace Walpole acidly appraising the chances of rival candidates, 'hates Fox; the Duke of Newcastle does not (I don't say love him, but to speak in the proper phrase, does not) pretend to love him; the Scotch abominate him, and they and the Jacobites make use of his connexion with the Duke to represent him as formidable; the Princess cannot approve him for the same reason; the Law as in duty bound to Chancellor and to Murray and to themselves, whom he always attacks, must dislike him.' The outlook was not promising, but the need for promotion was becoming urgent. Fox's methods on such occasions tended to be crude, and his reputation was not improved by his energetic canvass of ministers, which included a visit to his chief's brother within a few hours of Pelham's death. There followed a short struggle between Fox and Pitt for supremacy in the new government of the Duke of Newcastle, that unhappy states-man, who at his first audience 'lay there howling and embracing the King's knees'. Fox was fighting hard for advancement now, and it was current gossip that he 'must very soon be first Minister or be ruined'. In December 1754 he was offered a place in the Cabinet, which his friends feared would mean dignity without power. Sir Charles Hanbury

Williams even commemorated in advance his friend's escape
from the trap:

> 'Softly' quoth Reynard, 'if you please,
> I'll not be duped with words like these,
> I spy the snare, I see the danger,
> To others, Sir; go seek a stranger.
>
> . . . .
>
> My life would wither in your pow'r,
> And which I value ten times more,
> My yet unspotted reputation,
> Would sink at once with all the nation.'

But Fox could trust his own judgement in such matters. He
accepted the offer, and in the following year he became
Secretary of State for the Southern Department, with a
vastly extended field of patronage.

It was not quite what he had wanted, but he had beaten
Pitt, and, as far as he could foresee, the future would be
with him. Perhaps, if the future had offered nothing more
stirring than a dance of intrigue round the rather absurd
figure of the Duke of Newcastle, he would have been right.
But, although he had shown some activity in preparing for
war, he did not foresee how that war, when it came, would
affect his own position. To the last moment the country's
danger was not appreciated. 'I don't think', remarked
Lord Hertford, 'that a little war would do us any harm.'
So the Seven Years War began with that series of disasters
with which this country has so often opened its most victorious campaigns. It was the moment for a hero, and Fox,
with all his energy and ambition, was no hero. Besides, the
hero was already waiting, confident that he alone could save
the country. Within a few months Pitt was leading the
Empire from disaster to triumph, and Fox was swept aside,
to reappear in the inglorious, but very lucrative, post of
Paymaster. His career as a statesman was over.

Meanwhile he found in the Holland House nursery much
compensation for political disappointment, for Charles was
developing an intelligence which kept his father in a state

of respectful admiration. 'My sensible child' he called him at the age of three, and two years later found him 'very well, very pert, very argumentative'. Tradition has handed down many unauthorized anecdotes of the worshipping indulgence which Henry Fox offered to his brilliant child; of the garden wall pulled down in Charles's absence, and rebuilt because he had been promised the pleasure of seeing it demolished; of the state documents recopied, because Charles desired to smudge the originals; of the destruction of his father's watch, because 'if you must, I suppose you must'. The stories may be untrue, but they show something of the parental method as practised at Holland House. Probably it had no great effect at that age on Charles, because Lady Caroline was far from sharing her husband's views on the upbringing of children. 'Charles is dreadfully passionate,' she lamented, 'what shall we do with him?' 'Oh, never mind,' answered her husband, 'he is a very sensible little boy, and will learn to curb himself.' Charles, when he grew up, was fond of repeating this story with apparent approval of the educational principle involved, on the ground that 'I will not deny that I was a very sensible little boy, a very clever little boy, and what I heard made an impression on me, and was of use to me afterwards'. Confronted with what would now be called an infant prodigy, Lord Holland seems to have concluded that normal methods of upbringing were inappropriate. 'Let nothing', he proclaimed, 'be done to break his spirit. The world will do that business fast enough.'

Between his father's adoration and his mother's alarms Charles showed surprisingly few signs of becoming either a spoilt child or a prig. This can hardly be counted to the credit of his father's system. For the value of that interesting experiment was impaired at the outset by the corrective influence of the brother, his aunts, and his cousins. Charles, like most clever children, was fond of impressing his elders, and he soon found that his elder brother, his youthful aunt, Lady Sarah Lennox, only by four years his elder, and his cousin, Lady Susan Fox Strangways, were by no means tolerant of undue self-assertion in the young. Less apprehensive than his father of the danger of breaking his spirit, they saw to it that he should not be allowed to break theirs by establishing a domestic tyranny in the nursery of Holland House.

At a very early age he seems to have taken absolute control of his own education, which in his sixth year included play-going and voracious reading of dramatic literature. 'Stage-mad,' remarked his father, 'but it makes him read a good deal.' In 1756 the question of a school was debated. Charles wished to join his cousin, Lord Stavordale, at the very select establishment at Wandsworth kept by Madame Pampellonne, the widow of a French tutor. His parents were undecided, but Charles had no doubts. 'Charles', recorded his father, 'determines to go to Wandsworth.' The success of the experiment may be judged from the rather unduly complacent bulletin which his father addressed to Lord Ilchester in August of the following year: 'There is at present a great vying between Lord Stavordale and Charles. Your son intends, if possible, to recover the place he has lost as to making Latin, in which mine has got before him; and mine is determined he shall not. This do's Lord Stavordale good, but Mr. Davies seems pretty sure that Lord Stavordale's ambition (as he calls it) will not be durable, and that Charles's will. It seems Charles has more emulation than any boy ever had, and the pains he now takes that he may get into the 4th form next year at Eton as young as Faukner now is, who is just got there is surprising.'

It was not part of Charles's educational scheme to remain long at Wandsworth, and in the autumn of 1757 he instructed his parents to move him to Eton College.

CHAPTER II

1757–1766

Eton might almost have been designed for the education of Charles Fox as a statesman, so perfectly did it suit his tastes and character. That methodical standardization of the public schoolboy which became general towards the end of the next century was then almost unknown. This was fortunate for Charles, to whom the modern process of moulding to type would have been extremely distasteful. He was fortunate, also, in his headmaster, Dr. Barnard, an educationalist of independent mind, who knew the importance of allowing boys of character to educate themselves in their own way, and he was not bound to a curriculum by the tyranny of future examinations. Barnard's own enthusiasms, oratory and classic poetry, were exactly those which would appeal to Charles, and those which were then considered most suitable for a future statesman. He was placed in the Third Form instead of the Fourth for which his father had hoped; and he there began a career which, in spite of the frequent visits of his parents with their rather excessive hospitality, promised to be exemplary.

He was already a student of politics, and he knew better than most boys of his age would have known, that Pitt, a statesman among statesmen, was now the national hero, while his father, accumulating money at the Pay Office beyond his most golden dreams, had fallen low in public reputation. Rhymsters were already busy with Henry Fox's love of money, and it is possible that the lampoon on the occasion when the two statesmen received the freedom of the City in gold boxes may have reached Eton:

> The two great rivals London might content,
> If what he values most to each she sent;
> Ill was the franchise coupled with the box;
> Give Pitt the freedom, and the gold to Fox!

But Fox was a disappointed man in spite of his growing

fortune, and it was perhaps in echo of his father's disappointment that Charles at about this time expressed a passing doubt on the perfection of human happiness, when he informed his father, with a smile, that 'he wish'd his life was at end'. His father asked the reason, and was told in 'his merry odd good humoured way' that 'it is a troublesome affair, and one wishes one had this thing or that thing, and then one is not the happier; and then one wishes for another thing, and one's very sorry if one don't get it, and it does not make one happy if one do so'.

His progress up the school was not hurried. In 1759 Foxe mi., as the school list described him, was in the Fourth Form, and in the following year he reached Remove. An admiring group of friends and elders, Lord Carlisle, Lord Fitzwilliam, Lord Stavordale, James Hare, and Anthony Storer, followed a Form behind. In this year he had new grounds for his speculations on human happiness, for he was devoted with all the serious intensity of a schoolboy to his beautiful cousin, Lady Susan Strangways. He was writing Latin verses to her, and in the autumn term, when he had reached the Fifth Form, his aunt, Lady Sarah, reports upon the state of his affections: 'Charles Fox has made some Latin verses that were sent up for good; the purport of them is to discover a pigeon to fly to his love Susan, and carry her a letter from him, and that if it makes haste, it will please both Venus its mistress, and him. There now, are you not proud, to have your name wrote in a scholar's exercise?' The young Etonian writes to his cousin a rather different version of the incident: 'Th' other day I had, in an exercise I was sent up for good for, your Ladyship's name; therefore that envious girl, your fair friend, was very angry that I had not hers instead of it.'

When he came home for the Christmas holidays, Lady Susan was not at Holland House, and Charles's gloomy abstraction pervaded the rehearsal of the Christmas play. Last Christmas he had appeared successfully as Hastings, when she played Jane Seymour, but he was now, as his aunt observed, 'as disagreeable about acting this play as he can be, he won't learn his part perfect, won't rehearse, and, in short, shows plainly that your not being here is the reason he won't enter into it and be eager, which you know is the only way of going on with comfort.' It was a happy life in the Fifth Form for that cheerful group of friends, undisturbed by the stirring events of the day. For history was moving while Charles Fox polished his Latin verse at Eton. On a Saturday morning in October of 1760 the Prince was stopped in his ride by a note from Kensington Palace. He read it with no sign of agitation, and turned back to begin the reign of King George the Third.

His self-control that morning was habitual to him, but it concealed a strange conflict of emotions. Under the tuition of his mother and Lord Bute he believed that the country was sunk in corruption and dishonour, and it would be his mission as king to restore it to 'virtue, freedom, and glory'. He had set out this conception of his purpose and duty in an essay on Alfred the Great written a few years earlier. A passage from it shows the trend of his mind: 'When Alfred mounted the throne, there was scarcely a man in office that was not totally unfit for it, and generally extremely corrupt in the execution of it . . . he got rid of the incorrigible, reclaimed the others, and formed new subjects for to raise his own glory, and with it the glory and happiness of his country . . . when all this is carefully examined, we may safely affirm that no good and great Prince born in a free country and like Alfred fond of the cause of Liberty, will ever despair of restoring his country to virtue, freedom, and glory, even though he mounts the Throne in the most corrupted times, in storms of inward faction and the most threatening circumstances without.' He was convinced that, like Alfred, he would be surrounded by corrupt and designing men, who would wish to use him to their own advantage. He must trust none of them, and he must never allow himself to be ruled by his ministers as his predecessors had been ruled. This was his purpose, but he was tortured by fears that he had not the energy and firmness to carry it out. Again and again he wrote to Lord Bute in an agony of self-abasement and doubt: 'I am young and inexperienced and want advice. I trust in your friendship which will assist me in these difficulties. . . . As I have chosen the vigorous part, I will throw off that indolence which if I don't soon get the better of will be my ruin, and will never grow weary of this . . . I am resolved in myself to take the resolute part, to act the man in everything, to repeat whatever I am to say with spirit and not blushing and afraid as I have hitherto, I will also never show the least irresolution, and will not from being warm on any subject by degrees grow quite indifferent about it.' But in spite of his determination to make 'a good figure in the station it has pleased Almighty Providence to place me in', he returns to his constant apprehension that he is 'of such unhappy nature', and that he will 'make but a very poor and despicable figure'. This process of introspective self-development could only lead to a certain rigidity of mind. He must suspect every one, for to trust is to be deceived; he must never yield to pressure, for to yield would be to surrender in the fight; he must impose his will and not seek advice, lest he deliver himself into the hands of his advisers; and, above all, he must maintain his own opinions and suppress that sense of inferiority which tended to recur in spite of his resolutions.

His early experiments in imposing his will were not wholly encouraging, for they included an offer of marriage to Lady Sarah, whose age was then seventeen. But she could not at once decide to be Queen of England, and during the interval of her reflection the Princess and Lord Bute imposed upon him their joint will in the form of a German Princess. So much has been said to the detriment of Henry Fox, who was at that time angling for a peerage for his wife rather than for himself, because he doubted whether the Duke of Newcastle 'and perhaps others, would wish me out of the H. of Commons', that it is pleasant to record that notwithstanding the obvious advantages of such a marriage, he appears to have made no attempt to induce his sister-in-law to accept it. But the affair must have given him a glimpse of high honours and dignity, and it may have left him less content with the comforts of the Pay Office.

Henry Fox had again to consider the question of his future career in the following year when the King made his first move to free himself from the domination of the Whigs. It was a move to be expected from the pupil of Lord Bute, trained, on the example of King Alfred, to the task of 'attempting with vigour to restore religion and virtue when I mount the Throne' in order that the country might 'regain her antient state of Lustre'. Indeed any new king might have made a move against the Whigs without Lord Bute's tuition, for times had changed for a Hanoverian king. The Forty-five had made the throne secure; the Pretender need no longer be considered; and the King need no longer believe that the alternative to a Whig government might be a Jacobite plot. Another king might have found an easier way to independence, but King George, with his torturing doubts of his own ability and his suspicion of every adviser except Lord Bute, would have regarded any delay or compromise as a sign of that failure to assert himself which he most feared. The first move, if action must begin at once, was to end the war, which was a war of Whig ministers. In this he might expect support, for neither the Government nor the country was unanimous in supporting the war. With the help of Lord Bute he soon had his way. Pitt resigned after a year of the new reign, when he had lost his old supremacy, and the unhappy Duke of Newcastle was induced to give way to Lord Bute, who began his administration by negotiating preliminaries of peace with the French. After an interval of indecision the Duke declared himself against the Favourite, and the Whigs were in opposition.

The terms of peace were agreed, but they were not what the country might have expected after Pitt's victories, and

they had not been accepted by the House of Commons,
where, according to Fox, the Government must rely upon
'the Tories, the Scotch, and the loaves and fishes'. Lord
Bute, who combined in his person most of the causes which
then inspired dislike, realized that members would be induced to support the peace only if the leader of the House
possessed, in addition to skill in debate, extreme facility in
what was known as parliamentary management. They
turned to Fox, but he had now secured a peerage for Lady
Caroline, and was settling down to a comfortable old age,
to be divided between Holland House and his new estate,
purchased from his savings as Paymaster, at Kingsgate near
Margate. He was most unwilling to accept, but Bute and
the King were insistent. He wanted a peerage, and here
was a certainty of earning it. There was some conversation
about terms, an arrangement about his peerage, perhaps
some mention of an earldom, and the Paymaster joined the
Cabinet for the extermination of his former friends. He
knew exactly what was to be done, and in a few weeks of
concentrated intrigue he did it. Modern investigations
throw doubt on Walpole's stories of the purchase of honourable members with actual gold. But if coin did not pass,
posts, pensions, and reversions were freely offered, and the
holders of them were freely threatened; and by the end of
the year, when we have a glimpse of Charles at the play
'coiffé en aile de pigeon and powder'd', a solid majority of
the House of Commons was pledged to support the Peace.

When Parliament met, the majority voted obediently.
Mr. Pitt appeared, in the throes of gout, to make his expected protest; but 'it was not a day when his genius
thundered', and his voice was too faint to appeal to the
conscience of a House managed by Henry Fox. It was
natural that the King and his ministers should 'pursue the
victory without delay'. Patronage was a recognized instrument of government, and any new government might be
expected to establish itself by securing the offices and appointments of the enemy. The Duke expected it, but he

thought that the dismissals would not be many, and he even hoped that he might have some say in deciding who was to be sacrificed. No one foresaw that the pursuit would consist of displacing every pension and office holder, rich or poor, important or obscure, whose income could in any way be attributed to the defeated Whigs. In that massacre of the party with which he had worked for twenty years, Fox felt no embarrassment. He encouraged his leader to 'go on to the *general* rout' and 'leave none of them', recording with pride that he '*did His Majesty such honest and essential service*'. When the slaughter was finished, the victors had only to divide the spoil, which in Fox's case was to be the long-awaited peerage. He was then shocked to observe a general lack of sympathy. He was prepared for the hatred of colleagues whom he had betrayed after a long political friendship; he could face the fury of the people of London for the destruction of their hero, Pitt; but he had not expected ingratitude from the new Government, whose dirty work he had done, nor the contemptuous desertion of those personal adherents, Rigby and Calcraft, with whom he had shared his gains. When he claimed his peerage, he found that it was not to be an earldom, and that he was expected to resign the Pay Office. After acrimonious and humiliating negotiations he succeeded in keeping the Pay Office for three years more, and, as first Lord Holland, he was able to record, like some pilgrim of corruption who has at last reached the end of his acquisitive journey, that he had 'got that ease I always wish'd for, not with the grace I had a right to expect, but I am got there'.

He escaped from the public insults of London to his new estate at Kingsgate; but even there he was followed by the lampooners. Gray's poem, written four years afterwards, is typical of the rest:

> Old and abandoned by each venal friend,
> Here Holland formed the pious resolution,
> To smuggle a few years, and strive to mend
> A broken character and constitution.

The poem ends with a description of London, if Lord
Holland had been allowed to turn it into a picturesque ruin
of the kind which he was building on the coast of Kent:

> Owls would have hooted in St. Peter's choir,
> And foxes stunk and littered in St. Paul's.

But neither the air of Kingsgate nor the fashionable
diversion of building 'mouldering fanes and battlements . . .
turrets and arches nodding to their fall' could soothe his
feelings. His friends had deserted him, and his health was
failing. He could see nothing disgraceful in his conduct,
and he regarded himself as a victim of man's ingratitude.
He was hurt and bewildered by the general outcry against
him, and he looked for a means of escaping from it. Stephen
was already abroad, where his extravagance and gambling
losses were beginning to call forth mild protests from his
parents. Lord Holland decided that the rest of the family
should retreat across the Channel, and in May Charles was
withdrawn from Eton to set forth with them from the
private landing-stage at Kingsgate. It was a wise decision,
for Lord Holland's reputation abroad as a statesman and
philosopher was still unshaken. 'Le voilà qui pense,' remarked án admiring Frenchman when he fell asleep after
dinner. They were bound for Spa, where Lady Holland
was to drink the waters, but at Ghent they found news that
Stephen was ill, and they changed their plans to join him
in Paris.

What happened in Paris is obscure. We are told by tradition that Lord Holland deliberately accomplished his son's
moral downfall by sending him daily to the tables with a
supply of guineas, and by introducing him to resorts less
reputable even than the tables. But the story has nothing
but tradition to support it, and it is a story for which the
smallest foundation would invite fantastic development at
the hands of his enemies. No doubt Charles wanted to try
his luck at gambling, and no doubt Lord Holland's regret-
table principles of bringing up the young decreed that it
should be so, as they had decreed fourteen years before in

C

the affair of the broken watch that 'if you must, you must'.
It was, like many of Lord Holland's decisions, an act of
folly, for Stephen was already displaying a fatal enthusiasm
for gambling, and Charles's insatiable thirst for excitement
of every kind made him almost a predestined victim. But
it was exactly the kind of folly that was part of Lord Holland's system, and as folly rather than the systematic de-
bauchery perpetuated by tradition it may remain. There
is no record of any protest at that time from Lady Holland,
and there is nothing in Lord Holland's letter to George
Selwyn, when Charles went back to Eton, which might not
be written by the father of a modern Sixth Form boy:
'Charles is, I hear, again a perfect schoolboy in dress.
Madame de Coislin calls him *son jeune amoureux*, and in-
quires after him very kindly. . . . I tell her I am *amant* too;
but I am *le trop vieux*, she finds.'

The reversion of Charles from Parisian to Etonian was
not without its discomforts, for the boys laughed at his
French mannerisms, and Dr. Barnard is said to have celebrated his return by an Etonian beating. If the improbable
legend of the flogging be true, it was certainly not for idleness, for he was working with feverish energy to regain his
place, and he soon wrote to ask that the Parisian experiment
should not be repeated at Christmas, as he was afraid that
it might interfere with his work. It is hardly the letter of a
boy whose character has been ruined, and if the headmaster
had read it, he might have wished that more of his pupils
would try the effect of a gambling interlude in Paris:

'Dr. Barnard thanked me for his snuff box, and said it
was very much against his interest to advise me to be
absent in the summer rather than now, as by that means
the school lost so great an ornament at Election speeches.
I cannot help saying that I find Eton more disagreeable
than I had imagined; for which reason I think I am determined not to go to Paris at Xmas. My mother will be sorry
to hear this, I wish, however, I could contrive a way to see
Ste. I am so fully convinced of the use of being at Eton,

that I am afraid of running the risque of not returning. I am also resolved to stay there until Christmas twelve month; by this you may see that the petit maître de Paris is converted into an Oxford pedant. I am also satisfied that you will not disapprove of this resolution, and I hope therefore you will not endeavour to dissuade me from it, as I am convinced you will willingly consent to spend six weeks less agreeably to make me a much better scholar than I should otherwise be, which is a glory you know I very much desire.'
So the virtuous Etonian spent the Christmas holidays with his father at Holland House, reading the classics and listening to debates in Parliament. When he went back to Eton for his last half-year, he was still working and living at high pressure. He was in the Sixth Form now and fifth boy in the school. Of his group of admiring friends, only Bouverie, Hare, and Storer were with him in the Sixth. Carlisle and Fitzwilliam were in the Fifth, and Carlisle was metrically predicting that he would soon

> Shake the loud senate, animate the hearts
> Of fearful statesmen, while around you stand
> Both Peers and Commons listening your command.

He was doing his best to prepare for such a career, for he had learnt all that Dr. Barnard could teach him of oratory, and he was already attacking his father's political enemies in conscientious French verse:

> Longtemps, du peuple Pitt favori adoré
> Les méprisant toujours, en fut toujours aimé,
> Estimant leur amour, il prodigua leur vie,
> Et cherchoit leur gloire aux dépens de sa patrie.

But his last triumphant months at Eton were marred by the first shock of his life. In April 1764 the adored Lady Susan, to the horror and amazement of London, eloped with Mr. William O'Brien, an unsuccessful actor. 'Even a footman were preferable,' sighed Horace Walpole, 'the publicity of the hero's profession perpetuates the mortification.' Charles's despair was terrible. 'She likes him more than she likes me,' he sobbed again and again to Lady Sarah,

'Why does she like him more than she likes me?' He took his broken heart to Kingsgate for the summer, leaving his name in Upper School carved with an emphasis, which suggests no doubts of its future importance. Another relic of him remains at Eton, for Dr. Barnard had introduced the custom of 'leaving portraits'. Reynolds and Romney were the artists usually commissioned by Etonians, and the first of Reynolds's portraits of Charles Fox hangs in the Provost's house. He is dressed in a plain brown coat appropriate to his schoolboy status, his hair hangs straight, and his face has none of the plumpness which it soon acquired. He is surrounded by the portraits of Lord Carlisle and other contemporaries, some of whom were to suffer in fortune, if they gained in happiness, by their friendship with him.

Cricket and partridge shooting seem to have restored him to his usual cheerfulness, for when he went to Oxford in October as a gentleman commoner of Hertford College he showed no sign of the despairing lover. His chief anxiety, in one of his first letters, was to explain the rapid melting of a sum of £150 with which he had started his career. He had spent £50 of it in paying Eton debts, which he admitted to be extravagant. Then there were new shirts, new stockings, and one new frock, which had come to nearly £40; and six spoons ('I was told one must have some spoons at Oxford') cost £7; and the journey from Kingsgate and 'many other trifles' had reduced his balance to £34 11s., which, he feared, would soon need replenishment. And, sure enough, in less than a fortnight, his fears were realized, for he had to confess that he had been 'so foolish as to break all the good resolutions I had formed as to play, and have lost upwards of eighty guineas'. The letter ends with another good resolution of ominous uncertainty: 'I feel my imprudence will lessen your good opinion of me and justly; but I think I can answer for myself for the future, as I have made a most fixed resolution never again to play. I think I shall have courage enough to keep it, but cannot be sure enough of my strength to give an absolute promise.' But

these letters are far from conveying a true impression of
Charles Fox's life at Oxford. He might gamble away his
allowance, but during his two years at the University he
worked with the same energy which he had shown at
Wandsworth and Eton. He had always been an insatiable
reader, and from Dr. Barnard and Oxford he acquired that
love of the classics which remained with him through life,
and was often his only refuge in the stress of public and
private misfortunes. His reading at that time was not confined to the classics, for he was also working at French, 'as
I am thoroughly convinced of its utility', and at the same
time found that he could 'like vastly' the study of mathematics. 'I believe', he wrote, 'they are useful, and I am
sure they are entertaining.'

That Christmas was spent at Holland House, where he
consoled himself for the loss of Lady Susan by a passing
admiration for the Duchess of Hamilton, one of the beautiful
Gunnings. 'Charles', wrote his aunt, 'is in town and is
violently in love with the Duchess of Hamilton; think of
his riding out to see her. You know how he hates it; he is
all humbleness and respect and never leaves her. I am
vastly glad to see him improve so much, he is now quite
manly, and is very much liked, I think, in the world; he is
a sweet boy, and I hope will continue as amiable as he is.'

His appreciation of mathematics was undiminished when
he went back to Oxford, and he worked so hard that his
tutor could make no objection to a holiday in France during
May and June. 'Application like yours', wrote Dr. New-
come with scholastic enthusiasm, 'requires some intermis-
sion and you are the only person with whom I have ever
had connexion to whom I could say this.' So Charles set
out for Paris, fortified with the promise that the 'other
geometricians of the college' were more than willing to postpone their studies in that entertaining subject until his
return. 'He went over', wrote Lady Sarah, 'determined to
be in love with Madelle Coislin, who is beautiful, but he fell
in love with another lady and do you know the impudent

toad made love to both at a time.' In Paris he met David Hume, the historian, who ventured to hint that the amusements of that city were hardly the ideal preparation for public life. 'I told Charles this conversation between me and Hume,' wrote Lord Templetown to Lord Holland, 'and that I was obliged to own that the risk would be very great, 99 times in a hundred, but that I trusted to a noble and worthy ambition, which I thought I saw very strong in him, and which gave me the strongest assurance that he would neither disappoint the public nor his friends. Tho' Charles won't promise anything positively upon this subject, yet he acknowledges himself to be entirely of my opinion.' It was indeed a dangerous experiment, with Stephen already on the way to a gambler's ruin. But once more it seemed that Lord Holland was right, for Charles returned to Oxford for the long vacation, and toiled as if life could hold no object but academic distinctions.

CHAPTER III

1766–1774

At the end of the Easter Term of 1766 Charles Fox arrived at Holland House, hot, dusty, and dishevelled, explaining that he had celebrated the end of his University career by walking from Oxford to London with his friend William Dickson, but they had run out of money, and Lord Holland 'must send half a guinea or a guinea, without loss of time' to redeem the gold watch which he had left at Nettlebed in pawn for a pot of beer. He had worked with uncommon energy up to the last moment, and he left with the humble conviction that his education was far from complete. 'I employ almost my whole time at Oxford', he wrote to Sir George Macartney, 'in the mathematical and classical knowledge, so that I understand Latin and Greek tolerably well. I am totally ignorant in every part of useful knowledge. I am more convinced every day how little advantage there is in being what at school and the university is called a good scholar, one receives a good deal of amusement from it, but that is all.' This self-examination may have been due to a temporary depression of spirits, for Lady Sarah, still an enthusiastic chronicler of his affections, informed her cousin at that time that 'Charles . . . is in love with a Miss Burner'd, who he don't know, nor can he get presented to her; poor soul, he is in a piteous taking'.

Once more it seemed that Lord Holland's educational theory had been justified. With every inducement to become a useless idler, Charles Fox left Oxford with a reputation for hard work and a vigorous taste for poetry and classics. He was already one of the most popular young men of his time, with a diversity of friends ranging from young Mr. Burke, who had meditated on the Sublime and the Beautiful and was now Lord Rockingham's secretary, to the sporting Lord March, whose meditations and achievements were of a less exalted nature. But in spite of his successes,

Lady Holland still felt uneasy, and she continued sometimes to make her protest. 'I have been this morning with
Lady Hester Pitt,' she is reputed to have said in one of them,
'and there is little William Pitt, *not eight years old*, and
really the cleverest child I ever saw, *and brought up so strictly
and proper in his behaviour*,that *mark my words*, that little
boy will be a thorn in Charles' side as long as he lives'.

In August there was acting at Winterslow in which
'Charles would have done the Copper Captain well, if he had
known it, what he did know was very well indeed'; and in
September, after some hot tramps after the partridges at
Kingsgate, he set forth for France. He was followed in a few
weeks by the rest of the family on the way to Naples for the
winter.

He spent the whole of the next year abroad, travelling, as
a substitute for the more formal Grand Tour, with relays of
friends. In March his parents started for England, and he
went to spend the summer at Naples with his Eton friends,
Lord Fitzwilliam and Uvedale Price, who was to become
known as the authority on the Picturesque. In September
he was in Paris again with his parents, penitent, no doubt,
for the unfortunate advice, which he had recently given his
father. For Lord Holland, still hoping for recognition of his
services, had, at his son's suggestion, asked Lord Bute's
help to a step in the peerage. 'I hope I shall not mind it,' he
wrote, 'but your advice has been followed with as bad success as possible. It is my opinion Lord B's application did
more harm than good, and whilst he is cry'd out upon for
doing everything at Court, he *can* do nothing.' The letter
went on in a strain of maudlin self-pity:

> Of all Court service know the common lot,
> To-day 'tis done, to-morrow 'tis forgot.

'Don't ever, Charles, make an exception or trust as I did.'
The autumn was spent with Lord Carlisle in the south of
France and the Alps, to the almost hysterical alarm of Mr.
George Augustus Selwyn, the devoted mentor of Lord
Carlisle. 'The accident that had like to have happened to

you and Charles,' he wrote, '*m'a fait glacer le sang* . . . The wild boars, the Alps, precipices, felouques, changes of climate, are all to me such things as, besides that they *grossissent de loin*, that if I allowed my imagination its full scope, I should not have a moment's peace.' Charles joined his parents in Nice for the winter, and in April he was back in Italy with Uvedale Price, until he returned to England in August.

His chief interests of the moment, among others perhaps less admirable, were acting and Italian literature; and a letter to Richard Fitzpatrick shows how seriously he took both of them: 'Your letter has put me in mind of acting, and made me extremely eager for some more plays, though, to tell you the truth, the last time I acted I fell very short of my own expectations. However my spirit is not entirely broken, but I will avoid appearing in any conspicuous part, if possible. . . . I have so bad a taste as to differ from you very much about the French stage. I allow the French actors to be much better than ours, but I think our plays are infinitely better. Here at Florence the people are very clever at every other species of writing imaginable, but the dramatic. All the Italian plays are imitations either of Greek, Latin or French ones, but if the Italian plays are in this respect inferior to the French, English, etc., they are fully revenged in every other. For God's sake learn Italian as fast as you can, if it be only to read Ariosto. There is more good poetry in Italian than in all other languages that I understand put together. In prose too it is a very fine language. Make haste and read all these things that you may be fit to talk to Christians.'

Richard Fitzpatrick, to whom this letter was written, was two years younger than Charles Fox. They were not at school together, for Fitzpatrick chose Westminster and the Guards, instead of Eton and Oxford. But they met in their early days and found that in almost all respects their tastes and interests were identical. Fitzpatrick's *Dorinda* and his contributions to the *Rolliad* show that he had literary taste,

although his taste did not lead him to Fox's love of classical reading. They became the closest friends, and their friendship continued through Fox's life. In his letters to Fitzpatrick at all times Fox's mind is always most clearly revealed, for Fitzpatrick was probably the only man to whom he always confided his most intimate reflections and his most private affairs. When Fox was in Italy, they were both students of the drama, for they frequently appeared in private theatricals and had some reputation as actors. 'Mr. Fox', it was said, 'was preferred in tragedy, but Mr. Fitzpatrick was his superior in genteel comedy.'

With Uvedale Price, Charles Fox travelled slowly back to England, stopping at Geneva for a visit to Voltaire. But the great man did not seem inclined to conversation, and after a short stroll in the garden he dismissed them with a list of his principal works and the advice, which many authors might wish, but few would venture, to offer, 'Voilà les livres dont il faut se munir'.

Fox landed in England to find himself a member of Parliament, for a new Parliament had been elected, and Lord Holland, mindful of his own delays and disappointments, believed it impossible to begin the business of politics too early. He had joined forces with his brother to secure a seat in that election, for Lord Ilchester hoped that Parliament might provide some occupation for his son, Lord Stavordale, whose manner of living was beginning to cause anxiety. So the brothers opened negotiations with Lord Montagu's man of affairs, and the electors of Midhurst, nominees of Lord Montagu, to whom some plots of land were formally conveyed for the occasion, unanimously returned the Hon. Charles Fox as their member. He was in no great hurry to begin his new career. Foreign travel was still attractive, and he finished the summer in the Low Countries with his brother and his sister-in-law, for Stephen was now married to a sister of Richard Fitzpatrick. He waited until November to take his seat in Parliament, at the age of nineteen years and ten months.

It was in many respects an unfortunate moment for his début in London, for polite society was undergoing one of the occasional lapses from decorum which enliven social history. 'What is England now?' sighed Horace Walpole, 'A sink of Indian wealth, filled by nabobs and emptied by macaronis!... A gaming, robbing, wrangling, railing nation, without principles, genius, character or allies; the overgrown shadow of what it was.' It is the privilege of the older generation to discover fancied depravity in its successor, and Walpole was no enthusiast of new manners. But he could in the Seventeen-seventies point to noticeable changes in his world; and they were not changes for the better. There was, for example, an undoubted increase in extravagant spending and ostentation. It was not only in public amusements where masked balls at the Pantheon were added to the more sedate pleasures of Ranelagh, and competed with the round of 'balls, op'ras, concerts, Almack's and Soho', where, in days of hunger and high prices, it was said to be customary at the end of an indecorous masquerade 'to fling open the windows and pelt the eager, hungry, thirsty, and howling crowd below with half-empty bottles and the remains of the supper.' Ostentatious extravagance was increasing conspicuously in private life where no expensive eccentricity was thought excessive by the men of fashion, who seemed to compete in ruining themselves by building magnificent country houses to hold the pictures and marbles which they brought home from Italy. It was perhaps, as Walpole suggested, due to the increasing numbers of *nouveaux riches* from the West Indies and India, who at that time shared with the Scotch in popular opinion the blame for much that was undesirable in national life; but, whatever may have been the cause, it was an unfortunate tendency at the moment when a young man of Charles Fox's tastes and training was beginning his career.

More serious than the increasing extravagance was the practice of heavy drinking which seems then to have reached its highest point. Frequent drunkenness with consequent gout and premature old age was regarded in Walpole's world almost as a matter of course, and there was nothing unusual in a young man turning himself into a gouty invalid by a few years of fair drinking in London.

But the most dangerous innovation of all was the increase of gambling and the immense sums which were at that time won and lost. It surpassed anything that had been known, and the gossip of the day returns to it again and again. 'The gaming at Almack's,' wrote Walpole, 'which has taken the place of White's, is worthy the decline of our Empire or Commonwealth, which you please. The young men of age lose five, ten, fifteen thousand pounds in an evening there. Lord Stavordale, not one and twenty, lost eleven thousand there last Tuesday, but recovered it by one great hand at hazard; he swore a great oath—"Now if I had been playing deep, I might have won millions."' And as Walpole found to his cost deep gaming was not confined to men, for at a casual game with Lady Hertford he 'lost fifty six guineas before I could say an "Ave Maria"'.

Into this slightly demoralized world arrived Charles Fox at the age of nineteen. His temperament and training had provided him with many admirable qualities, but they had also produced in him an insatiable desire for emotional excitement of every kind. Lord Holland's system of education had its advantages, but it did not make for discipline or self-control, and it included little or no training in the prudent use of money. It was an unfortunate omission, for Charles Fox's desire for excitement was now to be fed by Lord Holland's new fortune.

His early youth gives an impression of speed, as if he were trying to take in those few years all that life could offer. He must hurry from Wandsworth to Eton and from Eton to Oxford, pursuing with immense energy all the interests and pleasures, high or low, which attracted him; and in each of them, classical reading, politics, gambling, amateur acting, he must take a full share, as if that particular occupation were the only purpose of his life. And if his early youth suggests speed, the velocity after his arrival in London became terrific. Faithful to his plan of living, he became at once a conspicuous devotee of each of the pleasures of London. It is fair to him to say that although he drank, as one of his contemporaries put it, 'what I should call a good deal', he was never a confirmed drunkard. But it must be admitted that this abstention may have been due in part to his preoccupation with other matters, notably gambling, which left him little time for frequent intoxication. For in gambling he was unsurpassed. He was already a member of Brooks's where they played high, and in a few months he had outstripped them all, and became by far the greatest plunger of his time. Many of the older generation were withdrawing from the game in alarm at the new tendency to higher stakes and deeper play, but others, to whom gambling was a profession rather than an amusement, remained to take fortunes from Charles Fox and his friends. If these men, 'the hounds', as Fox and Fitzpatrick called them, played fair, they have been much maligned, and Fox was the most unlucky of gamblers, for his almost invariable losses were proverbial and soon caught the attention of rhymsters:

> At Almack's of pigeons I am told there are flocks;
> But it's thought the completest is one Mr. Fox.
> If he touches a card, if he rattles a box,
> Away fly the guineas of this Mr. Fox.
> He has met, I'm afraid, with so many hard knocks
> The cash is not plenty with this Mr. Fox;
> In gaming, 'tis said he's the stoutest of cocks.
> No man can play deeper than this Mr. Fox,
> And he always must lose, for the strongest of locks
> Cannot keep any money for this Mr. Fox.
> No doubt such behaviour exceedingly shocks
> The friends and relations of this Mr. Fox. . . .

The full amount of his losses in this period of unrestrained gambling will never be known. It certainly exceeded £140,000. Lord Holland paid more than once with increasing despondency, as he saw his Paymaster's accumulations

melt to meet the urgent appeals of his sons, for his eldest son
was almost as reckless a gambler as his second. But appeal
to Lord Holland was not the usual method of payment. The
simpler way was to borrow from Jew money-lenders, who
attended so regularly on Charles Fox, as long as his brother's
bad health and childlessness made him heir presumptive to
the Holland estates, that he called the room where they
waited 'my Jerusalem Chamber'. And the pigeons borrowed
from one another as much as they borrowed from Jews.
Charles Fox and his friends, in different degrees losers to
the rapacious hounds, guaranteed each other's debts, bought
each other's annuities, and postponed each other's pay-
ments, until the collapse of one of the group might have its
repercussion through a series of great houses. Fox had not
been long in London before Lord Carlisle, to the indignant
despair of George Selwyn, had encumbered himself with an
annuity of £1,500 on his behalf, and an annuity of £1,200
was being paid by Mr. Crewe.

The name of Charles Fox is so closely associated with
gambling that the place and importance of gambling in his
life must be considered. He was certainly at that time a
reckless gambler, and, although he afterwards completely
gave up play, he was then quite unable to keep away from it.
But gambling, although his most spectacular interest, was
by no means his only interest. He might lose thousands in
the uninspiring society of the 'hounds', to whom cards were at
once a complete intellectual exercise and sufficient occupation
for life, but he could never be one of them. While he lost fortunes at Brooks's he was gaining the admiring friendship of
such men as Burke and Dr. Johnson, he was making a name
for himself as the greatest of debaters, and through even the
worst days he retained his faculty for intellectual detachment, which enabled him to go home and sit placidly reading Herodotus after a night of unlimited disaster, because
'what else should a man do when he has lost his last shilling?'
But although gambling was only a part, and never the most
important part, of his life, it had effects which make it diffi-

cult to follow the advice of another contemporary rhymster on Fox's character to 'revere the patriot and forget the man '. It is difficult to forget, for instance, that his father and mother were slowly dying, and their last days were made wretched by the behaviour of their two elder sons. Again and again Lady Holland would implore them to think of their father and give up high play, and Charles Fox in an agony of contrition would answer that the one desire of his heart was to give pleasure to his parents, that he had been guilty 'only of dissipation', and dissipation in itself was no crime, but for the future he would beyond question amend. And in a few days he was back at the tables. A letter from Lady Holland to Stephen Fox a few months before she died tells the story: 'Lord Holland is much the same; better I fear, I must never expect to see him. Oh! Ste—, this last attack, whatever it was, I'm confident has been owing to the disagreeable business he has of late been engaged in on your account. Lord Holland's state of health, I'm persuaded, is solely owing to the vexations of his mind, which have been too powerful for a benevolent friendly-feeling heart like his. Rigby Calcraft etc., etc. began; the Duke of Leinster, Lord Hillsbro, Sarah greatly contributed, and Charles Fox and you have put the finishing stroke. How painful this idea must be to you I know. Charles does not feel it, but he will severely one day, so he ought.'

And although we may agree that the possession of money, which he referred to as 'rascal counters', meant very little to Charles Fox, it is difficult to believe that it meant nothing, or that he thought it meant nothing, to the people who lent it. During his days of unrestrained play he lived chiefly on loans, and he borrowed money not only from money-lenders and from his friends, but from any one who could be induced to part with the smallest sum, including the waiters at Brooks's and the chairmen who stood outside Brooks's. If we may accept a most improbable story he even succeeded in borrowing from Casanova, himself a borrower of distinction. It is not easy wholly to excuse such a manner of living.

In one form of speculation the hounds could never catch him. He was devoted to racing, and his knowledge of horses (he was reputed to' be one of the best handicappers in the country) would have brought him winnings which would have seemed substantial, if they had not been swept into insignificance by his gigantic losses at cards. In partnership with Lord Foley he had as many as thirty horses in training, including the famous Pantaloon, a disappointing animal which rarely succeeded in taking the high place expected from its form and training. The well-known description of him at Newmarket might be a picture of his life as he was living it at this time: 'When his horse ran he was all eagerness and anxiety. He placed himself where the animal was to make a push or where the race was to be most strongly contested. From this spot he eyed the horses advancing with the most immovable look; he breathed quicker as they accumulated their pace; and, when they came opposite to him, he rode in with them at full speed, whipping, spurring, and blowing, as if he would have infused his whole soul into his favourite race.'

But he was by training and tradition a politician, and in politics he intended to make his name. Here everything was in his favour. He had ability of the kind which may be called genius; he had eloquence, the pride of Dr. Barnard, destined, as Carlisle had foretold, 'to animate the hearts of fearful statesmen'; he had that physical toughness on which a political career ultimately depends; and he had almost unlimited capacity for making and keeping friends. His seat was waiting for him, and there remained only the choice of a party. That choice, often so embarrassing and disastrous, was greatly simplified by his filial determination that he would not ally himself with his father's enemies. The Duke of Grafton did not fall within that almost universal exclusion, and Charles Fox took his seat as a supporter of the Government.

It was a strange Government, for the King, after experiments with a series of Whig groups—Bedfords, Rockinghams, and Chathams—had now, on the withdrawal of Lord Chatham into a retirement of gout and disappointment, obtained the services of a combined or coalition administration consisting of the remains of the Chatham group mainly sustained by Bedfords. It was, as Burke observed, 'a piece of joinery so crossly indented and whimsically dove-tailed; a cabinet so variously inlaid; such a piece of diversified mosaic; such a tesselated pavement without cement; here a bit of black stone, and there a bit of white; patriots and courtiers; King's friends and republicans; whigs and tories, treacherous friends and open enemies: that it was indeed a very curious show; but utterly unsafe to touch, and unsure to stand on'. Such a Cabinet might have been dominated by a strong leader, but at the head of this curious show was the Duke of Grafton, whose merits did not include either political wisdom or strength of purpose. Nor was it probable that the leader of the House of Commons would display the firmness and judgement which were lacking in his chief; for the leader in the Commons was Lord North, and force of character was not among the many admirable qualities of Lord North.

It was not a Government to face a crisis, and the life of the new Parliament began with the crisis of Mr. Wilkes. No Government of ordinary firmness would have allowed such an affair to become a crisis, still less to develop into one of the major events in the history of British liberty. But through sheer incompetence under the pressure of the King's obstinacy Ministers contrived to stumble from indiscretion to blunder, from blunder to folly, from folly to illegality and misgovernment, until they had drawn into the dispute not only Wilkes and his constituents, but the City, the press, and indignant mobs of Londoners, until riot and window-breaking became almost a commonplace of politics, and members became accustomed to see popular demonstrations outside their House, or as a contemporary satire put it,

> See the mad populace in swarms appear
> Inspired at once by liberty and beer.

It was indeed an age of riot, for demonstration by force of numbers was an almost necessary method of expressing popular feeling, and the riots of Charles Fox's early days in Parliament were not confined to the cause of Wilkes. 'We have', wrote Horace Walpole, 'independent mobs that have nothing to do with Wilkes, and who only take advantage of so favourable a season. The dearness of provisions incites, the hope of increase of wages allures, and drink puts them in motion. The coal-heavers began, and it is well that it is not a hard frost, for they stopped all coals coming to town. The sawyers rose too, and at last the sailors, who have committed great outrages on merchant ships, and prevented them from sailing.'

Charles Fox began to speak early in 1769, and in April he began to attract attention. The debate was on the expulsion of Wilkes after his re-election, and the motion was to declare his defeated opponent to be returned member. On that issue, in which the Government was manifestly wrong, the House was in a turmoil, and a new member could hardly expect a hearing. Stephen and Charles Fox both spoke, and both took the line of contemptuously dismissing the electors of Middlesex and the Wilkite demonstrators as rabble. Stephen began by 'indecently and indiscreetly' describing Wilkes as 'chosen by the scum of the earth'. But it was Stephen's misfortune to provoke irrepressible mirth on all occasions, and none took even his most solemn utterances seriously. But the effect was very different when the younger brother spoke. 'Charles Fox,' wrote Walpole, 'with infinite superiority in parts was not inferior to his brother in insolence.' He repeated his success a few weeks later in another of the Wilkes debates, and this time Walpole recorded that 'Charles Fox, not yet twenty-one, answered Burke with great quickness and parts, but with confidence equally premature'. Cavendish on that occasion begins his report with the words 'Mr. Charles Fox spoke very well'. The report is the barest summary, but the words of that dark eager young member sound through the *oratio obliqua*

in one sentence in which we are told that 'he would not take
the will of the people from a few factious demagogues, any
more than he would take the will of God Almighty from a few
priests who interpreted it for their own interests'.

The delight of Lord Holland was unbounded. Here was
something to compensate him for his own disappointments,
his lost friends, his failing health. His favourite son would
triumph exactly as he meant him to triumph, and if the appeals
for money became rather frequent and formidable, no one
would mind less than Lord Holland, although satirists
might use the son's losses for a sneer at the father's gains:

> Me let old Reynard still supply
> With thousands got or how, or why
> Concerns me not 'tis all the same,
> They're his from whence-soe'er they came.

During the winter Charles Fox was in Paris. Like most
men of fashion, he was almost as much at home in French
society as in English, and his letters, like those of Selwyn
and Horace Walpole, constantly break into French. He was
received with enthusiasm in Paris both for his own sake and
for the sake of the English guineas which he would lose to
French rooks as cheerfully as he had lost them to English
hounds. It was from this visit to Paris that Mme du Deffand
began writing to her friend Horace Walpole that well-known
series of Fox Bulletins which have so often been quoted as a
critical appraisement of his character. The impressions of this
venerable lady were important, for she had for generations
given the law of elegance and wit to the most brilliant society
of Paris, and she was by no means ready to resign her position. She was then, as Walpole wrote, 'now very old and
stone blind, but retains all her vivacity, wit, memory, judgement, passions, and agreeableness. She goes to opera, plays,
suppers, and Versailles; gives suppers twice a week; has
everything new read to her; makes new songs and epigrams,
aye, admirably, and remembers everyone that has been
made these four score years.' Many young Englishmen of
family, finishing their Grand Tour, were brought into her

formidable presence, and her opinions of them, retailed in
London by Walpole or Selwyn, were treated with respect.

At their first meeting this ancient oracle observed that 'Le
petit Fox a infiniment d'esprit, mais c'est de ces esprits de
tête', but her critical faculties were perhaps not at their best
on that occasion, for she proceeds in the same letter to compare the character of Horace Walpole, the urbane and worldly
wise, to that of Don Quixote. They met often during the
winter, and her impressions remained unfavourable. One
day she found that he had 'beaucoup d'esprit, mais il a pris
toute sa croissance, il n'ira pas plus loin'. A week later she took
the opposite view, and foretold that 'son imagination, son
feu, le mèneront loin, mais il croit trouver tout en lui et il
négligera toujours l'instruction et l'étude dont il n'aura pas
besoin pour la circonstance du moment. Enfin je ne vois pas
qu'il ait de la nature. Il y a du Jean Jacques.' Then she
wrote that although 'le petit Fox m'a étonnée, éblouie', and
they were 'fort bien ensemble', she had decided that 'son
esprit me paraît médiocre, et son caractère détestable'. Her
judgement was perhaps influenced by her dislike of high
gambling, and perhaps also by the fact that 'le petit Fox' spent
some of his time in the society of three ladies whom she knew
and disliked under the name of 'les oiseaux de passage'.
The impressions which he made in his travels that winter
were not all unfavourable. He again called upon Voltaire,
and this time the meeting was a complete success, as Voltaire
informed Lord Holland: 'Your son is an English lad, and I
an old Frenchman. He is healthy and I sick. Yet I love him
with all my heart, not only for his father but for himself.'

While Fox gossiped and gamed in Paris he missed a
dramatic moment in politics at home, for in these weeks
Lord Chatham made one of his spectacular reappearances in
public life, and the shock of it was too much for the Duke of
Grafton's government. A supreme crisis of gout had restored
him to a state in which he might once more 'lay himself with
all Duty and Submission at the King's Feet'; but the King
found that Lord Chatham's duty, as he conceived it, was to

utter a solemn warning on the dangers of misgovernment, and his submission included a destructive review of the course taken by the King and his ministers in the affairs of Wilkes. Then his voice was heard in the House of Lords with something of its old authority denouncing the failure of ministers to observe these first principles of honest administration and respect for law on which government depends. The effect was instantaneous. The Lord Chancellor, who had followed his colleagues in the affair of Wilkes much against his judgement and conscience, resigned on the spot, and after desperate efforts to fill his place the Duke of Grafton, remarking that his 'head turned', followed his Lord Chancellor. The King was prepared for a change; he had, indeed, been ready for weeks; and at the age of thirty-seven Frederick, Lord North, became First Lord of the Treasury.

The King might congratulate himself on his choice. He liked a gentleman, and Lord North was a gentleman; he liked respectability, and Lord North was respectable; and above all things he liked obedience, and Lord North was above all things obedient. Statesmen are labelled so successfully by their caricaturists that Lord North has come down to us in the image of somnolent and genial stupidity. At Eton his tutor had assured him that he was 'a blundering blockhead, and if you are Prime Minister, it will always be the same'. 'And', as Lord North himself would afterwards remark, 'it turned out to be so.' But the tutor was wrong, for Lord North turned out to be a first-rate parliamentarian and debater, as his opponents often found to their cost.

> When Barré stern, with accents deep;
> Calls up Lord North and murders sleep,
> And if his Lordship rise to speak
> Then wit and argument awake.

But the Government had lost some of its strongest members under Chatham's attack, and Lord North's wit and argument alone were insufficient to fill the void. It was a moment for promotions, and in a few days Charles Fox had his chance. Wedderburn, who was among the least popular of lawyers in the House, was saying that no precedent could be found for some proposal in the interminable troubles of Wilkes. Charles Fox jumped up and quoted an exact precedent of the year before. 'The House', said Walpole, 'roared with applause', and Fox became a junior Lord of the Admiralty.

The work of a junior Lord was certainly not onerous. It consisted largely of routine instructions and of adding a signature to those of two of his colleagues on official letters and orders. Charles Fox showed no signs of shirking his duties. From the 30th of March, when he first appeared at the office after his re-election for Midhurst, he took his full share of the work. His first official act was the purchase upon the best and cheapest terms of a schooner to survey the coast of Nova Scotia, and thenceforward his name appears in regular recurrence directing that Mr. Ford, the carpenter of the Royal George, be superannuated, that experiments (they proved successful) be made on the utility of Captain Bentinck's pump, that foreigners and strangers be excluded from the dockyard, that four midshipmen and a surgeon's mate, dismissed for smuggling at Cadiz, be reinstated at the request of His Catholic Majesty, that ships be paid off, refitted, and repaired, and that imprests be paid and accounts passed. No doubt his duties were mainly formal, but they must have taught him something of naval affairs, and perhaps laid the foundation for that interest in the Navy which he showed all his life.

But Lord North had not appointed him to sign minutes and routine letters at the Admiralty. He was wanted to defend the Government in Parliament, and in this his success was unquestioned. It was not only that he spoke brilliantly and could be extremely formidable to an enemy in debate, and it was not only that he was as indifferent to the denunciations of Chatham in the House of Lords as he was to the roars of Wilkite demonstrators in Whitehall. He had all these advantages in his favour, and he added to them the further advantage of discovering a political philosophy in his defence of the Government. His defence was based, by an ingenious paradox, on the principle of true Freedom, by which he meant the freedom and independence of Parliament. In his view Parliament alone represented the people, and the dignity of Parliament and the liberty of Parliament must be maintained against attack from any quarter, whether it be insults from printers, threat of force from a mob, or coercion by the King. True to this doctrine, he was able to invest the Government's contempt for Wilkites and printers with something approaching dignity and principle. 'I am not disposed', he proclaimed in a debate on the freedom of the press, 'to take the voice of a miserable faction for the voice of my country. Were the people really dissatisfied, I should be glad to know how I can ascertain the reality of that dissatisfaction. I must freely confess I know no other way but that of consulting the House.' In another debate on the same subject he declared that he would 'pay no regard whatever to the voice of the people: it is our duty to do what is proper, without considering what may be agreeable'. And the same speech contained a passage in his most stirring manner on the 'independency' of Parliament: 'Whether that independency be attacked by the people or by the Court is a matter of little consequence: it is the attack, not the quarter it proceeds from, which we are to punish; and if we are to be controlled in our necessary jurisdiction, can it signify much, whether faction intimidate us with a rabble, or the King surround us with his guards?'

His speeches at that time return again and again to the same doctrine. 'The only point therefore to be discussed', he proclaimed on a day when Whitehall was filled with a thunderous mob, 'is whether the people at large, or this House, are the best judge of the public welfare? For my part, Sir, I shall not hesitate to pronounce positively in favour of this House. What acquaintance have the people at large with the arcana of political rectitude, with the connections of kingdoms, the resources of national strength,

the abilities of ministers, or even with their own disposi-
tions?' And once more he utters his warning that the
threat to Parliamentary Government might come with equal
danger from King or mob: 'I will for argument's sake allow
that nine tenths of the people are at this moment in opposition to Government. But I shall at the same time insist,
that we have higher obligations to justice than to our constituents; we are chosen the delegates of the British electors
for salutory not for pernicious purposes; to guard not to
invade the constitution; to keep the privileges of the very
freemen we represent, as much within their proper limit,
as to control any unwarrantable exertion of the Royal
authority.'

It was a perverse and paradoxical defence of a Government which was living from hand to mouth with hardly a
pretence of political principle, but it was not a dishonest
defence; and it was not so sharply opposed to the principles
of his later life as might appear from a first sight of the
policy and practices which he then defended. His belief
in the independence of Parliament was genuine, as his long
conflict with the King was to show.

But such speeches, although they were highly effective,
were unlikely to make him a popular hero or to gain him
the affection of the King. 'I would not have them afraid,'
wrote his father, commenting on the terminology of his
sons, 'but I would have them more cautious of the mob than
they are. But calling them a mob is an offence and some
gentlemen in the House of Commons of great property were
very angry that the people of England (the dirtiest Black-
guards, I am told, and lowest rabble you ever looked at)
should be so term'd.' Charles Fox is reported to have
carried his defiance of the mob outside the House, for a
newspaper describes him as provoking a crowd with 're-
proachful words' from the window of a coffee-house in
Palace Yard, while Mr. Georgé Selwyn 'clapp'd him on the
back as if he was a dirty ruffian going to fight in the
streets'. He had certainly caught popular attention, for, as

the Black Boy or the Cub, he was now held up to execration
as the enemy of the people's rights, and on days of riot he
was one of the chief objects of attack. As to the King,
Charles Fox started with the handicap of being Lord Holland's son, his notoriety as a gambler increased the royal
disapproval, and his views on parliamentary independence
turned disapproval to aversion. He was popular in the
House, but his manner in debate was not always conciliatory. A wrangle with Wedderburn on an alleged misquota-
tion would have led to a challenge, if the Speaker had not
stopped him as he was hurrying from the House and patched
up a reconciliation. Later he came into conflict with his
friend Burke, but no mediation was needed to restore good
temper between them. He laughed while Burke was de-
claiming on the problem caused by the accidental inclusion
of a harmless but unauthorized spectator in a division;
Burke turned to snap at him that 'a gentleman capable of
laughing at this may make a laugh of anything'; but Fox
could endure reproof from Burke, and he restored peace by
a cheerful promise to admit himself wrong, 'if when I see
the honourable gentleman to-morrow he does not laugh too'.

His first year of office was spent at high speed on a round
which included Brooks's, Parliament, Newmarket, the Admiralty, cricket and partridges at Kingsgate, and some
country houses. The hounds were at him whenever they
had a chance, and his losses were the talk of London. He
was living with Fitzpatrick in lodgings over the shop of
Mackie, the grocer, in Piccadilly, and when doubts were
expressed whether the tenancy would be profitable to the
landlord, Selwyn was able to point out that Mackie would
at any rate be able to advertise that he kept the best pickles
in London. The elder brother, Stephen, was also a reckless
gambler, and it was well·for the family that the youngest
son, Henry, now gazetted to the Dragoons, did not follow
the example of his elders.

During the next year—it was 1771—the pace seemed to
increase. His speeches were more provocative, his gambling

wilder, and his losses heavier. It was an eventful session, and he took his full share in it. There was the unpleasant discovery that electors at New Shoreham had formed themselves into a 'Christian Club' for the purpose of collective bargaining in the sale of their votes, and he opposed the inquiry which led to the disfranchisement of members of the Christian Club. There was the matter of Nullum Tempus, when he intervened, 'the phenomenon of the age', as Walpole now described him, to discover a ground of principle in the case for Sir James Lowther and defeat a Bill which would certainly have become law if he had not spoken. And there was the long wrangle with printers developing from a reference to Colonel George Onslow, M.P., as 'little cocking George' by some obscure reporter, into a dispute with the Lord Mayor and Aldermen with riotous demonstrations round Parliament. The riot on the 27th of March surpassed anything known in the riotous history of that Parliament. The Lord Mayor had been ordered to attend, and 'accompanied by his committee and a vast number of merchants, tradesmen, and other citizens, proceeded to the House of Commons, amidst the acclamations of the populace'. The crowd was in a dangerous mood, and Charles Fox was the chief object of its fury. Only a few days before a large stone had crashed through both windows of his chariot, and now the same chariot was broken up and he was rolled in the gutter and pelted with mud. Lord North had the misfortune to be mistaken for Charles Fox, and was rescued with difficulty.

He ended the summer with some desperate losses, and retired to Kingsgate to reduce the increasing roundness of his figure by cricket and partridge shooting. During the winter he was again in Paris with Fitzpatrick and Lord Robert Spencer. Mme du Deffand was favourably impressed by le Fitzpatrick who had *douceur* and *souplesse*, but she was still doubtful about le Fox, although she was careful to record that he was not conceited and 'n'a point l'air méprisant ni vain'. This time she found him impetuous

and superficial. 'Pour le Fox', she wrote, 'il est dur, hardi,
l'esprit prompt; il a le confiance de son mérite; il ne se
donne pas le temps de l'examen, il voit tout à vue d'oiseau,
et je doute fort qu'il fasse la distinction d'un homme à
un autre.'

When Parliament met in January 1772 he showed that
the enforced silence of the recess had been distasteful to
him. He began at once by giving notice that he would introduce a new Marriage Bill to repeal and replace the Clandestine Marriages Act, on which his father had wasted so much
eloquence twenty years before. He had not apparently
read the Marriage Act when he moved its repeal, for his
attention was at the moment occupied by certain urgent
transactions with his money-lenders, but he could rely on
his father's help before the debates on his bill began. In
February he attracted some attention by his defence of
the Thirty-nine Articles against a petition urging that the
clergy should no longer be compelled to subscribe to that
formidable document. Religion, he opined, was 'best understood when least talked of'. 'He did not shine in this
debate,' wrote Horace Walpole, 'nor could it be wondered
at. He had sat up playing hazard at Almack's, from Tuesday evening 6th, till five in the afternoon of Wednesday
7th. An hour before, he had recovered £12,000 that he had
lost, and by dinner, which was at five o'clock, he had ended
losing £11,000. On the Thursday he spoke in this debate,
went to dinner at past eleven at night: from thence to
White's, where he drank till seven the next morning; thence
to Almack's, where he won £6,000; and between three and
four in the afternoon he had set out for Newmarket.'

If his time had been less actively occupied he might have
learned that his was not the only Marriage Bill on the
political horizon, for the King was meditating a rather
belated control of the matrimonial ventures of his family,
and on the 20th of February a Royal Message was conveyed to Parliament requesting that provision be made
that all future marriages of descendants of King George II

should be invalid unless approved by the King. It was evident in advance that such a Bill, however skilfully it might be drafted, would be used with effect by the Opposition, who would make the most of it as an insult to the English peerage and as a measure 'giving leave to the Princes of the Blood to lie with our wives, and forbidding them to marry our daughters'. It was an addition to the many unpleasant duties which Lord North was required to perform, and he undertook it with obedient despondency, which turned to dismay when he received Charles Fox's resignation as the first result of the royal message.

The Fox family was always peculiarly sensitive to any amendment of the Marriage Laws. In the present case the amendment would affect only the descendants of George II; but the powers which the King now claimed would have made impossible such a marriage as he had himself proposed to Lady Sarah Lennox. The Bill could not be approved at Holland House, and Charles Fox determined to oppose it. Walpole has suggested that he may have had other grounds for dissatisfaction, but the immediate occasion of his resignation was, as he himself said, the Royal Marriage Bill. 'I should not', he wrote, 'have resigned at this moment merely on account of my complaint against Lord North, if I had not determined to vote against this *Royal Family* Bill, which in place I should be ashamed of doing. Upon the whole I am convinced I did right, and I think myself very safe from going into opposition, which is the only danger.' No doubt he had in mind his future career and his chances of returning to office; and it was no doubt pleasant to his gambling instinct to lay the foundations of success and promotion, and then hazard his future at a moment when he was faced with financial ruin. But it was something more than either a conscientious declaration of principle on Royal Marriages or a magnificent gamble. His resignation showed that, although his political ambitions were high, his political freedom came first, and he would not surrender it for security of office or hope of promotion. He

would choose his own course, submitting neither to Court
nor party.

Meanwhile he was moving at his highest speed towards
the inevitable crash. Transactions with money-lenders were
becoming more frequent; the anxiety of friends who had
given security for his debts was becoming graver; and the
taunts of lampoons were becoming sharper:

> By turns solicited by different plans,
> Yet fixed to none, Fox dresses, games, harangues,
> Where varying fashion leads the sportive band,
> And whim and folly bound it hand in hand,
> Behold him ambling through those flow'ry ways,
> A model macaroni, à l'Angloise.

In spite of his increasing bulk he remained for a few years
longer a model macaroni, with his 'little odd French hat,
shoes, red heels, &c.' in which he could be seen any day in
St. James's Street. It was rumoured that his fortunes were
to be restored by marriage with an heiress, and his father
was asked whether the story could be confirmed. 'I only
hope it is true,' said Lord Holland, 'for then he will have
to go to bed for at least one night in his life.'

He opposed the Royal Marriage Bill, but it was observed
that he avoided offending Lord North. The world waited
for April, when the debate on his own Marriage Bill was due,
and that debate, when it came, brought Horace Walpole
hobbling goutily back to the House to record his impression
of the new prodigy:

'Though I had never been in the House of Commons
since I had quitted Parliament, the fame of Charles Fox
roused my curiosity and I went this day to hear him. He
made his motion for leave to bring in a bill to correct the
old Marriage Bill, and he introduced it with ease, grace, and
clearness, and without the prepared or elegant formality
of a young speaker. He did not shine particularly; but his
sense and facility showed he could shine. . . . Lord North,
who had declared he would not oppose the introduction of
the new bill, now unhandsomely opposed it to please the

Yorkes and Peers, and spoke well. . . . Burke made a long and fine oration against the motion. . . . Two-thirds of this oration resembled the beginning of a book on speculative doctrines, and yet argument was not the forte of it. Charles Fox, who had been running about the House talking to different persons and scarce listening to Burke, rose with amazing spirit and memory, answered both Lord North and Burke; ridiculed the arguments of the former and confuted those of the latter. . . . Charles Fox had great facility of delivery; his words flowed rapidly but he had nothing of Burke's variety of language or correctness, nor his method. Yet his arguments were far more shrewd; he was many years younger. Burke was indefatigable, learned, and versed in every branch of eloquence. Fox was dissolute, dissipated, idle beyond measure. He was that very morning returned from Newmarket, where he had lost some thousands of pounds the preceding day. He had stopped at Hockerel, where he found company, had sat up drinking all night, and had not been to bed when he came to move his bill, which he had not even drawn up. This was genius—was almost inspiration.' So thought Walpole, and the House agreed with him, for they supported the Bill, defeating Lord North by a majority of one vote, and causing that statesman the most anxious reflection to devise some means of getting this dangerous deserter back to the ministerial fold.

The Bill had produced its effect, and it was allowed to die a few weeks later, when its author arrived from Newmarket just as it was rejected.

Lord North saw no hope of tranquillity with Charles Fox out of the Government. There was a desperate shuffling of places. A well-paid Vice-Treasurer of Ireland was induced by the offer of a special salary to become Captain of the Band of Pensioners; a junior Lord was promoted to be Vice-Treasurer of Ireland; and Charles Fox became a junior Lord of the Treasury at £1,600 a year. His critics accused him of taking it in the hopes of becoming Chancellor of the Exchequer if Lord North succeeded his father, but they consoled themselves with the reflection that 'the *odds* (to use a language he is not wholly a stranger to) are much against him'.

It was an important post, for, although the Treasury demanded less attendance to the routine of office by its Junior Lord than had been expected at the Admiralty, the political duties were greater, and it was a recognized step to promotion. But if by giving him political duties Lord North hoped to reduce him to obedience, he was quickly disappointed. In his second term of office Fox seemed anxious above all things to show that by accepting office he did not surrender his independence or bind himself to support his chief. In February they were back at their old subject of the Thirty-nine Articles, and Charles Fox spoke and told against his chief. During the summer they discussed the affairs of the East India Company and Lord North had to endure the agony of hearing Lord Clive, the owner of at least ten seats and the possible purchaser of more, denounced by his Commissioner of the Treasury as 'the origin of all plunders, the source of all robbery'; and in a later debate Lord Clive was driven from the House 'with anger or shame' by the invective of the same speaker.

It was a bad year for Charles Fox, for the money-lenders no longer waited with accommodating offers of cash in his Jerusalem Chamber. They knew that his sister-in-law, Lady Mary Fox, was expecting a child, and, if it should be a son, there was the end of their debtor's hope of the Holland estates. They awaited the event anxiously and cut off the supply of loans, leaving him to borrow what he could from any one who could be induced to lend. Meanwhile creditors were drawing in, and the hounds were at him night after night. His father was manifestly dying, and must not be asked for money even by a favourite son at his wits' end. During that desperate summer, when any night a run at Brooks's might still put everything straight, he seems for a moment to have lost his head. There was a scandal.

A shady adventuress, calling herself the Honourable Mrs. Grieve, was arrested for fraud and, in the course of the hearing, a story was revealed, which Walpole lost no time in proclaiming: 'In a word the famous Charles Fox had been the bubble of this woman, who undoubtedly had uncommon talents and a knowledge of the world. She persuaded Fox, desperate with debts, that she could procure him as a wife, a Miss Phipps, with a fortune of £80,000, who had just arrived from the West Indies. There was such a person coming over, but not with half the fortune, nor known to Mrs. Grieve. With this bait she amused Charles for many months, appointed meetings, and once persuaded him that, as Miss Phipps liked a fair man, and as he was remarkably black, he must powder his eyebrows. Of that intended interview he was disappointed by the imaginary lady's falling ill of what was afterwards pretended to be the small-pox. . . . Had a novice been a prey of those artifices, it would not have been extraordinary, but Charles Fox had been in the world from his childhood, and been treated as a man long before the season. He must have known that there could not have been an Hon. Mrs. Grieve nor such a being as she pretended to be. Indeed, in one stroke she had singular finesse; instead of asking him for money, which would have detected her plot at once, she was so artful as to lend him £300, or thereabouts, and paid herself by his chariot standing frequently at her door, which served to impose on her more vulgar dupes.'

Most of this, the powdered eyebrows and the pretence of small-pox, may be treated as mischievous gossip, and it would be pleasant to dismiss the whole story in the same way. The deliberate pursuit of an unknown heiress for her money is so remote from the principles and practice of Fox, as to be almost incredible. But unfortunately the most partial of his apologists could never entirely reject the story, and his solitary reference to it ('She got nothing out of me') is certainly not a denial. He was, as Walpole says, desperate. He believed, as gamblers always believe, that with a little more rope everything could still be saved. Mrs. Grieve gave him a small loan with a vague prospect of more, and that prospect would be enough to entrap him for the moment without any bait of a mythical heiress.

The final crisis came on the 21st of November, when an heir was born to his brother, 'a little Messiah', as Charles Fox cheerfully remarked, 'born for the destruction of the Jews'. In a moment every creditor was upon him. There were the money-lenders claiming debts which he could never pay; there were his friends who had stood him security and would now be crippled; there were tradesmen and servants who had trusted him and were faced with ruin. Everything was involved; the racing partnership with Lord Foley was dissolved; the famous Pantaloon, who so nearly won him fortunes at Newmarket, was sold; the chariot so impressive to the clients of Mrs. Grieve was taken; and still the debts poured in until it seemed that he would be forced to join other distinguished plungers in exile abroad. There could be no question of keeping it from his father, who now worn out in mind and body was wearily hoping for a speedy death. Lord Holland did not hesitate for a moment in the last magnificent gesture of his life. He ordered his agents to 'pay and discharge the debts of my son the Honble. Charles James Fox not exceeding the sum of one Hundred Thousand pounds', and he went on paying when the debts far exceeded the first estimate.

Charles Fox was free, chastened, and repentant, but by no means cured. The thought of his mother's reproaches and his father's anxiety was unbearable, and he began urgently to plan a new career. He would earn his living; he would be called to the Bar; and his friends at Brooks's began to exchange bets on the probability and date of his call. He was at the same time considering an alternative plan, hardly less laborious, to restore his fortunes by means of 'a kind of itinerant trade, which was of going from horse race to horse race, and so, by knowing the value and speed of all the horses in England, to acquire a certain fortune'. No doubt he felt ashamed and no doubt he intended to reform his life, but his resolution did not endure, and he never went farther in the experiment of earning his living.

In Parliament he was as arrogant as ever. The House was again in conflict with a printer, Mr. Woodfall, who had printed an attack on the Speaker written by the cantankerous parson Horne. Their recent experience of printers had been unfortunate, and Lord North would thankfully have left ill alone. But Fox, invoking the privilege and dignity of Parliament, persisted in the attack and committed his suffering chief to decisions which could only lead to trouble. The climax came when Lord North found himself pledged against his convictions to support his junior Lord in a motion that the offending printer should be committed to Newgate instead of to the custody of the Sergeant-at-Arms. There were precedents to the contrary, but Charles Fox would not withdraw, and Lord North was forced to vote with him in a minority of 68 against 152. The King was furious. 'I am greatly incensed', he wrote in one of that procession of notes which made his Minister's life a burden, 'at the presumption of Charles Fox in forcing you to vote with him last night, but approve much of your making your friends vote in the majority. Indeed, that young man has so thoroughly cast off every principle of common honour and honesty that he must become as contemptible as he is odious. I hope you will let him know that you are not insensible of his conduct towards you.'

Between the relentless discipline of his King and the levity of his subordinate, Lord North groaned in spirit. This combination of oppressions was beyond bearing; and, gloomily reflecting upon the uncongenial future, he decided to rid himself of that of his two tyrants who was amenable to dismissal. If tradition may be accepted, his decision was conveyed in a form which he must have known would earn a twinkle of appreciation from the recipient:

'His Majesty has thought proper to order a new Com-

mission of the Treasury to be made out, in which I do not
see your name.

28th February, 1774.   NORTH.'

To Lord Holland it was the last of his life's disappointments. His whole teaching had been directed to one great
purpose, that his son should begin early, climb to the top,
and stay there. And here was his son turned out in disgrace with no prospect of getting back. The old man wished
for death more ardently than ever. His mind was failing and
his body was nearly worn out. The end came peacefully on
the 1st of July, and Lady Holland followed him three weeks
later. For months she had suffered an agony of pain, and
had lived only by an effort of will to nurse her husband.

'Does the world talk of our orators, poets or wits?'
wrote Walpole a few months later. 'Oh, no! It talks of vast
fortunes lost at play! It talks of Wilkes at the top of the
Wheel and of Charles Fox at the bottom: all between is a
blank.'

CHAPTER IV

1774–1782

CHARLES FOX at the bottom of the wheel was hardly an over-statement in the spring of 1774. In his short career he had soared high, the phenomenon of the age, and his fall had the same superlative quality of his rise. It seemed to be final. He could look forward to nothing but enmity from the King; with that enmity he could hope for nothing from Lord North; nor did it seem probable, after his declarations during the last four years, that either of the Opposition groups, Rockinghams or Chathams, would hold out a hand to him.

His fall was great, but his years in London had not been wasted. He had shown that he could become one of the most notable members of a House of Commons in which he was the youngest; and he had made some friends. At the moment when his fortunes seemed lowest he was made a member of The Club, and admission to that society was a distinction which might well restore his self-confidence. And he had the friendship of Edmund Burke.

It was not a new friendship, for they had known and liked one another from the days when Charles Fox came up from Eton to hear debates, and they found that, in spite of obvious divergences in tastes, they had much in common. Burke had made surprising progress since those early days when Horace Walpole had noticed his meditations on the Sublime and the Beautiful ('a sensible man, but has not worn off his authorism yet, and thinks there is nothing so charming as writers, and to be one. He will know better one of these days.') From the Sublime and the Beautiful he had turned to the Present Discontents; he had sat nearly ten years in Parliament; and as Lord Rockingham's secretary he was now preaching to the Whigs that political philosophy from which subsequent generations have drawn inspiration. It was not an easy task, for he had to devise anew, rather than revive, the political principles of his

party. They had ruled the country for so long without
any effective opposition that policy and principles had been
lost in the conviction that a group of Whig families could
claim, almost unchallenged, the government of the country.
This long-established security and failure of political principles, which came from security, was one of the causes of their
collapse when the extinction of all Jacobite hopes made it
possible for the King and Lord Bute to turn to other supporters. But the qualities of Burke were peculiarly suited
to his task. He had an unusual facility for defining abstract
principles and at the same time complying with the demands
of expediency. By this process he was able with complete
honesty of thought to devise a policy which would appeal to
'the Great' who led his party. Under his guidance they
could, for example, oppose electoral reform, but they could
demand the reform of government by the removal of corruption. This accorded with Burke's respect for the existing
structure of the constitution, and it accorded also with the
feelings of the Whig noblemen, who had no fancy to surrender their pocket boroughs, but were delighted to attack the
system of corrupt government, sinecures, pensions, places,
contracts, which had been their own weapon and was now a
weapon of the Court. But even when their principles were defined for them, the Rockingham Whigs were not enthusiastic
politicians, and Burke had to struggle against the superior
attractions of Newmarket, hunting, and country houses.
They believed that activity in Parliament would achieve nothing, and they were not disposed to exert themselves at Westminster to no purpose, when life could be more pleasantly
spent elsewhere. In his efforts to instil new life and energy
into his party Burke may often have wished for such a recruit as Charles Fox, but Walpole's ridiculous story, that
Fox's quarrel with North was the result of an elaborate intrigue by Burke, has nothing to support it. Their friendship
was a real one, and it did not depend upon political sympathy.
Their views on general principles were not far apart, and no
intrigue was needed to bring them together.

Their political alliance was finally brought about by chance. At the moment Fox left office a great political issue was beginning to overshadow the questions on which he had so vehemently declared his views. In the matter of the American colonies he agreed with Burke, and in that matter he had not committed himself when he was with the Government. He had perhaps found the subject distasteful, for the immediate question arose on the payment of a war debt of £70,000,000 on the Seven Years War, and the discharge of debts was not a subject which attracted him. It was, indeed, a subject for which few members of Parliament could feel enthusiasm, for the glory of victory remained with Lord Chatham, while the payment for it, coupled with Lord Chatham's criticisms, were the portion of his successors.

But the real issue was a matter more important than the payment of war debts, and more important than the power of Parliament to tax colonists and put down smuggling. The machinery of the British Empire was out of date, and a new British Empire must be built up. The old system of the Acts of Trade, which made the trade of a colony subject to the convenience of traders at home, and compelled colonists to trade only with Britain or with such other countries as the British Government might decide, was out of date. It was still one of the usual conditions which European countries imposed on their colonies, but it was unsuitable to modern trade, and it was evaded by a general system of smuggling. Great measures of reconstruction were needed to realize a new vision of Empire, but it was unlikely that such a view of the question would commend itself either to the King or to the ministers of his choice.

The immediate issue was less edifying. The war debt had been incurred largely in defence of the colonists, and the colonists showed no sign of either taxing themselves or of providing for their own defence. In the absence of agreement the King and his Ministers proposed to enforce what they believed on good advice to be the right of Parliament to

tax the colonies. But their proceedings during the last ten
years almost invited opposition. Grenville had imposed a
stamp duty, and Rockingham had repealed it with a declaration that the right of Parliament remained unaltered. Then
Charles Townshend had imposed duties on five commodi-
ties, and three years later they were all withdrawn except
the trifling duty on tea, which was the occasion of the present
trouble. Opinion in London was divided on the right of
taxation, and it is not surprising that the colonists felt themselves encouraged to resist. Nor is it surprising that they
should make their stand on the question of taxation rather
than on the Acts of Trade and the suppression of smuggling,
which were in fact the more important of the government
measures; for a call to arms against taxation without
representation was at once more inspiring and more dignified
than a national uprising in defence of smuggling.

In his short terms of office Charles Fox had seen something of the American trouble. He was at the Admiralty
when news arrived of the Boston massacre, in which some
bewildered soldiers, surrounded and pelted by a hostile mob,
at last fired off seven muskets without orders; and he was at
the Admiralty when inquiries were made as to the extent of
smuggling and the force which would be needed to suppress
it. At the Treasury he could examine other aspects of the
problem—the war debt, the cost of a defence force, the
revenue to be expected from duties—and at every stage
there was Burke with his illuminating comments. But he did
not need Burke's persuasion to make up his mind to support
the colonists. All through his life he intensely disliked the
idea of coercion by force of arms, and he could not easily endure the thought of an army crossing the Atlantic to reduce
the Americans to submission.

In March Lord North decided—it was his answer to the
Boston tea party—to close the Port of Boston, and on the
19th of April Burke and Fox spoke on the same side. It was
one of Burke's greater speeches, and he reviewed the history
of the dispute, defining the principles of taxation and the

principles of government. A few passages convey something of his manner:

'Never have the servants of the state looked at the whole of your complicated interests in one connected view. They have taken things, by bits and scraps, some at one time and one pretence, and some at another, just as they pressed, without any sort of regard to their relations or dependencies. They never had any kind of system, right or wrong; but only invented occasionally some miserable tale for the day, in order meanly to sneak out of difficulties into which they had proudly strutted. And they were put to all these shifts and devices, full of meanness and full of mischief, in order to pilfer piecemeal a repeal of an Act which they had not the generous courage, when they found and felt their error, honourably and fairly to disclaim. By such management, by the irresistible operation of feeble councils, so paltry a sum as 3d. in the eyes of a financier, so insignificant an article as tea in the eyes of a philosopher, have shaken the pillars of a commercial empire that circled the whole globe. . . .

'No man ever doubted that the commodity of tea could bear an imposition of three pence. But no commodity will bear three pence, or will bear a penny, when the general feelings of men are irritated, and two millions of people are resolved not to pay. The feelings of the colonies were formerly the feelings of Great Britain. Theirs were formerly the feelings of Hampden when called upon for the payment of twenty shillings. Would twenty shillings have ruined Mr. Hampden's fortune? No! But the payment of half twenty shillings on the principle it was demanded, would have made him a slave. . . .

'Let us, Sir, embrace some system or other before we end this session. Do you mean to tax America, and to draw a productive revenue from thence? If you do, speak out; name, fix, ascertain this revenue; settle its quantity; define its objects; provide for its collection; and then fight when you have got something to fight for. If you murder—rob! If you kill, take possession; and do not appear in the character

of madmen, as well as assassins, violent, vindictive, bloody
and tyrannical, without an object. But may better counsels
guide you.'

Fox followed with a short speech, putting his point forcibly in two sentences:

'A tax can only be laid for three purposes: the first for a
commercial regulation, the second for a revenue, and the
third for asserting your rights. As to the first, it has clearly
been denied that it is for either; as to the latter, it is only
done with a view to irritate and declare war against the
Americans, which, if you persist in, I am clearly of opinion
you will effect, or force them into open rebellion.'

He renewed his attack a few days later with a sarcastic
review of Rigby's suggestion that until 'things were returned
to a peaceable state' the colonies should not be taxed:
'So I find that taxes are to be the reward of obedience;
and the Americans, who are considered to have been in open
rebellion, are to be rewarded by acquiescing in their measures.
When will be the time that America ought to have heavy
taxes laid upon her? The right honourable gentleman tells
you that that time is when the Americans are returned to
peace and quietness.'

From Rigby he turned his attack on Lord North, whom he
charged with 'impudent and shameless silence', but the victim scored a point by remarking that he had never heard of
impudent silence, but he had 'seen gentlemen on their legs
whose shameless impudence shocked all mankind'.

The death of his parents left Fox in precarious solvency.
Lord Holland, who had already paid the debts of his two
elder sons, left, according to Walpole, 'everything to his
wife, and £400,000 of public money. She paid all the debts
of her two eldest sons; so Stephen remained possessed of
£10,000 a year; Charles had a place of £600 a year, an estate
of £200 and £10,000 in money; Henry, the youngest, had
£20,000 and £900 a year.' It was a short-lived solvency, for
the new life, which was to begin with his father's payment of
debts, was haunted by inconvenient creditors whose claims,

forgotten in that great liquidation were now merged in a new burden of debts. He was still gambling, and still losing. The losses were no longer on the old spectacular scale. Indeed he sometimes won now, and it was sometimes possible for an alert creditor to secure a share of the winnings before the whole was swept away in the next loss. But the luck, or the play, was still against him in the long run; his friends shook their heads over his future, and Selwyn could see no hope 'till he is less intoxicated than he is with the all-sufficiency, as he imagines, of his parts. I think that and his infinite contempt of the *qu'en dira-t-on*, upon every point which governs the rest of mankind are the . . . chief causes of all his misfortunes.' Carlisle still feared that his friend's career would be devoted to a fretful search for loans to discharge gambling debts, instead of 'following the natural bent of his genius'. 'I believe', he said, 'there never was a person yet created who had the faculty of reasoning like him. His judgements are never wrong; his decision is formed quicker than any man's I ever conversed with; and he never seems to mistake but in his own affairs.'

He was opposing the Government, but he was not a member of the Opposition; and the General Election put him in a difficulty, for seats of the Whig connexion were not for him, and he could not find the ready money for Midhurst. As he hurried from seat to seat, missing most of the partridge shooting in his anxiety, Walpole observed that 'Charles Fox, like the Ghost in *Hamlet*, has shifted to many quarters; but in most the cock crew, and he walked off'. It was an uneasy position for a penniless candidate, when nabobs and planters were bidding for seats, and the secret service fund was available to support Lord North. At last, after much negotiation he was elected by the thirteen voters of Malmesbury who then had the privilege of returning two members. It has never been made clear by what interest or arrangement he got the seat. His colleague was Strahan, the King's printer, a supporter of the Government and a friend of Dr. Johnson. Strahan was a rich man and he might have been willing to spend enough in the constituency for both members; but Strahan could not bring Fox in as a candidate, and it is unfortunate that the history of that transaction should be lost.

In November the new Lord Holland died of dropsy, a disease evidently dangerous to that family. Charles Fox succeeded to the sinecure, granted for the three lives, of Clerk of the Pells in Ireland. It was worth £2,300 a year and it had been granted to the first Lord Holland, according to the malevolent gossip of Walpole, 'in the late reign, and which Princess Amelia told me she had heard the late King give him on condition of his never asking a peerage'.

The first session of the new Parliament began with some slight encouragement to the critics of Government on the American question. The closing of ports and the diversion of trade may produce repercussions which ministers do not always foresee, and protests and petitions were reaching Parliament from traders all over the country and from the West Indian plantations. In the Lords Chatham made an earnest appeal for conciliation before it was too late:

'I contend not for indulgence, but justice to America; and I shall ever contend that the Americans justly owe obedience to us in a limited degree—they owe obedience to our ordinances of trade and navigation; but let the line be skilfully drawn between the objects of these ordinances, and their private, internal property; let the sacredness of their property remain inviolate; let it be taxable only by their own consent, given in their provincial assemblies, else it will cease to be property. . . .

'We shall be forced ultimately to retreat; let us retreat while we can, not when we must. I say we must necessarily undo these violent oppressive acts; they must be repealed— you will repeal them; I stake my reputation on it:—I will consent to be taken for an idiot if they are not finally repealed.—Avoid, then, this humiliating, disgraceful necessity. With a dignity becoming your exalted situation, make the first advances to concord, to peace, and happiness. . . .'

He ended with a warning that a war would not be fought in Massachusetts only. He saw 'foreign war hanging over your heads by a slight and brittle thread: France and Spain watching your conduct and waiting for the maturity of your errors'.

In the Commons the petitions from trading communities gave Burke and Fox the opportunity of repeated forecasts of 'defeat on one side of the water, and ruin and punishment on the other', and in March Burke made that speech on Conciliation, from which sentences—'I do not know the method of drawing up an indictment against a whole people', is one of them—remain among the familiar quotations of the English language.

But the Whig opposition did not respond to the inspiring lead of Burke and Fox. Lord Rockingham and his friends were ready to govern the country, but they saw no hope of returning to power, and, unlike the Bedford group, they had no personal ambition for office. Their minds were, indeed, more often occupied in finding excuses for remaining out of London than in devising attacks on North. An alliance with the Chatham group would no doubt have strengthened the Opposition, but neither Lord Rockingham nor Lord Chatham was remarkable for ease or pliancy in negotiation, and after a meeting Lord Rockingham could report only that he 'thought his countenance denoted more than a transient appearance to something like cordiality'. But nothing came of that transient appearance, and at the beginning of 1775 it seemed that the opposition, 'poor souls who can do no harm', were doomed to remain in a state of languid despair. As to the trouble in America, they believed that the Government was wrong and that unbounded disaster might be expected; but they saw no hope of inducing the King or North to alter his views; and they were not disposed to exert themselves in a cause which seemed hopeless. 'I confess', wrote the Duke of Richmond, who was one of the more active among them, 'that I feel very languid about this American business. The only thing that can restore common sense to this country is feeling the dreadful consequence which must soon follow such diabolical measures.' Another eminent Whig soothed his conscience by the reflection that active opposition would only make matters worse by making 'the driving more furious'. They would only be like 'a child pulling against a runaway horse; let him alone and he will stop the sooner'.

While the Whigs meditated on their futility, and Fox charged his former chief with 'every species of falsehood and treachery', General Gage, behind his earthworks at Boston, tried to decide whether he was blockading America or enduring a siege. The question became clearer in April when he sent a column of infantry to seize some stores at Concord, and his soldiers struggled back along the road from Lexington under incessant fire from American volunteers. During the spring, while London was entertained by a 'new diversion borrowed from the Venetians, a race of boats called a regatta', and by thrilling gossip on the Duchess of Kingston's approaching trial for bigamy, reinforcements slowly accumulated at Boston. They were less than half the number required by General Gage, and they were accompanied by three major-generals—Howe, Burgoyne, and Clinton—whose arrival indicated that serious business would now begin. The other actors in the tragedy were already in their places. Lord Sandwich, the notorious Jemmy Twitcher of contemporary letters, was at the Admiralty, and Lord George Germaine at the Colonial Office was anxious to show how great a statesman and strategist had been maligned when the court martial after Minden declared him 'unfit to serve His Majesty in any capacity whatever'. Beyond the earthworks of Boston Colonel Washington was anxiously facing the difficulties of improvising an army out of 'a mixed multitude of people under very little discipline, order, or government'. A few days later the generals made their plans to 'find elbow-room', as Burgoyne put it, by occupying a neighbouring hill, on which the colonists were entrenched. It was called Bunker's Hill, and it was taken on the 17th of June in the first battle of the war after a day of disastrous losses, which disposed of the comfortable belief that the rebels would run as soon as they saw a red coat.

It was a pleasant summer in London, and Charles Fox made the most of it. He was playing again with Fitzpatrick as his partner, and sometimes with success, to the indignation of Selwyn, who tried in vain to intercept some of the winnings in the interest of Lord Carlisle. 'When I spoke to him the other day about your demand,' reported that veteran gossip, 'I was answered only with an élevation de ses épaules et une grimace dont je fus tant soit peu piqué.' But the winnings were far from meeting the losses. He was in debt again, and borrowing from any one who would lend. Lord North, no doubt, knew something of the position when he suggested that the Clerkship of the Pells, with its income for life might be exchanged for an annuity for a term of years. It was not an act of philanthropy on the part of Lord North, who wanted the sinecure for the purposes of government, and it is difficult to believe, as has been suggested, that it was an act of friendly accommodation on the part of Charles Fox to help the Government out of a difficulty. The sinecure of £2,300 for life was exchanged for an annuity of £1,700 for 31 years, and the annuity for a fixed term may have been considered a better security for ready money than the sinecure. He was known to be a ruined gambler, and some of his opponents tried to bring it against him in the House. His Tory cousin, Captain Acland, incautiously retorted during a debate in the autumn that the control of the militia 'was fitter in their hands than in those of men who had ruined themselves by the most scandalous vices'. Charles Fox got up at once and said that he confessed his errors and wished he could atone for them. It was a disarming reply, and in the clash between Acland and Lackland, as the House called them, the latter was the winner.

During the autumn the question of reinforcements became acute, for the soldiers at Boston were putting their needs above anything contemplated by Lord George Germaine,

and in Whitehall the Adjutant-General was gloomily fore-
casting that 'our Army will be destroyed by damned drib-
lets'. Burke and Fox maintained their attacks, while
Montreal was lost, while the generals discussed evacuation
of Boston, and the King bargained with the Grand Duke for
the hire of Hessian soldiers. In a long course of denunciation it is not easy to be original, but Fox could still find something new to say of Lord North: 'Not Lord Chatham, not
the Duke of Marlborough, no not Alexander, nor Caesar, had
ever conquered so much territory as Lord North had lost in
one campaign.'

The year 1776 began drearily for the Opposition. Lord
George Germaine was, as Selwyn found him, 'in very great
spirit . . . is quite persuaded that all this will end after the
first campaign, and that he himself, as I take for granted,
shall establish his reputation as a minister by it'. But the
spirits of the Whigs were far from buoyant. 'What little
life there was', lamented Horace Walpole, 'existed in the
Duke of Richmond and Charles Fox. The latter bustled,
tried to animate both the Duke and the Marquis, conferred
with Lord Shelburne, but neither abandoned his gaming
nor rakish life. He was seldom in bed before five in the
morning, nor out of it before two at noon.' Walpole himself
had been trying his hand at 'bustling' the Duke of Richmond, and, when his efforts produced no response, he
relieved his feelings with a bitter analysis of Lord North's
Government: 'Lord North was a pliant tool without system
or principle; Lord George Germaine of desperate ambition
and character; Wedderburn a thorough knave; Lord Sandwich a more profligate knave; Lord Gower a villain capable
of any crime; Elliot, Jenkinson, Cornwall, mutes who would
have fixed the bowstring round the neck of the constitution.'

The Army withdrew from Boston, and the Americans
occupied it in triumph. It was a victory, but it did little
to relieve Washington's anxieties. His armies, without
training or equipment, tended to melt away as fast as they
were raised, while the King's army at Halifax was now being

reinforced by a stream of bewildered but obedient Germans. In the spring matters became worse. Benedict Arnold was driven back from Quebec, and it seemed hardly possible that the colonists could hold out. It was then that Charles Fox showed the true character which lay behind his manner of cheerful irresponsibility, by proclaiming to the Whigs that now, if ever, must they stand by their cause.

'Whatever happens,' he wrote to Lord Ossory in June, 'for God's sake let us all resolve to stick by them as handsomely (or more so) in their adversity as we have done in their glory, and still maintain the Whig cause, however discredited by defeat, to be the only true principle for this country.'

'I am still convinced', he wrote in the same letter, 'the Americans will finally succeed, whether by victories or defeats'; and, as he wrote, a document was being drafted in America, which became known ten days later as the Declaration of Independence. In October he wrote in the same terms to Lord Rockingham, who was then playing with the idea of a Whig secession from Parliament: 'A secession at present would be considered as a running away from the conquerors, and we should be thought to give up a cause which we think no longer tenable. . . . Above all, my dear Lord, I hope it will be a point of honour among us all to support the American pretension in adversity as much as we did in their prosperity, and that we should never desert those who have acted *unsuccessfully* upon Whig principles, while we continue to profess our admiration for those who succeeded in the same principles in the year 1688.'

The Rockinghams were learning that their new ally was something very different from the political adventurer and ruined gambler for whose adoption they were derided. It was true, as Walpole remarked, that he had not abandoned his gaming; and Selwyn was still watching for those occasional turns of luck, when he 'contrived to wrench out of Charles' black hands 50 pounds for Spencer, by watching the opportunity of his play'. But he was now becoming known as a moving spirit in opposition to the American war; and, although the Government majority was safe, the Opposition was gaining in strength. The mercantile interests affected by the loss of American trade were, of course, seriously concerned; their representatives in Parliament were becoming restive; and independent members were beginning to hesitate. This uneasy body of dissent and doubt might look to Fox as a spokesman. He had already brought over Fitzpatrick and his brother, Lord Ossory, and if the war went on, he might expect to gain more supporters.

For his own part, he had not joined the Rockingham group, but he was now allied with them, and he liked them more and more. They were surprisingly unlike the Bedford group and the hungry place-hunters whom he had met when he was in office. Many of them were not only indifferent to the rewards of office, but regarded it as a grievous burden that they should miss their hunting and shooting, forego Newmarket, and leave their beautiful houses in the country for the unwelcome duties of governing the country. In these beautiful houses they now welcomed Charles Fox, and never was a guest more popular or more contented. The new Duchess of Devonshire, the famous Georgiana, was making Devonshire House and Chatsworth Whig strongholds, and she has left on record her early impressions of Charles Fox: 'I have always thought', she wrote to her mother, 'that the great merit of C. Fox is his amazing quickness in seizing any subject—he seems to have the particular talent of knowing more about what he is saying and with less pains than anybody else—his conversation is like a brilliant player of billiards, the strokes follow one another, piff paff.' They became devoted friends and allies, and their friendship lasted until her death. He was no less popular with other ladies of the great Whig houses, who vied with their husbands and brothers in offering him that affectionate loyalty which he inspired in all his friends. His poem to Mrs. Crewe, printed by the Strawberry Press, shows

F

how attentively he could make himself pleasant to his Whig
hostesses:

> When the loveliest Expression to Feature is join'd,
> By Nature's most delicate pencil design'd,
> Where Blushes unbidden and Smiles without Art
> Speak the sweetness and feeling that dwell in the heart;
> Where in Manners enchanting no Blemish we trace,
> But the soul keeps the Promise we had from the Face,
> Sure Philosophy, Reason, and Coldness must prove
> Defences unequalled to shield us from Love.

The poem, thirty-eight lines long, was regarded as one of
the most successful efforts of an author who could seldom
convey in verse the charm which was his when he spoke.
It had, at any rate, the merit of civility, which could not
be claimed for the more familiar lines which he is said to
have addressed to another Whig lady:

> She loves truth, but she lies till she's black in the face;
> Praises virtue, but none in her conduct you'll trace.
> Her delicate feelings all wickedness shocks;
> But her lover's Lord Robert; her friend is Charles Fox.

He would probably have been drawn to the Opposition
without the attraction of Whig friendships, for he meant to
make a career of politics, and although he never saw those
frequent notes from the Queen's House by which the royal
criticisms of his behaviour were conveyed to Lord North
('cast off every principle of common honour and honesty . . .
as contemptible as he is odious . . . aversion to all restraints'),
he knew well enough that the King was against him, and
that no party which enjoyed the King's favour could offer
any future to him.

In October he spoke on the King's speech, and some of
his words were a warning addressed straight to the King
himself: 'It has been well said that the speech is an hypo-
critical one; and in truth there is not a little hypocrisy in
supposing that a king . . . I except His present Majesty,
who really loves liberty—but a common king should be
solicitous to establish anything that depended on a popular

assembly. Kings, Sir, govern by means of popular assemblies, only because they cannot do without them; to suppose a king fond of that mode of governing, is to suppose a chimera. It cannot exist. It is contrary to the nature of things, it is hypocrisy to advance it.'

A few weeks later the King, with an obvious sigh of relief, informed Lord North of a rumour that Charles Fox was going abroad at once and would not be back until after the recess. In that case it would be wise, suggested His Majesty, to 'bring as much forward before the recess as you can, as real business is never so well considered, as when the attention of the House is not taken up by noisy declamation'.

The rumour was true. Fox went to Paris with the inseparable Fitzpatrick, and Mme du Deffand resumed her disparaging bulletins to Horace Walpole. Her feelings on this occasion seem to have been affected by stories of their gambling losses, for, like many of her compatriots, she took a serious view of transactions involving money, and she could neither understand nor forgive the levity with which the two young Englishmen treated losses and gains alike. 'J'entends dire', she wrote in January, 'qu'ils perdent toujours, et qu'ils payent. Quelle est leur ressource? Je ne comprends pas. Ce sont deux bien mauvaises têtes.' A week later she attempted another character study of le Fox: 'En effet j'en pense à de certains égards, il n'a pas un mauvais cœur, mais il n'a nul espèce de principes et il regarde avec pitié tous ceux qui en ont; je ne comprends pas quels sont ses projets pour l'avenir, il ne s'embarrasse pas du lendemain. La plus extrême pauvreté, l'impossibilité de payer ses dettes, tout cela ne lui fait rien. Le Fitzpatrick paroîtroit plus raisonnable, mais le Fox assure qu'il est encore plus indifférent que lui sur ces deux articles; cet étrange sécurité les élève à ce qu'ils se croient au-dessus de tous les hommes. Ces deux personnages doivent être bien dangereux pour toute la jeunesse. Ils ont beaucoup joué içi, surtout le Fitzpatrick; il a perdu beaucoup.' But she seems to have realized that le Fox was beyond her powers of analysis, for she concludes that 'il joint à beaucoup d'esprit, de la bonté, de la vérité mais cela n'empêche pas, qu'il ne soit détestable'.

There were other visitors in France during that winter, whose interests were of a different kind. Benjamin Franklin was at Passy negotiating secretly with Vergennes on the possibility of help from France. His reception was encouraging, for Vergennes was waiting for the right moment to bring France into the war. That moment, in his view, must be before the colonists were crushed, and after the war had reached a point where it would be no longer possible for Britain to patch up a peace with them and turn in full force on France. It would be necessary to strike at the exact moment, and an arrangement in advance with Franklin would be invaluable. It was improbable that Charles Fox met any of the American agents in Paris, but he could hardly avoid noticing how well Dr. Franklin and his fur cap were received, and how remarkable was the general enthusiasm for the cause of America in a society in which democratic aspirations were not encouraged. He would have been unobservant if he returned to England without a strong suspicion that Lord Chatham did not exaggerate in his warning of 'France and Spain watching your conduct and waiting for the maturity of your errors'.

They returned to find the country frost-bound and the spirit of the Whigs hardly less chilled. The Opposition had adopted Lord Rockingham's favourite plan of showing disapproval by withdrawing from the proceedings of Parliament. The plan had no support from Charles Fox, who saw every reason for increasing rather than reducing his activity in Parliament. It was a depressing prospect, but if the Opposition would not act with him, he must act alone. He had another reason for depression, for Fitzpatrick was about to join the Guards in America, where Henry Fox, now a captain in the Thirty-eighth with Bunker's Hill to his credit, was hoping for promotion.

He persuaded a few of the Whigs to emerge from retreat in February and join him in denouncing Lord North's

suspension of the Habeas Corpus Act, when he again warned
the House of the impending extinction of public liberty, if
the cause of the colonists were lost: 'The tone of the minister
is become loud, firm, and decisive. He has already assured
us in this House, that he has nearly subdued America; and
by what we are able to collect from this bill, we may presume, he means to extend his conquests nearer home.' It
was the absolute conviction of the Opposition that if the
King succeeded in defeating the Americans, he would proceed to restore in England the arbitrary power which the
Whigs had overthrown in 1688. If the people of England
resisted, the Hessians, who had been so useful in subduing
the colonists, might be called in to sweep away liberty and
establish His Majesty's conception of the Patriot King.
But Fox had a more urgent argument than the possible
extinction of English liberties. In the debates on the Bill
he warned the House from his own knowledge and observation that French Ministers were meeting American agents,
and that the French were waiting only for a favourable
moment to declare war.

It was a busy winter at the Colonial Office, for Lord
George Germaine was elaborating the plan by which he
hoped at once to re-establish the King's authority in America
and his own military reputation. The plan was based on a
theory of General Burgoyne, who was spending the winter
in London, that the colonists might be forcibly subdued
if the line of the Hudson River could be seized and held. It
depended for success on the arrival of greater reinforcements than Germaine could contemplate and on a successfully timed combination, whereby an army moving south
would join hands with an army marching from New York.
It was much discussed in London society, and it is unlikely
that none of the many American agents in London failed
to convey a hint of it to Washington.

At the end of the session Charles Fox began his annual
round of visits for partridge-shooting to the Whig country
houses. It was one of the greatest delights of his life.

Endowed with that abnormal energy which sometimes goes with excessive fat, he was never happier than when he was panting through the stubble under a hot September sun. His execution was probably marred by his excitement, but his enthusiastic presence was a memorable experience for each member of the party, and the Whig country houses competed for the privilege of entertaining him. His friends found him more delightful than ever in that autumn, although he was no longer the exquisite in dress who had once driven across France in search of new patterns for waistcoats. No longer *coiffé à l'aile de pigeon*, with the magnificence of a model *macaroni à l'angloise*, he had gone to the other extreme of studious neglect of appearance. His hair fell in uncombed disorder, and his usual dress was now the blue coat and buff waistcoat which he had adopted, it was said, as the colours of the American colonists. His clothes, owing perhaps to exhaustion of credit with his tailor, were seldom new or clean. The *Diaboliad*, which appeared in that year, portrays him in his new style:

> In order due, Volpone next appear'd;
> Loose was his hair, unshaven was his beard:
> O'er his whole face was spread a yellow hue,
> Borrow'd perhaps from some relenting Jew
> Not anxious to be paid. Gold he had none:
> The inverted pocket told that all was gone.
> But 'ere he made his claim to Hell's rewards,
> His right hand waved aloft the fatal cards.

In September he went from Chatsworth with Lord John Townshend to Ireland. There he saw the sights in heavy rain, and began a friendship, which was to have its importance, with an attractive barrister named Grattan, who was making a name for himself as an eloquent speaker in Opposition in the Irish House. He aroused the admiration of his Irish hosts by bathing—an unusual and an unpleasing exercise to Charles Fox—in the chilly water of the Devil's Punch Bowl.

He returned to London to hear news from America, for

The COMPOUND MEDALLION.

FOX · NORTH · GEORGE III

From a cartoon in the author's possession

Burgoyne, after lecturing his Indian allies in the most polished language on the extent to which the practice of scalping was permissible in the King's army, had begun the great converging march, and reported a victory at Ticonderoga. Parliament met in November, and within a few days the attack on the Government was opened by one of Charles Fox's most memorable denunciations of Lord George Germaine, as 'that inauspicious and ill-omened character' whose 'ignorance and presumption, whose ignorance and inability' were ruining the country. Lord North gallantly came to the rescue, and congratulated Charles Fox on abandoning him, an old hulk, to attack a man of war. But the ruffled feelings of the man of war were by no means soothed when Charles Fox strolled over to the Treasury bench in the course of the debate, and Lord North cheerfully remarked, 'Charles, I am glad you did not fall on me to-day, for you was in full feather'.

'I am clear', wrote Fox to Lord Ossory, 'the *opinion* of the majority of the House is now with us. I cannot help flattering myself that *opinions* will, in the long run, have their influence on votes.' He was not wrong in his estimate. The war was not yet unpopular, but its effects on trade and credit were becoming more serious; prices were rising; bankruptcies and unemployment were increasing. The traders were not alone in their alarm; in Parliament the independent members, the members in the commercial interest, and many of the country members were tending to that state of mind in which they would first listen to, and finally vote with, a leader who had force enough to rally the opponents of the war. That leader, who might now change opinions into votes, was Fox. Three years had passed since Walpole saw him at the bottom of the wheel with Wilkes at the top. He was very far from the bottom now. His speeches and opinions were no longer treated as the flourishes of a brilliant youth. They were taken seriously as the pronouncements of a statesman who was proving himself every day to be right. His reputation was rising, and he might soon find himself at the top of the wheel before he had reached the age when most statesmen would think themselves lucky to get their first step.

In December Parliament heard the result of Lord George's converging march. Howe, it was said, did not receive his orders to move, because Lord George was unwilling to postpone a journey to the country while a fair copy of the dispatch was prepared. That tradition is not supported by evidence. In fact a copy of Burgoyne's orders was sent to Howe, but no direct instructions were given to him. So Howe decided upon another plan, and Burgoyne, moving on Albany alone, was surrounded at Saratoga, and surrendered on the 17th of October with an army of two thousand. Charles Fox at once moved for an inquiry with some well-deserved comments on the suffering Germaine. 'Charles', wrote Fish Crauford, 'spoke with great violence, but the House for this time went along with him. We were not shocked at his talking of bringing Lord George to a *second* trial, nor were we shocked at being asked if we could patiently continue to submit to see this country disgraced by him in *every* capacity.' The disaster was worse than they imagined. It produced the moment for which Vergennes was waiting, when a peace with the Americans could no longer be patched up, and King Louis might appear in the unfamiliar role of a champion of freedom and an ally of the oppressed. In the first days of 1778 Horace Walpole sent to his friend Mann a gloomy but accurate impression: 'The Parliament, when it shall meet, is to go into great inquiry, which, I conclude, will end in nothing at all, or rather, not end. The talk of the day is that France has signed a treaty with the provincials, and the Stocks look pale upon it; but all these rumours only fill up the chinks of time, and will be forgotten when great events happen. By *great events* I mean foreign war and domestic calamity. We are on the high road to both. The present moment is only like the half-hour at the theatre before the play begins: the galleries are riotous, pelt the candle snuffers, or bawl for the overture;

when the curtain is drawn up, nobody thinks but of the tragedy.'

Charles Fox lost no time in going into the great inquiry which Walpole predicted. In January he was clamouring for the orders which had been given to Howe and Burgoyne, and, a few days later, he made one of his usual attacks on the unhappy Lord North, who tried to disarm criticism by describing himself as an 'unfortunate minister'. But these were only preliminaries to the great encounter on the 2nd of February, when the Duke of Richmond in the Lords and Fox in the Commons moved that 'no more of the Old Corps be sent out of the Kingdom'. Their object was not only to declare that the Government had failed and would fail again in America, but to point out that the danger of war with France was now so great that no more of the Regular Army, as it would now be called, could be spared for America.

On that day the House and galleries were packed to hear Fox. Some one thought fit to call attention to the presence of strangers, and the galleries were cleared of men. Then a member, still dissatisfied, observed that a number of ladies had been allowed to remain, and proceedings were delayed for nearly two hours until the Duchess of Devonshire and her friends could be induced to depart. Fox spoke for two hours and forty minutes, and his audience listened with concentrated attention to every word. He took the House through the history of our disastrous negotiations with America, the war, and its failures. He concluded that victory in America could not be expected, and the removal of more regular troops from England would only leave the country defenceless. When he sat down the ministers looked at one another—and remained silent. The Opposition vote, which a month before had been 89, rose to 165.

It was a real triumph for Fox, and he at once wrote his impressions to Fitzpatrick, to whom he always revealed his mind. His conclusion from the debate was that he might expect 'great divisions', but he could not hope to turn out the Government. He then discusses his own future:

'With respect to my own share, I can only say that people flatter me that I continue to gain, rather than lose, my credit as an orator; and *I am so convinced that this is all that I shall ever gain (unless I chose to become the meanest of men), that I never think of any other object of ambition.*

'*I am certainly ambitious by nature,* but I really have, or think I have, totally subdued that passion. I have still as much vanity as ever, which is a happier passion by far; because great reputation I think I may acquire and keep, great situation I *never* can acquire, nor if acquired, keep without making sacrifices that I never will make. If I am wrong, and more sanguine people right, *tant mieux,* and I shall be as happy as they can be, but if I am right, I am sure I shall be the happier, for having made up my mind to my situation. I need not say how happy I am at the thought of your coming; I should be so at all times, but I really want you at present to a great degree. I have other friends whom I love, and who I believe love me, but I foresee possible cases where I am determined to act against all the advice that they are likely to give me. I know they will not shake me, for nothing ever shall; but yet it would be a great satisfaction to have you here, who I know would be of my opinion. You guess, I dare say, the sort of cases I mean, I shall be told by prudent friends, that I am under no sort of engagements to any sort of men. I certainly am not, but there are many cases, where there is no engagement, and yet it is dishonourable not to act as if there was one. But even supposing it were quite honourable, is it possible to be happy in acting with people of whom one has the worst opinions, and being on a cold footing (which must be the case) with all those whom one loves best, and with whom one passes one's life?' The letter ends with some gossip of London, including the pleasant news that George Selwyn, that anxious and painstaking gambler, 'has been cut up for a large sum, after having been fattening for a month'.

Fox's warning of danger from France had better grounds
than he knew, for on the 6th of February Franklin signed
a Treaty of Amity and Commerce, which provided that
France and America should be allies if France should engage in war with Britain. North had good reason to know
the danger without any warning from Fox, and he would
long ago have given way, if his master had not made up his
mind that 'England gained nothing by granting indulgence
to her dependencies'. But it was no longer a question of
gaining anything. The only hope of avoiding a war with
France lay in making terms with America, and on the 17th
of February, 'a day ever memorable as one of the most
ignominious in English annals', he introduced what he
described as 'conciliatory propositions'. They were unexpected, and the astonished House heard him propose the
surrender of almost all the British claims. He sat down in
a 'dull melancholy silence', which continued until Fox got
up to assent to the propositions with a suggestion that the
concession, which was almost identical with Burke's proposals three years ago, was now too late. Horace Walpole's
story of the debate is more dramatic than the official report.
He and his cousin, Thomas Walpole, had news from Paris
that the treaty was signed. They decided not to tell Burke,
whom they distrusted, nor Rockingham, whom they considered unreliable by reason of his 'childish fluctuations',
but to keep their news a secret until shortly before the House
met, and then tell Fox and no one else. Fox made the most
of his advantage by asking Lord North whether a treaty
had not within the last ten days been signed in Paris, because 'if so, the Administration is beaten by ten days, a
situation so threatening that in such a time of danger the
House must concur with the propositions though probably
now they would have no effect'. The unhappy minister
tried desperately to avoid answering, but at last he had to
mutter something about having heard a report but having
no official intelligence.

The crisis was too much for Lord North's habitual

serenity. He had already tried to resign, but the King had made it a personal matter, indicating that he 'should have been greatly surprised at the inclination expressed by you to retire, had not I known you may now and then despond, yet that you have too much personal affection for me and sense of honour, to allow such a thought to take a hold on your mind'. Confronted with a war with France and probably with Spain, Lord North again asked to be released. This time the appeal to personal affection was not enough, and the King, shuddering with horror, had to consent to negotiations with Lord Chatham. To call for the man who had already saved the country in a great war seemed an obvious step, but the King saw in it 'the road opened to a set of men who would certainly make me a slave for the remainder of my days'. Chatham might come in if North would not otherwise remain, but he must come as the subordinate and the supporter of North. 'I will only add,' wrote the King, 'to put before your eyes my most inward thoughts, that no advantage to this country nor personal danger to myself can ever make me address myself to Lord Chatham, or any other branch of the Opposition. Honestly I would rather lose the crown I now wear than bear the ignominy of possessing it under their shackles. I might write volumes, if I would state the feelings of my mind, and what I will never depart from. Should Lord Chatham wish to see me before he gives his answer, I shall most certainly refuse it.'

With this doubtful sanction negotiations were opened by Mr. William Eden, who thus began a long career of diplomacy. He first approached Charles Fox, who declared himself to be 'unconnected and at liberty'. He gathered that Fox would not object to any of the existing ministers except Germaine, but there could be no question of his joining the government 'alone and singly', and it was doubtful whether he would join at all. With this faint encouragement Eden hurried to Lord Shelburne, as the representative of Chatham, and found that, if any arrangement was to be made with the Opposition, 'Lord Chatham must be the dictator'. Even on these terms an arrangement would be difficult, for the Rockingham party insisted on conceding American independence, and Chatham was entirely opposed to it. The King became voluble in his indignation at the thought of Chatham in power. In a series of agitated notes he assured Lord North that 'whilst any ten men in the Kingdom will stand by me, I will not give myself up to bondage', that 'no consideration in life shall make me stoop to Opposition', that 'rather than be shackled by those desperate men' he would lose his Crown.

The negotiations dragged on, while in the House the Whig orators poured out their denunciations of Lord North. There were debates on the Conciliatory Bills, and Fox told him that he had broken his word; on the state of the Navy, and Fox treated him 'with the utmost contempt and indignity'; on the negotiations with France, and Fox, boiling with indignation at the infamous treatment of Burgoyne by the Government and the languid efforts of the Opposition, became so angry that 'in his passion he tore the paper and went away'. On the question of American independence he went with the Rockinghams, persuaded thereto by Burke and perhaps influenced by his family tradition of feud with Shelburne. Perhaps if he had joined Chatham he might have taken a following with him; but the chance of alliance was not long open to him. In April, as Lord Carlisle and his commissioners were starting on their mission of conciliation, the Duke of Richmond spoke in the House of Lords in favour of conceding independence. Lord Chatham came forth in the last and greatest of his returns to public life, protesting that 'as long as I can crawl down to the House, and have strength to raise myself on my crutches, or lift my hand, I will vote against giving up the dependency of America on the sovereignty of Great Britain'. The effort was too great for him, and he fell dying as he tried to speak. When they voted him a public funeral, as the statesman who had saved England in the Seven Years

War, the King was 'rather surprised', opining that 'this compliment, if paid to his general conduct, is rather an offensive measure to me personally'.

Meanwhile the country was being roused by something more potent than oratory. With the threat of invasion the people of England were preparing in earnest. New corps were being raised, the militia was embodied, and volunteers were pouring in. Whig leaders, who had cheered American victories, were by no means ready to cheer a French invasion, and many of them were in camp with their regiments. It was an anxious summer with Paul Jones landing in Kirkcudbrightshire to raid Lord Selkirk's house, and Admiral Keppel, with the rather uncertain support of Sir Hugh Palliser, in the Channel holding his own against superior forces of the French. The Commissioners were on their way to America, but in June Fitzpatrick came home with dismal views on the prospects of conciliation. The session ended on the 3rd of June, and the King took occasion to hint to his distracted minister that he could hardly expect support in Parliament, 'whilst you have not yourself decided the path you mean to take'.

Charles Fox made his usual round of the Whig country houses for cricket and partridge-shooting. As a cricketer he displayed the same enthusiastic activity which made him the delight of a shooting-party, but both his score and his bag suffered sadly from that impulsive zeal which usually got him run out at cricket, and tempted him to useless fusillades at distant partridges. His hosts, as always, wanted nothing more than his company; but it was not always easy for him to accept their invitations, for travelling needed ready money, and the sources from which he could hope to obtain ready money were now very few.

There were many consultations that summer in the Whig country houses, for the Opposition was by no means united. The British armies were inactive in America, and d'Estaing's squadron threatened their communication with England. In the Channel the position was no less dangerous, although

the Navy, shamefully outnumbered, was for the present
holding its own. Fox, who had as good information on the
subject as any one outside the Government, had long been
doubtful whether the Americans could be conquered, and
he was now convinced that the only hope of safety was to
withdraw at once from America and concentrate the whole
resources of the country in a war with France and Spain.
It was by no means a policy of despair. If France were
beaten, the Americans were likely to make a much more
favourable settlement than Lord North could produce with
his Conciliatory Acts, while d'Estaing was manœuvring
off Cape Delaware.

When Parliament met in November the question was
still unsettled, and the session was devoted to the usual
attacks on Lord North, in which Charles Fox's speeches
were, as usual, said to be the best he had ever made. They
had now a new target for invective, for Lord Sandwich at
the Admiralty was proving no less disastrous than Lord
George Germaine at the Colonial Office. He had constantly
assured the House that the Navy was ready, that fifty
cruisers were available; but when Admiral Keppel put to
sea in June to save the country from French invasion, he
had only twenty ships of the line to face thirty-two ships
of better condition waiting in Brest. In August the Jamaica
convoy of seventy-five merchant ships was captured by the
French, and Lord Sandwich could do nothing to save it.
The year ended with the Navy outnumbered and faced with
the prospect of the Spanish fleet being added to the French.

The Government began the next year, it was 1779, with
a scandal, which Lord North would have thankfully avoided.
It was one of the difficulties of Lord Sandwich that most of
the better naval commanders were Whigs, who could not
be expected to appreciate the system of political promotion
then practised at the Admiralty. The climax of indignation
was reached when it was announced that Keppel, the hero
of the Navy and the favourite of the Whigs, was to be tried
by court martial, because his own subordinate officer, Sir

Hugh Palliser, had made after an action a report to Lord Sandwich accusing him of cowardice and incompetence. The court martial opened at Portsmouth in January with a strong attendance of eminent Whigs in the court, and thither hurried Charles Fox both to support Keppel and to enjoy the unaccustomed spectacle of the Rockingham Whigs in a state described as 'finely warm'. The trial dragged on for weeks, and every day brought confusion to Sandwich and Palliser and exultation to the Whig leaders who filled the court. At last, on the 11th of February, the news of Keppel's acquittal arrived in London, and the streets were filled by a crowd which showed its feelings by breaking any windows which were not illuminated. Late in the evening Charles Fox and a party of his friends, who had all drank as much as they could conveniently carry, sallied out of Brooks's to observe the proceedings. In the street they waylaid the Duke of Ancaster of the Court party, who was beyond question drunk, and with his enthusiastic approval they suggested to the crowd that Lord George Germaine's windows might as well be broken. When this pleasing task had been performed, they called attention to the windows of Lord Sandwich. The response was overwhelming, and the First Lord, with his mistress, Miss Ray, who lived with him at the Admiralty, had to escape through the garden into the Horse Guards. A few days later Keppel dined in the City, and the same crowd turned out again to demonstrate. But this time they responded to other influences. 'It was believed', said Walpole, 'to be at the instigation of the Court, to make the Opposition sick of such rejoicings, for many windows of the Opposition were broken, particularly Charles Fox's.'

The windows of the Admiralty had hardly been reglazed before the First Lord found himself in the thick of another scandal. His mistress, Miss Ray, was murdered in the street by a curate named Hackman, who had left the Army and entered Holy Orders in the hopes of obtaining through Lord Sandwich such preferment as would enable him to induce

Miss Ray to leave the Admiralty and share his life and living. It was hardly the fault of Lord Sandwich that, when
his mistress refused to join in this ingenious plot, the disappointed curate should waylay and murder her; but the
affair was made the occasion of further demonstrations
against the First Lord and the Government. Walpole
records the end of the episode: 'The poor assassin was
executed yesterday. The same day Charles Fox moved
for the removal of Lord Sandwich, but was beaten by a
large majority; for in Parliament the Ministers can still
gain victories.'

But Keppel's trial had not entirely dominated the whole
of political life. Lord North was once more trying feebly to
resign, and once more the King's refusal was accompanied
by grudging permission to approach members of the Opposition. This time Fox believed that something might be done.
It was hardly a question of political advantage. The country
was in danger, and the best hope of safety was to get rid
of Lord Sandwich and Germaine. If they could be replaced
by good Whigs, the ultimate preponderance of the Whig
party would follow. He discussed the idea with his friends,
but he could arouse only the mildest interest in the official
leaders of the Opposition. 'In short,' he wrote to Lord
Rockingham in January, 'our difference of opinion is quite
complete. You think you can best serve the country by
continuing in a fruitless opposition; I think it impossible
to serve it at all but by coming into power, and go even so
far as to think it irreconcilable with the duty of a public
man to refuse it, if offered to him in a manner consistent
with his private honour, and so as to enable him to form
fair hopes of doing essential service. I know there are some
people, and perhaps you may be one, who will say that these
opinions are the consequences of my particular situation,
or, at the best, that I am warped towards them by that
situation.' He went on to implore his reluctant leader not
to reject all possibility of compromise. 'Supposing', he
asked, 'an Administration should be formed partly of those

who now act in Opposition, and partly of the present people (always understanding the most exceptionable to be removed, particularly North, Sandwich, and Germaine), whether you would give such a Ministry any countenance, whatever? By *countenance*, I mean whether any of your friends would take employment in such a Ministry, if they were such as were suitable to them in other respects, and the men with whom they had to act, such as they could have no other objection to them than of coming in contrary to your opinion?' The Duke of Richmond undertook the avuncular duty of explaining over a sheaf of closely written pages the disastrous enormity, the impossibility, of a coalition in any form. His letter ends with a hint that any Whig who took a place in the Government would do so as a deserter; and once more Lord North was disappointed.

Charles Fox, though a leader of Opposition, had not yet become a member of the Whig party. But the Opposition drew its life and inspiration from him, and he was now attracting it to men who came as Foxites rather than as Whigs. There was the clever Mr. Sheridan, who was already a favourite at Devonshire House. Fox had proposed him unsuccessfully for Brooks's, and was now hoping to bring him in both for Brooks's and for Parliament. There was young Mr. Pitt, tall, angular, and eager, whom Lady Holland had foreseen thirteen years ago as 'a thorn in Charles' side as long as he lives', now seeking Charles Fox with the most thornless deference to discuss the debate with, 'But surely, Mr. Fox, that might be met thus', or 'Yes, but he lays himself open to retort'. And there was the young Prince of Wales, who was already causing the gravest anxiety to his father by his adherence even in the nursery to the attractive leadership of Charles Fox.

The national danger became graver during the spring, for an alliance against England was made between France and Spain, and in June Spain declared war. The news produced, according to Fitzpatrick, 'a very general consternation, and a most universal acknowledgement of the necessity of changing the ministry which most people think must take place, though in point of voting the numbers were much as usual in both Houses'. But votes and majorities seemed of little account as the summer wore on, and the combined fleets of France and Spain sailed up the Channel, sixty-six ships of the line, and appeared before Plymouth, which was almost defenceless against attack. A change of wind which turned to a gale, drove them down the Channel again, and saved Plymouth for the moment; but Hardy's fleet, less than half the enemy's strength, lay somewhere off the Scilly Islands, and if Hardy's fleet were destroyed, nothing could prevent an invasion. Meanwhile a desperate attempt was being made to fortify Plymouth, and Charles Fox, determined to miss none of the excitement, came posting down to Saltram. He was always a friend of the Navy, and he had many friends among the sea captains, who were waiting at any moment to put out for the last defence of their country. Such was his enthusiasm that he is said to have extracted a promise from Captain Jervis of the *Foudroyant*, that if the fleet went out to fight he should sail in the *Foudroyant*. Only one thought marred the exaltation of living with such heroes in such days. If only another Government were in power, with whom a Whig might rejoice in victory; if only Keppel were in command, and Sandwich gone; for it was a bitter reflection that if the Navy saved the country, they would be saving first and foremost Jemmy Twitcher. 'The fleet to-day', Fox wrote to Fitzpatrick in August, 'was a most magnificent sight. It was formed in order that, in case of attack, they may not be found in the confusion that Johnstone was; and faith, when one looks at it and thinks there is a possibility of its coming to action in a day or two, *on se sent ému beaucoup*. If some things were otherwise at home, and the fleet were commanded by Keppel, one should feel very eager indeed, when even in the present damned state of things, who can help feeling something at the sight of it. It seems to be the opinion that, if they do come, Hardy will make some sort of fight with them in the narrow part of the Channel. At all events, if the French should come again I cannot think that they will go away as they did before and that there must, either at sea or land, be *quelque chose à voir*; in which case I should be very much vexed indeed to have left this country just before the sight begins.'

There could be no partridge-shooting for active statesmen with d'Orvilliers in the Channel, but at the beginning of September they might, if they had known it, have shot partridges in complete security, for the danger was past. The fleets of France and Spain were defeated by small-pox and putrid fever, and in the middle of the month they put back to Brest with their plan of a joint invasion abandoned. In other respects matters were improving at sea. Merchant fleets were arriving safely, and English seamen were repaying to the Americans and French all that our mercantile marine had suffered at the hands of Paul Jones.

The winter session was remarkable for the first and only duel fought by Charles Fox. A newspaper misreported him in such a way as to imply an insult to another member, Mr. Adam, who demanded that he should publish a notice disclaiming any intention of insult. Fox replied that to issue contradictions to the press of a statement which he had not made was contrary to all his ideas, and a meeting with pistols was arranged in Hyde Park for the early morning of the 29th of November. Fox was accompanied by the faithful Fitzpatrick, and showed himself unmoved by the obvious danger of exposing so wide a target. He gave the first shot to his enemy: 'Sir, I have no quarrel with you, do you fire.' They both missed, and Adam asked, 'Will Mr. Fox declare he meant no personal attack on my character?' But Mr. Fox would declare nothing of the sort. 'This', he retorted, 'is no place for apologies.' Shots were again exchanged, and the affair ended in compliments. Fox then remarked casually that he believed the first shot had hit him. It was indeed the case; but the buckle of his waist-band, 'which', Sir George Trevelyan has observed, 'in the case of Charles Fox, was necessarily an article of solid construction', had turned the bullet. A slight abrasion of the skin gave the world of fashion excuse to throng the house, in which the duellist restored himself after the discomfort of rising at what was too often his bedtime.

Lord North had new grounds for despondency during the winter. From America Clinton was begging for reinforcements for his next campaign, and, so far from sending reinforcements, ministers were wondering whether part of Clinton's army would not be wanted for home defence. A general election was in sight, and the freeholders were already showing signs of that pent-up disapproval for which Prime Ministers must always be on the watch. Petitions demanding reform, peace with America, economy, were arriving, and vast gatherings of freeholders were beginning to speak their collective mind. It was disquieting to hear of Yorkshire freeholders petitioning against waste of public money, sinecures, and personal government, and it was disconcerting to find Westminster electors not only adopting the Yorkshire petition but adopting Charles Fox as their candidate. In the House, too, the Opposition was gaining and the Government majority was falling. Burke introduced in February his plan for 'Oeconomical Reformation' with its abolition of offices and sinecures. In March he actually carried a resolution that the Board of Trade, a sanctuary of literary pensioners, was useless; and the King had hardly recovered from the shock before Mr. Dunning got a majority of eighteen to support the subversive opinion that 'the Influence of the Crown has increased, is increasing, and ought to be diminished'. The Government was unpopular, not only for its failures in the American War; there was a general feeling that the country was on the brink of disaster. Taxes were rising, trade was failing, distress was serious; and crowds, which in the past had playfully broken windows, began to show signs of more aggressive activity. Stocks were falling dangerously, and there were signs of a financial panic, although the wealthy sufferers did not always appreciate what was happening to them. 'Lady Melbourne', wrote Walpole, 'was standing before the fire and adjusting her feathers in the glass; says she, "Lord, they say the stocks will blow up: that will be very comical".'

In the spring, while Clinton was taking Charleston, the end seemed very near, and members of Brooks's began to think of themselves as ministers. A debate on the Yorkshire petition for the reform of expenditure gave Fox an opportunity of proclaiming his confidence in the people in terms which reversed the contemptuous declarations of his early days. The people, he pointed out, were not in arms and did not threaten war; their petition should be treated with respect or they would 'lose all confidence in their representatives, all reverence for Parliament'. He spoke, as he always spoke, with extraordinary animation; his voice was harsh and his delivery rapid. Such a style suffers sadly in reported form, but a passage from his speech on that day may suggest something of his impetuous manner:

'I wish most anxiously that gentlemen would consider what they are when they sit in this House. Insignificant in themselves, they derive their importance from the appointment of their constituents. It is the duty of members of Parliament to conform to the sentiments, and in some degree even to the prejudices of the people. In their legislative capacity, the wishes and wants of the people ought in this land of liberty to be their grand rule of conduct. I say in that legislative capacity; for I make a distinction between that and their judicial capacity; in which last they must give judgement according to the letter of the law, and in this too, they consult the interests of liberty. Suppose the people should be of the opinion there is no longer any need of a very expensive Board of Trade and Plantations, when that trade and those plantations, for the sake of which the Board was first established, no longer exist, would it not become the noble Lord's duty to sacrifice his particular opinion to theirs, and to act agreeably to their notions and instructions? . . . I cannot imagine that any objection can possibly be made to this petition. But some may say, "Are we sinners above all that went before us, like those on whom the tower of Shiloh fell? Are we more corrupt than other Parliaments who were never pestered with petitions of this kind?" No, I do not suppose you are; but though former Parliaments were as bad as you, and you know the severity of that comparison, yet the people did not know it. Now they perhaps do not see it, but they feel it; they feel the pressure of taxes; they beg you not to lay your hand so heavily on them, but be as economical as possible. . . .'

It was a little disconcerting after this democratic outburst to see the tottering Government unexpectedly saved by a popular upheaval. London was well accustomed to riots of different degrees of violence, but no one could have foreseen that the most violent of them all would be aroused by the old bogy of No Popery, or that it would be led by such an oddity as Lord George Gordon; and no one could have foreseen that Lord George Gordon and his ragged Protestants would be the means of saving the detested Government. But the Gordon riots gave polite society a shock, and frightened many a wavering courtier back to his allegiance. The King, too, emerged from the crisis with credit. While magistrates and aldermen listened trembling to the crash of broken windows and the roar of burning houses, while Burke and Fox mounted guard at Rockingham House and Fox relieved the tedium by charging out to arrest a rioter, while Lord North with a bodyguard of friends was watching the fires from the roof of his house, observing that he was 'much more afraid of Jack St. John's pistol than of the rioters', the King showed that indomitable courage, which was his greatest quality, and himself issued the orders which saved London.

The crisis gave new life to the ideas of collaboration between Government and Opposition, and officious enthusiasts managed to arrange a secret meeting between North and Fox, choosing behind the scenes at Drury Lane Theatre for the place of encounter. Nothing came of their conversation, but projects for a coalition were revived, and in the debate on the riots Fox was distinctly complimentary to the Minister. The King consented grudgingly to the negotiation, observing on the possibility of office for Fox that 'if any lucrative, not ministerial office, can be pointed out for him provided he will support the Ministry, I shall have no objection to the proposition. He never had any principle, and can therefore act as his interest may guide him.' But the King was not thinking of a coalition. For months he had prepared for a general election and, after some astute manœuvres to put the Opposition off their guard, he dissolved Parliament on the 1st of September. Charles Fox had postponed his usual visits for the partridge-shooting, to go, on the urgent advice of his physician, to Bath. His manner of living was not conducive to good health, but he would probably not have troubled himself to drink the waters of Bath, if he had not been seriously alarmed by the occasional failure of his voice. He was making a leisurely progress towards Bath, when he heard the news of the dissolution. This time there was no difficulty about a seat. He had the choice of all that Whig aristocracy could offer. His first act was to secure for himself the safe seat of Bridgwater, where the local Whigs had invited him to stand. He then raced to London to fight the uncertain seat of Westminster. His opponents for the two seats at Westminster, both supporters of the Court, were Admiral Rodney, who was at sea, and Lord Lincoln, who was known as the nominee of Lord Sandwich. The Westminster hustings exactly suited Charles Fox. Every day he poured out his 'letters and paragraphs and a thousand clever things', and at all hours he was to be seen, 'bowing and sweltering', haranguing the crowd, and making himself the chief subject of interest to the population of Westminster. The ladies of Devonshire House drove out to support him, and the Whig aristocracy were whipped up to show unaccustomed affability to voters. At last the poll for the two seats was declared:

Rodney   4,230
Fox   3,805
Lincoln   3,070

The Man of the People, as he was now called, was uproari-
ously chaired with a special demonstration of exuberance
as the procession passed the Palace of St. James.

It was a sensational victory for Fox, but the country did
not follow Westminster. Lord North was still the reluctant
leader of a majority, and Mr. Dunning might again observe
that the power of the King, supported by the Civil List and
the Secret Service Fund, had increased, and, far from being
diminished, was fortified by the news of a real victory by
Lord Cornwallis over Gates in South Carolina. Burke had
lost his seat at Bristol, but Lord Rockingham gave him
another at Malton. There was some new blood in the
House, which promised well. Fox found a seat at Stafford
for his clever friend Sheridan, and he had succeeded also,
with rather more difficulty, in getting him into Brooks's.
Young William Pitt was in for Appleby, and his friend
Wilberforce was member for Hull.

There was small attendance of the Opposition when the
House met in November, and the weary game of baiting
Lord George Germaine began again. In the New Year they
turned from Germaine to Sandwich, who had appointed the
discredited Palliser Governor of Greenwich Hospital; and
on the reduction of the Civil List Mr. Pitt made his first
speech. It was a complete success, and Charles Fox hurried
up to pour out his delighted congratulations, while one of
the patriarchs of the House quavered sentimentally that
'old as I am, I expect and hope to hear you both battling
within these walls as I have done your fathers before you'.

Fox had now completely recovered voice and health, as
a pair of highwaymen discovered when they tried to stop
him near Highgate on a thick night in February. He was
directing his renewed energy to an elaborate attempt to
restore his fortunes by a faro bank at Brooks's with Fitzpatrick as his partner. It was a highly organized and, for

a time, a highly successful venture, and until Parliament
rose in July it was the talk of London. The effect of prosperity was soon apparent, and in February Selwyn observed
'Charles, dressed, as clean, and with as good a coat, and gold
buttons, as if he had been at the head of affairs'. A few
weeks later the successful banker was said to be in 'prodigious affluence', and had laid the foundations of a new
racing stable by buying 'Truth, a racehorse, for the Lord
knows what: he would not own what he gave for it, so
most probably it was for a sum of which he was rather
ashamed'.

But creditors soon heard of the prodigious affluence, and
Charles Fox was 'accablé de demandes comme de dettes,
et avec la reputation d'avoir de l'argent, il ne sait où don-
ner de la tête'. Many of them were paid, but some were
ignored, and, to the infinite diversion of London, a creditor
of Fitzpatrick, whose claim was not admitted, proceeded
to an execution. Walpole and Selwyn hurried to Arlington
Street to see the 'two carts at Charles' door filling by the
Jews with his goods, clothes, books, and pictures. He was
waked by Basilio yesterday, and Hare afterwards by his
valet de chambre, they being told at the same time that the
execution was begun and the carts were drawn up against
the door. Such furniture I never saw.' Walpole had even
more to tell: 'As I returned full of this scene, whom should
I find sauntering by my own door but Charles? He came
up and talked to me at the coach window, on the Marriage
Bill, with as much *sangfroid* as if he knew nothing of what
had happened.'

He could afford to treat the execution coolly, for the
Bank was still winning, and it was easy for his house to rise
'like a phoenix from the flames, is new painted, and is going
to be new furnished, with certain precautions to keep his
furniture *à l'abri de ses créanciers*'. All through the summer, while Rodney and de Grasse manœuvred in the West
Indies, and Washington confessed himself to be 'at the end
of his tether', the bank was held by the partners, with Lord

Robert Spencer, recently ruined, to deal for a small fee
when the eminent bankers were resting. Selwyn gives us a
glimpse of their methods: 'Yesterday about the middle of
the day, passing by Brooks's, I saw a Hackney coach, which
announced a late sitting. I had the curiosity to enquire
how things were, and found Richard in his Pharo pulpit,
where he had been, alternately with Charles, since the evening before and dealing to Adm. Pigott only. I saw a card
on the table. . . . Received from Messieurs Fox & Co. 1,500
guineas. The bank ceased in a few minutes after I was in
the room; it was little after 12 at noon, and it had won
3,400 or 500 guineas. . . . This Pharo Bank is held in a
manner which, being so exposed to public view, bids defiance to all decency and police. The whole town as it passes
views the dealer and the punters, by means of the candles
and the windows being levelled to the ground. The Opposition who have Charles for their ablest advocate, is quite
ashamed of the proceeding, and hates to hear it mentioned.'
They were still winning at the end of the session, when
Selwyn found 'Charles . . . at the Quinze table, and seemed
to be winning. I never saw him but with heaps of gold
before him. His house, I mean the place of execution,
where he is to go soon, is the sprucest to look at from the
street I ever saw; I never knew such a transition from distress to opulency; or from the dirt to cleanliness.'

Parliament rose on the 15th of July, and Fox, magnificent
in his new clothes and free from all difficulty about travelling expenses, departed for his usual round of cricket and
partridges. There was gloom that autumn in the Whig
country houses, for it seemed the Americans must be worn
down, and Government remained as strong as ever. Charles
Fox once more defined his position to Fitzpatrick: 'I agree
with you in thinking that the people of this country in
general deserve no pity, and certainly the King still less. But
it is not a little hard upon us, who expected to play some
part upon the stage of the world, and who had certainly
at least the shares of individuals in the greatness of the

country, to be obliged to bound our hopes, nay, our wishes, to being able some way or other to heal the wounds made by others, and to put this country, which was the first in Europe, upon a footing to be one amongst the many nations of the world. I dare say you think this more than we can do; but to those who ever had any ambition, good God! what is this? Indeed, indeed, it is intolerable to think that it should be in the power of one blockhead to do so much mischief. . . . Read the speech of Richard Plantagenet in *Henry VI* when France is lost, and if I do not forget (for there is no Shakespeare here) it is very consonant to our feelings upon this wretched state of affairs.'

But two days before the House met, the final disaster in America was known. For reasons which have never been clear Cornwallis moved north from Carolina. At Yorktown he established a defensive post, where he was cut off ·by Washington and Lafayette. He surrendered with an army of 6,600, and Lord North received the news 'as he would have taken a bullet through his breast, for he opened his arms, exclaiming wildly . . . "O God, it is all over!"' He knew well enough that he had lost America, and once more he begged that he might resign. But the King would have none of it; he saw no reason for the resignation of Germaine or Sandwich, and the onslaught of Fox began again. 'What should or could I add', wrote Selwyn in those days, 'to the account which the papers now give of the debates? Charles is for my part the only one I can bear to hear, but although it be impossible for him to do anything, but go over and over again the old ground, make the same philippics, it is entertaining to me, and I can hear him (which is a singular thing) with the same pleasure and attention as if I gave ample credit to what he said, with such talents, and with such good humour, as is at the bottom of all that pretended ceremony. It is as impossible not to love him as it is to love his adversary. . . . Charles aims sometimes at humour; but he has not an atom of it, or rather it is wit which is better, but that is not talent neither, and they are indeed but despicable ones to my mind, *et de tous les dons de la nature celui qui est le plus dangereux et le moins utile*, but Charles' poignancy and misapplication of truth, make the most known falsehoods serve his purpose better: in all that he is admirable. His quotations are natural and pleasing and à propos, and if he had any judgement or conduct or character he would, and ought to be, the first man in this country.' But alas for judgement, conduct, and character! Charles Fox and his friends were now trying to revive the famous bank; but they 'had so few and such poor punters that Charles and Richard was obliged to sit down from time to time as decoy ducks'.

It was an unhappy winter for the King, who was beginning to realize that he had lost America and must soon lose his Government. It was small comfort to him that the stocks did not fall, because the market believed that the Government would do so. Not least of his troubles in those unhappy days was the Prince of Wales, who seemed to be fashioned by nature for his disappointment, for the Prince had now adopted both the politics and the society of Charles Fox, without acquiring his mentor's kindness of disposition. 'When we hunt together,' complained His Majesty, 'neither my son nor my brother speak to me; and lately when the chase ended at a little village where there was but a single post-chaise to be hired, my son and brother got into it and drove to London, leaving me to go home in a cart if I could find one.'

The surrender came gradually. At the end of the year the King agreed that Germaine should give up office, and the failing majority showed that the end was near. On the 18th of February and the 9th of March the Government was defeated, and North reported uncompromisingly that it was 'totally impossible for the present Ministry to conduct His Majesty's business any longer'. The King could hold out no longer, and on the 20th of March Lord North had the profound satisfaction of announcing the resignation of his Government. It was a freezing night and the House

adjourned after the announcement some hours earlier than
was expected. Only Lord North's carriage was waiting,
and, leaving his friends and enemies shivering in the cold,
he drove off murmuring contentedly, 'You see, gentlemen,
what it is to be in the know'.

CHAPTER V

1782–1783

A N interregnum between ministries provides much opportunity for rumour, and the pause which followed Lord
North's resignation was unusually full of gossip. Mr. Selwyn,
in an agony of anxiety for his pension, hurried from club to
club to see the Whigs at Brooks's 'fancying themselves
Ministers, and going into the place of them, as they think,
and to drive the King from every shadow of power and
dignity', and to hear the courtiers at White's gloomily speculating on the places and sinecures which would vanish under
Burke's Plan of Economy. London was full of rumours.
The King would not see Lord Rockingham; the King would
not have Charles Fox; the King would leave England; there
would be a republic. At last the truth was known. The
King had sent for Lord Shelburne, Lord Holland's old enemy.
But Lord Shelburne could not make a Government of the
remains of the Chatham group, and he could only refer to
Lord Rockingham, and Lord Rockingham could only tell
the King through Lord Shelburne on what terms the Whigs
would form a Government. There were anxious consultations with Lord Shelburne smooth and conciliatory, the
intermediary between the Court and the majority, until at
last a compromise was reached, and Lord Rockingham took
office on the 27th of March. The new Ministers went to kiss
hands; and on that day Mr. Selwyn stayed at home. 'I
could not go to Court,' he wrote mournfully, 'my temper
would not permit. I could have seen my Royal master on the
scaffold with less pain than insulted as he has been to-day. . . .
From my parlour window I saw Mr. Secretary Fox step into
his chariot from his office, and Lord Shelburne and Dunning
from the other office.' But Selwyn had no need to mourn
the humiliation of his royal master. The King had certainly
passed through a time of anxiety. He had even a message of
abdication in draft, announcing that 'His Majesty therefore

with much sorrow finds that he can be of no further utility to his Native Country, which drives him to the painful step of quitting it for ever.' But when Lord Shelburne had finished the negotiations, and the Ministers came to kiss hands, the draft could safely be laid aside, for the offices were distributed as follows:

First Lord of the Treasury	Lord Rockingham
Lord Chancellor	Lord Thurlow
Chancellor of the Exchequer	Lord John Cavendish
Secretaries of State	{Lord Shelburne / Mr. Fox
Lord President	Lord Camden
Lord Privy Seal	Duke of Grafton
First Lord of the Admiralty	Admiral Keppel
Master General of the Ordnance	Duke of Richmond
Commander-in-Chief	General Conway

It was evident that the Ministry was divided in advance. Lord Thurlow could be trusted only as long as he believed himself to be on the winning side, and Lord Shelburne had secured posts for two of his friends, Lord Camden and the Duke of Grafton, besides getting a peerage and a pension for his supporter Dunning. The exalted spirit of Burke might have upheld Whig principles in the Cabinet, but no place was found for him. His omission was probably due less to the aristocratic exclusiveness of a Whig administration than to the fact that the Whigs doubted whether Burke, with all his inspiring genius, possessed either the self-control or the judgement necessary for a cabinet minister. Young Mr. Pitt was of the quality to strengthen an administration, but he had announced that he would never accept subordinate rank, and no one would make way for this uncompromising young man of twenty-three, whose advanced views on Parliamentary Reform could arouse little enthusiasm in Whig palaces. If, as was expected, Lord Shelburne and his friends were to form a Court party in the Cabinet, the burden of opposing them would fall chiefly on Charles Fox. No wonder Horace

Walpole could 'see such seeds of mischief already sown, and
the vanquished are so far from wearing an air of defeat, that
I have not the smallest expectation of duration to the new
system. . . . I shall be much surprised if the present Administration receives a quarter's salary.'

Even without dissensions the prospects of the new Government were by no means easy. The aim of the Whigs was to
limit the power of the King over Parliament, and this was
the purpose which underlay the three Bills which they were
preparing for the reform of Parliamentary Government.
These were the Bill to exclude contractors from the House
of Commons, which would remove an obvious method of
Parliamentary corruption, the Bill disfranchising Revenue
Officers, who numbered at least 40,000 obedient or coercible
voters in an electorate of 300,000, and Burke's Economy
Bill with its reductions in sinecures and Civil List, which
had already plunged George Selwyn into the gloom of impending loss. The victims of these measures were preparing
for war, and were already spreading the rumour that the
new Ministers were reckless republicans who would stop at
nothing short of a general upheaval.

Ministers were faced also with new and alarming tendencies among the citizens and races whom they governed, for
the War of Independence had produced its repercussions in
places far from Boston. Irishmen were pointing out that all
the principles for which the colonists were fighting applied to
Ireland no less forcibly than to America, and in the matter
of misgovernment they could express their grievances with
a cogency which would reduce the American complaints to
insignificant grumblings. And Englishmen, clamorous in
the case of Yorkshire freeholders and countless petitioners,
were demonstrating unanswerably that, if the American
demand for 'No taxation without representation' contained
the approved principle of government, some drastic electoral
reforms must be made before tax-payers in England could
consider themselves represented in Parliament. Across the
Channel, French pamphleteers were most disrespectfully

H

comparing the strange enthusiasm of their King for the principles of Liberty in America with his apparent indifference to the constitutional aspirations of his own subjects. But King Louis was in a better position than the Whig ministers. He could afford for a few years longer to disregard pamphlets, protests, and popular clamours, while the new ministers in England, who had vehemently applauded all the claims and principles of the colonists, were expected without delay to apply those principles to the whole system of British Government.

And above all things it was necessary to make peace, for, although Lady Melbourne had not been entertained by the blowing up of the stocks, the financial position was precarious, and the new Ministry could hardly call for money to carry on a war which they had so long opposed.

Peace might be urgent, but it was not easy, for England was defeated and disgraced, and our enemies were pleasurably awaiting the moment when they might repay some of the humiliations which they had suffered in the days of Lord Chatham. But our enemies, though united by treaty, were by no means united in purpose, and it might be possible for a government of firmness and skill to get better terms than Lord North and the King had earned. It was a situation full of possibilities for skilful diplomacy. It might offer an opportunity to the experienced urbanity of Lord Shelburne or to the more impulsive and energetic methods of Fox. But it was essentially a task for one directing brain, and it could offer little prospect of success to the competing efforts of both statesmen. The department of Fox was responsible for all negotiations with foreign countries, and the department of Lord Shelburne was responsible for the colonies. Until American independence was recognized, the Americans were technically colonists, and Lord Shelburne could and would claim to negotiate for peace with them, while the department of Fox negotiated with our enemies in Europe. The demarcations of departmental powers and the intrigues and feuds which arise out of such demarcations have always provided one of the recreations of official life, and no one acquainted with the pleasures of interdepartmental warfare will fail to appreciate the possibilities offered by the conflicting claims of the two Secretaries of State. It was, of course, the duty of the Prime Minister to put his foot on such mischievous bickering, but Lord Rockingham had never been a strong leader, and his foot was now in the grave.

With this unpromising outlook the new Ministers set to work. Their first recorded decision disclosed their divisions. Fox believed that a separate peace might be made with Holland, and possibly even a League of Northern Nations might be formed, if the friendship of the Empress Catherine could be obtained. When the subject was before the Cabinet, it became clear that Lord Shelburne was entirely opposed to the scheme, and, originating perhaps a family tradition, was aiming at a better understanding with France. From that moment Fox, writing to Fitzpatrick, who was in Ireland as secretary to the Duke of Portland, the new Lord Lieutenant, began to predict an explosion. Early in April he writes of 'something very like a warm debate' on the Economy Bill and a 'very teasing and wrangling Cabinet' on the same subject. By the end of the month he had little hope: 'Shelburne shows himself more and more every day, is ridiculously jealous of my encroaching on his department, and wishes very much to encroach on mine. He hardly liked my having a letter from Grattan, or my having written one to Lord Charlemont. He affects the Minister more and more every day, and is, I believe, perfectly confident that the King intends to make him so. Provided we can stay in long enough to have given a good stout blow to the influence of the Crown, I do not think it signifies how soon we go out after, and have him and the Chancellor to make such a Government as they can, and this I think we shall be able to do.'

The stout blow lost much of its violence before it fell, but none the less the Rockingham Whigs succeeded in carrying their three great measures to uphold the independence of Parliament and diminish the power of the King, although the Economy Bill became law in much enfeebled form.

They were less successful when they negotiated an Irish Settlement under pressure of urgency. Fox's correspondence with Grattan and Lord Charlemont, which had displeased his fellow Secretary of State, was not an exchange of current gossip. The pressure of Irish claims became critical from the first days of the new Government, and in May they were driven to arrange a temporary settlement on the basis of abolishing the right of Great Britain to legislate for Ireland and abandoning the appellate jurisdiction of the British House of Lords. Fox would have preferred to negotiate more deliberately for a lasting settlement, but there was little hope for deliberation with Irish volunteers under arms, and, faithful to his principle that he would 'rather see Ireland totally separated from England than kept in obedience only by force', he carried the settlement through Parliament.

He was putting his whole energy into the task of his office. He never touched a card; he was never seen at Brooks's, to the disappointment, it was said, of several gentlemen who had paid up their arrears of subscription and hurried to the club in the hope of hobnobbing with a real Secretary of State. His powers of work astonished his former friends, who had 'sat often with Mr. Fox at a green table, but never before at one covered with green velvet', and Walpole was pointing to him as the 'master genius' who might still gain the ascendant. 'He already', wrote Walpole, 'shines as greatly in place as he did in Opposition, though infinitely more difficult a task. He is now as indefatigable as he was idle. He has perfect temper, and not only good-humour but good-nature; and, which is the first quality in a Prime Minister in a free country, has more common sense than any man, with amazing parts, that are neither ostentatious nor affected.' He was on the crest of the wave, and Dr. Johnson saw him at this moment as the man 'who has divided the kingdom with Caesar; so that it was a doubt whether the

Private

Mr. Fox presents his Compts. to Miss Mary Bouverie, He would not press her about coming to the Office this morning as he found she wished so much to take leave of her Mother; but Mr. Fox hopes She will not take it amiss if he acquaints her that it is indispensably necessary that she should be at the Office by four o'clock P.M. exactly as there are two dispatches to copy which can only be trusted to a confidential hand.

St. James's 19m past 1. P.M.
D. June 1782

A LETTER FROM THE SECRETARY OF STATE TO MISS MARY
BOUVERIE, AGED 6

In the possession of MRS. HENRY LASCELLES

nation should be ruled by the sceptre of George III, or the tongue of Fox'.

But the end was in sight. Lord Shelburne was an old friend of Benjamin Franklin, the American agent in Paris. The Cabinet agreed that his friendship should be used to open negotiations, and early in April a Scotch merchant named Oswald, selected for the mission by Lord Shelburne, was sent to Paris to approach Franklin. Mr. Oswald, whom Lord Holland had recommended for office some twenty years ago, seems to have possessed no great qualification for diplomacy except that of honesty, for at an early stage in the conversations he confided to Franklin that England was in a desperate state and must accept almost any terms, and he seems to have shown neither surprise nor indignation when Franklin suggested, as a means of ensuring real reconciliation and providing compensation both to injured Americans and expropriated loyalists, that Canada and Nova Scotia should be ceded to America. This remarkable proposition was put in writing and given to Mr. Oswald to be taken to London and shown to Lord Shelburne in confidence. Mr. Oswald also bore a letter expressing Franklin's hope, which we may well imagine to have been sincere, that all future negotiations would be entrusted to Mr. Oswald. Several courses were open to Lord Shelburne when this embarrassing document reached him. But one course he could hardly take with propriety as a member of the Cabinet, and that was to conceal the proposals from his colleagues, to answer them in a private letter to Franklin, and to obtain the Cabinet's sanction to Mr. Oswald's return for further negotiations. Lord Shelburne took that course.

On the 8th of May the agent selected by Fox to negotiate for a general peace reached Paris. If Fox had been a little more experienced in the conduct of departmental strife he would have chosen a representative of such importance that Mr. Oswald and his mission would have been swept into insignificance. But he appointed Mr. Thomas Grenville, a young gentleman whose qualifications for the post, beyond the fact that he was the son of the statesman whose stamp duties had caused the war, were less obvious than those of Mr. Oswald. A few days after Grenville had arrived in Paris, the news reached London that Rodney had totally defeated the French fleet at the Battle of the Saints, and taken prisoner the French commander-in-chief, de Grasse. There was a sigh of relief from England, accustomed for years to news of a very different kind, and hopes were high that it might lead to a better peace. But Grenville, although he had, as he thought, authority to concede American independence, found progress unexpectedly difficult. He soon found, when Oswald came back to France at the end of May, that Franklin preferred to negotiate with 'Lord Shelburne's ambassador', as he was called by the French, and a few days later 'Lord Shelburne's ambassador' let out to him the story of the secret paper. Tempers began to rise. Grenville wrote to Fox privately to complain and to suggest that he should be replaced by a 'dignified peer'. Fox asked for further 'proofs of this duplicity' and prepared for a battle in the Cabinet. But the position was less clear than it seemed. The Cabinet had caused a real misunderstanding about the powers of the rival envoys, and Lord Shelburne had his answer ready on the affair of the secret document. His supporters have, indeed, said that he behaved with transparent honesty in this and in every other transaction of his career. In that case he was unfortunate in the impression which he made on his contemporaries, for they regarded him, almost without exception, as a dangerous intriguer, named with good cause Malagrida and the Jesuit of Berkeley Square. He was, no doubt, in many respects the ablest of statesmen, but his ability included little or no power to inspire confidence, and his position with the King gave further grounds for suspicion. There was a wrangle in the Cabinet on the 31st of June in the absence of Lord Rockingham, and Fox found himself outvoted. He said something about resignation, but decided not to bother Lord Rockingham, who was seriously ill; and on the next day Lord Rockingham was dead.

There followed the usual consultations and hurried journeyings between the great houses. But there was little use in consultations. On the day of Lord Rockingham's death the King asked Lord Shelburne to be First Lord of the Treasury. The Rockingham side of the Cabinet proposed the Duke of Portland. Their choice was based on the unfortunate tradition of their party that membership of one of the great Whig families was in itself a qualification for high office. His other qualifications were not conspicuous, for he was far below Lord Shelburne in ability, and he would not have been proposed if the party had believed that either Fox or the Duke of Richmond would have been acceptable to the King. If the Whigs meant to assert a right to nominate the King's First Minister they would have been wiser to have put forward a candidate who could be rejected for no reason but political bias. The King refused the Duke. There were more consultations in the great Whig houses, and Mr. Secretary Fox resigned, celebrating his release from the cares of office by an immediate return to Brooks's. 'The Prince of Wales', recorded Walpole, 'dined with Mr. Fox yesterday by previous engagement; they drank royally. Charles went thence to Brooks's, stayed till four in the morning, and it being so early, finished the evening at White's with Lord Weymouth—and the evening and the morning and the next day were the first day!'

In that carouse he could celebrate something more than his freedom from the cares of office. Reflecting upon the last three months, he could, as he believed, look to the future in the best of spirits. He had shown to the world that he could turn his back on his less respectable life and assume all the qualities of a successful minister, and Walpole was announcing 'aloud and everywhere' that he was the fittest man in England to be Prime Minister. He had shown the King the danger of opposing his strength to the Whig party. For he was to-day the virtual leader of the Whigs, and he had no doubt that to-morrow all true Whigs would follow his example and desert the perfidious Malagrida. There might be a revival of the old system for a time. But sooner or later, after the King had exhausted his ingenuity in contrivance and conciliation, there must come the Government in which Charles Fox would be leader in fact if not in name.

But the vision faded during the next few days. There was a meeting of Whigs at Lord Fitzwilliam's house, and after acrimonious discussion it became evident that they were not all prepared to follow their impulsive leader. The Duke of Richmond refused to resign, and Lord Keppel felt it his duty to remain in office while the country was at war. In the end only Lord John Cavendish resigned from the Cabinet, accompanied by Burke and some of the devoted Foxites in minor office. It was a little disconcerting, also, to the orthodox Whig to find Lord Shelburne filling the vacancies in the Cabinet more easily than was expected. Fox had for some time had his doubts of his young friend William Pitt. He had hinted to him, when Lord Rockingham died, that Malagrida would 'look to *you*; *without you* they cannot succeed; *with* you I know not whether they will or no'. And that inscrutable young man had answered, 'If they reckon upon *me*, they may find themselves mistaken.' But Fox still had his doubts: 'I *believe they do* reckon on Pitt, and I believe they will *not* be mistaken.' And sure enough, Mr. William Pitt at three-and-twenty became Lord Shelburne's Chancellor of the Exchequer. 'That', wrote Walpole, anticipating the language of a later generation, 'is some glory.'

Charles Fox consoled himself with the society of Perdita Robinson, who had recently held the young Prince of Wales in thrall. His relations with that beautiful but rather tedious lady are unimportant. He explained his constant presence at her house in Berkeley Square by the necessity of keeping an eye on the movements of her neighbour, the Prime Minister, the Jesuit of Berkeley Square; while George Selwyn, insisting a little unkindly on her obscure origin, asked, 'Who should the *Man of the People* live with, but with the *Woman of the People*?' The affair did not last long.

He reverted, on leaving office, to that untidiness of appearance which had preceded his short career as a Secretary of State and his opulence in the days of his famous bank. There is a description of him in his lodgings in St. James's Street as he rose very late in the morning after a heavy night at Brooks's to receive his followers and the Prince of Wales: 'His bristly, black person, and shagged breast quite open and rarely purified by any ablutions, was wrapped in a foul linen night gown, and his bushy hair dishevelled.' The adoring Lord Holland had to admit that this description 'though of course a strong caricature' had nevertheless some truth to recommend it. No wonder the King, who had good reason for anxiety at his son's manner of life, wrote with horror of 'the Activity of Mr. Fox, who every honest Man and those the least interested in the support of their Constitution must wish to the utmost to keep out of Power'.

The exclusion of Fox was for the present the King's first object. The death of Lord Rockingham had left three parties in Parliament: Lord Shelburne governed with his precariously balanced Cabinet; Fox with the remnant of the Rockingham Whigs was in opposition; and as a third party sat Lord North with his large but uncertain following. Lord North had been silent and depressed since he left office. The loss of America seemed more serious on reflection than in the heat of action, and he had been troubled by difficulties in balancing the accounts of money which the King had given him for electoral purposes. It is not always easy to put such transactions on paper, and some of his explanations would have delighted his old enemies. 'Perhaps', he wrote in April, 'it may be answered that the sums paid to gentlemen who have the command of Boroughs, for their interest, are to be considered as Bribes. But these bargains are not usually called by that name and the money disbursed in that manner does not exceed what has been disbursed on all former occasions.' No doubt he fully appreciated the possibilities of a third party holding the balance of power, but he showed no apparent desire to negotiate with either side, and he was careful not to commit himself when the King wrote in August imploring him to support Lord Shelburne. 'Many strange scenes', wrote His Majesty with impressive gravity, 'have occurred in this country, but none more so than the present contest, it is no less than whether the sole direction of My Kingdom shall be trusted in the hands of Mr. Fox; Lord North has long known my opinion of that gentleman, which has been if possible more riveted by three months' experience of him in Office, which has finally determined me never to employ him again, consequently the contest is become personal and he indeed sees it also in that point of view.' Lord North, who had long experience of his Sovereign's epistolary style, answered with the respectful hope that he would be able to inform His Majesty of the views of his friends before the meeting of Parliament.

Meanwhile, the new Prime Minister found his task almost as difficult as his enemies could have wished. Most of the work of Government fell on him alone, and he had to give his personal attention to the negotiations for peace, which were now entirely in his hands. Fitzherbert, a diplomatist of experience, was sent out to reinforce the impressionable Oswald. It was clear enough that the Americans and their allies were far from being united, and that much might be gained by the adroit use of their dissensions. But it was no less clear that the treaty of peace would be one of defeat, and that neither the treaty nor the minister who made it would be received with enthusiasm by the defeated nation. Meanwhile, it was pleasant to bar the door against the Opposition by sending papers to the King with complacently acid notes to the detriment of his former colleagues. 'The contents', ran one of them, 'must decide on Mr. Fox's character with the Public, if they are ever called for by Parliament, I am afraid Mr. Fox has none to lose with your Majesty.' And it was no doubt consoling to both Lord Shelburne and his master when negotiations looked unpromising to assure one another that the difficulty was due to 'Mr. Fox's precipitation on the head of Independency' or to 'the strange, undigested opening of the Negotiation by Mr. Grenville, under the direction of Mr. Fox'.

The attack on the Government was opened on the 9th of July, when a pension of £3,200 awarded to the Prime Minister's friend, Colonel Barré, was challenged. The case of the Opposition was not strong, for Lord Rockingham had consented to the pension; and Burke did not improve the case, or improve his own reputation, by announcing that 'if Lord Shelburne was not a Cataline or a Borgia in morals, it must not be ascribed to anything but his understanding'. In the House of Lords the Prime Minister retaliated by affirming the right of the King to choose his own ministers, vowing that he would never consent 'that the King of England should be a King of the Mahrattas, among whom it was a custom for a number of great Lords to elect a Peishwa, who was a creature of the aristocracy, and was vested with the plenitude of power, while the King was, in fact, nothing more than a royal pageant, or puppet'. When Parliament rose on the 11th of July the King and Lord Shelburne had on the whole strengthened their position.

During that August Lord North went on a progress 'into the Tory regions of Oxford and Staffordshire', ending in Manchester with the unfamiliar experience of being drawn in his coach through the city by a cheering crowd. His triumph was observed without enthusiasm by Government and Opposition.

It was a wet and dismal summer for England. The Dutch fleet stood off the Thames to intercept a British convoy from the Baltic which was bringing much needed equipment to the naval yards, and the combined forces of France and Spain were preparing another attack on hard-pressed Gibraltar. Fortunately for the country, Lord Keppel had replaced the hapless Jimmy Twitcher at the Admiralty. In the early days of September he expounded to the Cabinet his plan to relieve Gibraltar and rescue the Baltic convoy, which had taken refuge in a Norwegian port. Admiral Millbank's squadron was to be detached from Lord Howe's fleet at

Spithead and make a feint of attack against the Dutch, which would drive the Dutch back into harbour. Then, on the first favourable wind, Millbank's squadron would sail down the Channel, before the Dutch could guess that he had left the Thames, and the combined fleet would dash to relieve Gibraltar. With the same favourable wind the Baltic convoy would run for home before the Dutch put out to sea. Almost miraculously it happened as Keppel had planned. The convoy escaped, and by the end of the month news reached London that Gibraltar was safe. The Whigs might well claim that the war would have ended very differently if Conway and Keppel had been in the place of Germaine and Sandwich.

But even with Gibraltar safe the peace negotiations moved heavily. Weeks were wasted before negotiations could be opened with America. A new American agent, Mr. Jay, who 'was a lawyer and might think of things that did not occur to those who were no lawyers' made difficulties about discussing terms until America had been recognized as an independent nation. At last, by making full use of French and Spanish dissensions, agreement was reached with America at the price of deserting the loyalists, whose property had been confiscated; and with America out of the way the negotiations with France and Spain seemed more hopeful. In September, while Fox was blazing at partridges with Coke of Norfolk, Lord Shelburne in Berkeley Square was conversing with Rayneval on a possible surrender of Gibraltar. The English terms stiffened a little when Gibraltar was saved, and through October and November Oswald and Rayneval hurried backwards and forwards between London and Paris. There were disputes in the English Cabinet, quarrels between the French and Spaniards, suspicion of all parties by the Americans. At the last moment an effort was made to soften the blow to the loyalists, but nothing could be got from Franklin but a promise that Congress would recommend the States to show mercy. There was a final wrangle with Rayneval and Vergennes over Dominica, and on the 20th of January the Preliminary Articles of Peace were signed.

Probably it was as good a peace as any one could have made at that moment, but it was a peace of defeat, and it was unlikely that the nation, exulting over the Battle of the Saints and the relief of Gibraltar, would accept it with enthusiasm. The new boundary of Canada, the new American fishing rights in the Gulf of St. Lawrence, the loss of the Floridas, Tobago, and St. Lucia, and above everything, the desertion of the loyalists, would be attacked with fury, and the Prime Minister was conscious that his party was in a minority and that he was losing friends.

The peace treaty was not his only difficulty. The new schemes of economy were rousing an agitation among place-holders; the possibility of electoral reform was contemplated with grim suspicion by some of the borough owners, who could calculate exactly the value of their property and joined the Duke of Richmond in the hope that 'a Committee, doing but little, will satisfy'; and there were new troubles in Ireland, for Lord Mansfield had decided a case which had indeed been put down before the settlement removed such cases from his jurisdiction, and nothing would satisfy the Irish but a new Act explicitly repudiating British supremacy.

And, to add to his difficulties, his Cabinet was melting. Keppel had never intended to remain, and he resigned when the war at sea was ended. Lord Carlisle resigned out of sympathy with the loyalists, and, it was suggested, with other more personal grievances against the Prime Minister. The Duke of Richmond would not attend the Cabinet, and was complaining to the King of 'Lord Shelburne's assumption of too much power'. Other ministers, the Duke of Grafton and Lord Camden, were becoming restive, and might resign at any moment.

A change was imminent, and managers were anxiously calculating the strength of parties. According to Mr. Eden the forces were 'Minister, one hundred and forty; Reynard, ninety; Boreas, one hundred and twenty; the rest unknown or uncertain'. Would it end in a coalition of parties, or would one of the parties break? Boreas had the whip hand, but he showed no sign of asserting himself, and would only, as his discontented supporters complained, 'by self or agents talk too much of absence, neutrality, moderation'.

The moves which led to the final solution of the problem were complex, and they were accompanied by the host of rumours, denials, evasions, and tentative approaches which are usual in such transactions. North was approached by the Ministry with the unflattering suggestion that his followers, without their leader, should join the Shelburne party. The move failed, and the Ministry next tried an overture to Fox. Pitt was the emissary, and the conversation was broken off when Fox made it clear that he would join only if Shelburne retired. Pitt stood by his chief, and the King relieved his feelings by attributing the failure to 'the hastiness and impoliteness of Mr. Fox'. But the Government agents were not alone in the field. George North was anxious to see his father in office again, and Eden, Lord Loughborough, Adam, and Lord John Townshend were sounding the possibilities of an arrangement between Fox and North. It did not seem a promising enterprise, for the political life of Fox had been mainly directed to the extinction of North, and North showed no great anxiety to be resuscitated. But the intermediaries persevered, and at last had the mild success of carrying to Lord North the rather unconvincing message that Mr. Fox had always thought well of him. They renewed their efforts and were authorized to inform Lord North of Pitt's overture for a coalition with Fox. At last, after many comings and goings of agents, underlings, and self-appointed negotiators, an interview between the leaders was arranged. They agreed to unite in opposing the peace treaty, and they discussed vaguely a coalition. Fox urged that the King 'should not be suffered to be his own Minister', and Lord North became quite voluble in his opinion that 'the King ought to be treated with all sort of respect and attention, but the appearance of power is all that a

King of this country can have'. The Ministers made desperate efforts at the last moment. Lord Shelburne talked
of retiring and leaving the Government to Pitt and Fox.
Finally he made through Rigby an offer of coalition to
Lord North. But it was a day late. 'I cannot meet Lord
Shelburne *now*,' said North, and Rigby went back with the
news that Lord Shelburne's administration was doomed.

If the moves and countermoves which led to the coalition
were complicated, the motives of the two leaders concerned
in that disastrous venture are even more obscure, and the
obscurity is increased by the reluctance of some of the disappointed actors to discuss after the event the considerable
parts which they had played in the tragedy. Indeed one
eminent Whig, who was regarded at the time as an ardent
advocate of coalition, assumed with some success in later
years the role of the wise counsellor whose advice had been
rejected.

But what was in the mind of Charles Fox? It is easy
enough to dispose of the motive attributed to him by his
enemies that he was tempted by the spoils of office. His
whole political career is an answer to that suggestion, and
he had in any case a definite offer of office from Shelburne
before he turned to North. At that time the dominant idea
of Fox's politics was to drive home the 'good stout blow' at
the power of the King. He believed that his business as a
Whig statesman was, above all things, to defend the power
of Parliament against the encroaching power of the King;
he believed that in Lord Shelburne the King had found an
agent if not an ally; and he believed, with some reason, that
at any moment Lord Shelburne's precarious majority might
be reinforced by Lord North with his hundred and twenty
certain votes, and if that happened, the triumph of the
King and the discomfiture of the Whig cause would be
complete.

The idea of an alliance with political opponents was not
then so remarkable as to carry its own condemnation. In
the eighteenth century the principles which underlay the

divisions of party could not easily be defined. The Tory
group was associated with High Church principles, and the·
Whigs had an undefined claim to the support of the nonconformists. But this distinction was traditional rather
than real, and the growing mercantile interest brought new
problems into politics which tended to obliterate the old
distinctions. A change of allegiance did not necessarily
mean a change of principle; and negotiations for alliance
between apparently hostile groups had been the commonplace of public life since Fox had known Parliament. The
real question in such alliances was, which of the allies should
have control; and Fox was complacently confident that in
a coalition with Lord North the power would be with Fox.
He knew well enough that this alliance was of no ordinary
kind, that he would be accused of inconsistency, lack of
principles, dishonesty; and his speeches of the last nine
years would be quoted against him. There were some unfortunate passages in those speeches. He had, for instance,
referred to his new ally as 'a lump of deformity and disease,
of folly and wickedness, of ignorance and temerity, smitten
with pride, immediately breaks all measures of patience;
it being hardly conceivable that so much pride, vice, and
folly could exist in the same animal'. This, no doubt, could
be gracefully ignored, as an example of those rhetorical
flourishes which so notoriously do not destroy friendship
and good feeling in British public life. But he had made
some remarks about coalition which would be less easy to
explain. 'What!' he had thundered in 1779, 'What! Enter
into an alliance with those very ministers who had betrayed
their country. . . . Gentlemen must have foregone their principles and have given up their honour before they could
have approached the threshold of an alliance so abominable,
so scandalous, and so disgraceful.' And the Parliamentary
Reports as recently as March 1782 showed a no less forcible
reference to the same subject: 'Mr. Fox said, from the
moment when he should make any terms with one of them,
he would rest satisfied to be called the most infamous of

mankind. He could not for one instant think of a coalition with men who, in every public and private transaction,
as ministers, had shown themselves void of every principle
of honour or honesty.'

But the recollection of such utterances left him unmoved.
He had certainly said some hard things of Lord North, but
the real quarrel had not been with Lord North, but with the
King, whom he had attacked through Lord North. It was
well known that at the height of their quarrel he had retained
some personal feeling for Boreas, for he was, as he said, a
'bad hater', and could never bring himself to carry on a
personal feud for long. At the moment all the hostility of
which he was capable was directed against Shelburne, and if
North could be used against Shelburne, so much the better
for the country. It was on this newer enmity that Loughborough relied in his intrigue for a coalition, when he wrote
that Fox would 'feel his ancient resentment totally absorbed
in his more recent hostility, which I think he has no other
probable means of gratifying'.

There was one other aspect of the coalition pre-eminently
attractive to Fox. It was a gambler's hazard. It could be
justified only by success, and success, if attained, would be
complete. 'Unless', wrote Fitzpatrick, '*a real good Government* is the consequence of this juncture, nothing can justify
it to the public.'

There were critics in plenty after the event to convict him
of lack of judgement. He should have reflected, they said,
that even before the coalition he was under suspicion. His
reasons for resigning when Shelburne became Prime Minister
had been misrepresented, even to the extent of suggesting
that his sense of aristocratic dignity was such that he would
serve under a Duke but not under an Earl. He should have
considered the effect on public opinion, and he should have
known that the 'unnatural junction' with North would
never be understood or forgiven. No doubt they were right.
Fox's judgement as a party leader was by no means infal-
lible, and the coalition was one of his mistakes. He did not

appreciate the extent to which his motives would be misrepresented and misunderstood. But it was an error and not a crime, and the error was shared by a statesman whose name is honoured by many to whom the character of Fox least appeals. Burke believed no less firmly than Fox that alliance with North was essential if the objects of the Whig party were to be accomplished.

The motives of Lord North have also given rise to conjecture. Contemporary writers have suggested that the unhappy Boreas, oppressed by the gloom of defeat, had reflected apprehensively on the threats of impeachment which had so often been hurled at him. He had pictured himself at the Bar of the House, in the Tower, perhaps even before the fatal block, and he welcomed an alliance with his most dangerous enemy as a certain escape from any possibility of impeachment. No doubt he had more than one motive for his decision, and an anxious desire to find safety in what had been the camp of his enemies may have been among them.

The first act of the new alliance was to oppose the terms of peace. It was not a happily chosen ground for attack, for Lord Shelburne might well retort that one of the new allies was responsible for losing the war, and the other had resigned when the chance of making a better peace was in his hand. The Address upon the Peace was moved on the 17th of February, and the amendment was moved by Lord Carlisle in the Lords and Lord John Cavendish in the Commons. In the Lords Shelburne defended his peace terms with skill, and the address was carried. In the Commons the main attack was made by Lord North, who spoke after Lord John Cavendish. Fox spoke later and made his public defence of the coalition:

'I am accused of having formed a junction with a noble person whose principles I have been in the habit of opposing for the last seven years of my life. That I shall have the honour of concurring with the noble Lord in the blue ribbon upon the present question is very certain, and if men of

honour can meet on points of national concern, I see no
reason for calling such a meeting an unnatural junction. It
is neither wise nor noble to keep up animosities for ever.
It is neither just nor candid to keep up animosity when the
cause of it is no more. It is not my nature to bear malice,
or to live in ill will. My friendships are perpetual, my enmities are not so. "Amicitiae sempiternae, inimicitiae placa-
biles." I disdain to keep alive in my bosom the enmities
which I may bear to men, when the cause of those enmities
is no more.'

This was quite in conformity with Fox's character, but
he was perhaps less convincing when he reviewed the
criticisms which he had so recently directed at his new
friend, and tried to turn them into an attack on Lord
Shelburne:

'When I was the friend of the noble Lord in the blue
ribbon, I found him open and sincere: when the enemy, I
found him honourable and manly. I never had reason to say
of the noble Lord in the blue ribbon that he practised any
of those little subterfuges, tricks, and stratagems which I find
in others; any of those behind-hand and paltry manœuvres
which destroy confidence between human beings, and which
degrade the character of the statesman and the man.'

The debate was remarkable as being one of the few occasions on which Pitt lost his self-control in public. He was
imprudent enough to suggest that Sheridan would do well
to reserve his epigrams for the theatre, where they were
appreciated, and leave the House to the consideration of
more serious matters. Sheridan answered with a gibe which
stuck to him for years: 'Flattered and encouraged by the
right honourable gentleman's panegyric of my talent, if
ever I again engage in the compositions he alludes to, I
may be tempted to an act of presumption, to attempt an
improvement on one of Ben Jonson's best characters . . .
the character of the Angry Boy in the Alchemist.' The
result of the division had never been in doubt. The Ministry
was in a minority of 16.

For four days the world waited, while the Prime Minister meditated on the chance of a dissolution. On the whole he thought not. He had only to look at the cartoons in Piccadilly to realize that he was not the idol of the nation, for they were now depicting him, with the most untrustworthy face, as Judas Iscariot, denounced by a triumphant Fox. And in making his decision the Prime Minister did not rely only on his own impressions. He had the advice of the most experienced authority in the country, Mr. John Robinson, who, as Secretary of the Treasury, held a position in some respects like that of a modern Government Whip. He had administered the Secret Service money and the royal contributions to political corruption, and he had 'managed' for Lord North the elections of 1774 and 1780. It was part of his duty to know the political ambitions of each member of the House, and the means, often in terms of cash, by which constituencies could be secured for the Government. The position of an official entrusted with the duties of bribery for the Government may become a little difficult when the Government changes, but Lord North, on leaving office, had defined Mr. Robinson's duty as being 'to inform, to assist, and to support His Majesty's Government, in whose hands soever it was, so far as it could be done with propriety and consistency'. He was free, therefore, to compose a memorandum on the State of Representation when Lord Shelburne asked for it, a request eagerly seconded by the King on the ground that 'this will be very material to counteract the activity of Mr. Fox'. But Mr. Robinson had to confess that he was puzzled. 'Nothing can be more difficult', he wrote, 'than to form a state of the political sentiments of the House of Commons in the present Juncture. In a stable permanent government . . . conjectures may be formed with tolerable certainty of the opinions which gentlemen will entertain on particular questions, but in a state so rent as this has lately been, torn by intestine divisions, and split into different parties, with an administration to be established, after one had been overturned and another

divided, it is the hardest task that can be to classify them.'
An election would evidently be a leap in the dark, and Lord
Shelburne prudently declined it.

On the 21st of February the final blow was struck by a
vote of censure in the Commons, and Lord Shelburne resigned.   The inevitable result was postponed while the
King, who had decided that 'no consideration shall make me
throw myself into the hands of any Party', distractedly rang
the changes of possible Prime Ministers.   He approached
Lord Weymouth and Lord Gower in vain, and for one day
he induced William Pitt to consent.   Meanwhile the Whigs
were trying to persuade the Duke of Richmond to remain in
office, and Brooks's and Devonshire House were hives of
rumour, while the Prince of Wales was announcing that his
father had not yet agreed to the plan of the coalition, 'but,
by God, he should be made to agree to it'.

Mr. Grenville, calling at the Queen's House during the
crisis, records for his brother a specimen of the King's
voluble incoherence, in which courtiers had not yet detected signs of impending tragedy: 'This, I think, was the
main gist of the conversation to this point; though I have
thrown it much more into form than it was spoken—as it
was interrupted by a great variety of digressions; upon the
coalition, in the reprobating of which I took care to join
with him most heartily; upon Fox, whom he loaded with
every expression of abhorrence; upon the Duke of Portland,
against whom he was a little less violent; upon Lord North,
to whose conduct he imputed all the disasters of the country;
upon American Independence, which seems to have been a
most bitter pill indeed; upon associations and reforms, clubs,
gaming-houses, aristocratic cabals, etc., etc.; together with
much enquiry into the state of Ireland, and the characters
and conduct of people there; and a long detail about Lord
Bellamont, who he believed was crack-brain'd and of whom
he told two curious stories of audiences which he had asked,
and in which he at last insisted that unless the King would
make him reparation for the second disgrace he had suffered

by the nomination of Lord Arran, by suffering him to kiss his hands, on or before St. Patrick's Day, for an English Baronage or an Irish Marquisate, given to him, or given to Lord Montrath and entailed upon him, he would come no more to Court; which curious condition, you may believe, has not been complied with; and consequently, said the King, I shall be delivered from the trouble of seeing him.'

At last the King gave way and sent for Lord North, who advised him to send for the Duke of Portland. There was another delay while the King tried to insist that the Duke should send in writing a full list of his proposed Ministry, and at one stage of that negotiation the Duke was imploring the King to discuss a list of the chief appointments, while the King, with his hands behind him, nimbly evaded his new minister in his refusal to look at the proffered document. 'The Administration', wrote Walpole on the 10th of March, 'that was thought settled, is not. The Duke of Portland was invited, and refused in the same breath; that is, was ordered to send his list *in writing*, and would not, and, lest any party should be in the right, he and his new friend Lord North are not agreed on their list; and yet they and their Sovereign have squabbled about part of that unsettled list. He has insisted on keeping the Chancellor, they on dismissing him. Why? oh! thereby hangs a tale, more serious than all the rest. George the Fourth has linked himself with Charles Fox. The Chancellor was consulted (by the King) and is said to have expressed himself in terms that would be treason, if the present tense were the future; but, that I may be in the praemunire I leave to your nephew to expound the rest by word of mouth.' The story which Walpole so prudently suppressed was typical of the Lord Chancellor. Consulted by the King, he had growled out the opinion that His Majesty would 'have no peace till your son and Fox are secured in the Tower'.

On the 2nd of April the Coalition Government was formed and Charles Fox was once more a Secretary of State. There

was nothing unexpected in the distribution of the principal
offices:

First Lord of the Treasury	Duke of Portland
Secretaries of State	{ Lord North { Mr. Fox
President of the Council	Lord Stormont
Lord Privy Seal	Lord Carlisle
Chancellor of the Exchequer	Lord John Cavendish
First Lord of the Admiralty	Lord Keppel

The King struggled hard to keep Lord Thurlow, but he had
to give way, and the Great Seal was put into commission.
Lord Townshend was present when the new ministers came
to kiss hands, and his description of the scene became
famous. He had, he said years afterwards, foreseen that
the Coalition Ministry could not last, for he was at Court
when Mr. Fox kissed hands, and he 'observed George III
turn back his ears and eyes just like the horse at Astley's,
where the tailor he had determined to throw was getting
on him'.

The new Government, as Fitzpatrick had said, could succeed only by success, and the prospect of success was far
from bright. The immediate problem was the peace treaty
on which they had defeated Shelburne, and much depended
on the hope of improving the terms of peace. It was a faint
hope; for the League of Northern Nations, which had long
been the dream of Fox's foreign policy, would at best be a
plant of slow and uncertain growth. Its progress was at the
mercy of the 'incurable levity of the Empress Catherine',
who was by no means a person to be hurried. Meanwhile
there was nothing for it but a gallant attempt to make a
better bargain where Shelburne had already tried and failed.

Political symptoms at home were also disquieting. The
demand for electoral reform, with its growing multitude of
freeholders and petitioners in support, was no ephemeral
agitation to be soothed by fair words. It was to persist for
half a century, unappeased by promises and undeterred by

force, until it achieved its triumph in the Reform Bill. For the present the cause had William Pitt as its spokesman in Parliament, and ministers were gloomily aware of its possibilities as a weapon of opposition, while they realized that a Reform Bill which satisfied the petitioners would be far from satisfactory to the Whig aristocracy.

In Ireland, too, affairs were full of anxiety. The volunteers, who had done so much with Whig applause to achieve Irish liberty, remained obstinately under arms with most alarming prospects for the independence of the new Irish Parliament. Agitated dispatches were flying between Dublin and London, and the Ministry was faced with the unwelcome necessity of making a decision. Their dilemma was as unpleasant as it was familiar, for it was the choice between resistance or submission to a threat of force. The subject belonged to Lord North's department, but the burden of it rested on Fox, who knew well enough that Boreas was unlikely to take any decision until disaster was beyond repair.

India, like Ireland was the affair of Lord North, and, like Ireland, it was swept into the net of Lord North's more energetic colleague, although Lord North had more personal experience of Indian affairs than any member of the Cabinet. It was a difficult and urgent problem, but it was one of the few problems from which the Ministry hoped to acquire merit. The House was not uninformed on Indian affairs. In the last three years the difficulties of the Court of Proprietors of East India Stock had been constantly debated, and, assisted by no less than eighteen reports of select committees, members could show a more detailed knowledge of the subject than might be found among legislators of a later generation. The Court of Proprietors and India House could expect little sympathy from either party in Parliament. Nabobs, with their enviable but obnoxious wealth and their no less obnoxious purchases of seats, were already unpopular with the governing class, and the Court of Proprietors was liked no better than its servants. In 1781 a new charter had been negotiated on terms which provided for a payment of £400,000 by the Company in discharge of all debts. In the following year Dundas put before the House the report of his Committee of Inquiry, and moved a series of resolutions against the high officers of the Company, Sir Thomas Rumbold, Sir Elijah Impey, and Mr. Hastings himself. The House directed that Mr. Hastings should be recalled, but the Court of Proprietors took advantage of the confusion which followed Lord Rockingham's death to cancel the order of recall. At the same time the Chairman of the Court of Proprietors was accused of deliberately withholding evidence from the Select Committee. It was unfortunate for the Court of Proprietors that within a few months of these acts of defiance they should be forced to throw themselves on the mercy of the House. But in 1783 they had to make the melancholy confession that, instead of paying the last £100,000 of their debt of £400,000, they would need help to the tune of £900,000 to carry on their work for another year. The whole future of the government of India and the relation between the trading corporation and the British Government were in the melting-pot, and the statesman who could achieve a solution would gain the applause of all parties.

Fox began his new duties with the zeal which he had already shown in office. His first concern was the Peace Treaty, and he conducted negotiations with a keenness which drew from Vergennes, accustomed to the suavities of Berkeley Square, the rueful admission, 'c'est un fagot d'épines que ce M. Fox'.

Once more he had abandoned gambling with the same abrupt renunciation, and once more he astonished London by his reappearance as the model of industry. He had already broken his allegiance to Perdita Robinson; but for this he had motives other than the desire to assume the gravity of the senator. During his nine months out of office something had happened to him which was to change the whole course of his life. He had met Mrs. Armistead, and in her society he was moving towards that life of placid domesticity which was to become his ideal existence. She was a lady of obscure origin, and much conjecture has been wasted on the manner of her past life. That question, so attractive to contemporary gossip, has little interest to-day. From all the gossip and unconfirmed rumour one fact alone emerges. However she may have spent her earlier life, she spent the rest of her days in an existence which, except for the temporary omission of a marriage ceremony, had all the appearance and circumstances of the most staid and blameless respectability. Her appearance, as Reynolds has portrayed it, suggests the well-known picture of Mrs. Fitzherbert. Her face was of the same type, and, like Mrs. Fitzherbert's, it suggests good nature and sympathy rather than acute intelligence. Even the celebrated Mr. Lavater, whose estimates of character from physiognomy were sometimes as disconcerting to his contemporaries as the revelations of psycho-analysts have been to the present generation, would have found it difficult to discern any trace of selfishness or spite in the features of Mrs. Armistead.

Under her influence Charles Fox's conception of the life of an Englishman was changing. The pleasures and emotions of Brooks's, Devonshire House, Westminster, and even Newmarket, were beginning to pall, and in their place a vision was forming of an existence surprisingly repugnant to anything associated with him in the past—a little house in the country with a small farm, a placid existence with Mrs. Armistead, his books, the nightingales in the garden. Many of the friends of his youth would have recoiled in horror from the thought of such a life; few of them could have appreciated it; and probably none of them at that time, except Fitzpatrick, realized that their leader's increasing weariness of the life of London and his increasing devotion to rural domesticity were the explanation of many of his perplexing moods and actions.

Meanwhile history was repeating itself. Once more the King was drafting and re-drafting his message of abdica-

tion, in which Parliament was, if all went ill, to be informed
that, notwithstanding His Majesty's 'pleasing hope' that
he 'might have proved the happy Instrument of conciliating all Parties and thus collecting to the Service of the State
the most respectable and most able Persons this Kingdom
produced', his efforts had been frustrated 'by the obstinacy
of a powerful party that has long publicly manifested a
resolution not to aid in the service of the Empire unless the
whole Executive management of Affairs is thrown entirely
into its hands', and he was 'therefore resolved to resign my
Crown and all the Dominions appertaining to it to the Prince
of Wales, my Eldest Son and Lawful Successor, and to retire
to the care of my Electoral Dominions the Original Patri-
mony of my Ancestors'. His Majesty seemed to have
better occasion for alarm than he had a year ago, for the
Opposition was cutting a poor figure. 'The ousted ministers',
wrote Walpole, 'do not attempt a division in either House
of Parliament. In the Lords, where most vigour was expected, Lord Shelburne and the late Chancellor made so
ridiculous a figure, that even they themselves appear
ashamed. Mr. William Pitt, though little supported, in-
dulges himself in shining, and does shine marvellously. His
language is thought equal to his father's; his reasoning much
superior; and no wonder, if at all good! He is less deficient,
even when speaking on affairs of money; and in his last
speech, had more fire than usual. Is not all this wonderful
at twenty-three? Is it not wonderful, when he can shine,
though within the orbit of Mr. Fox, and opposed to him?'

It was perhaps an indication of the poor prospects of the
Opposition that Lord Thurlow should intimate to Lord
North that his restoration to the Woolsack might be a
means of overcoming the King's objection to new peerages,
and might even lead to some show of royal favour. This
explanation of Lord Thurlow's venture was a not unfair criticism of his character, but the Whigs suspected in it something more than the opening move of a veteran place-hunter.
The King had broken their last Government by the intrigues

of one of his friends in the Cabinet, and they did not mean
to give him another chance.

The spring began without danger to the new Government. In May Pitt made a 'very long, guarded, and fluctuating speech' on his favourite subject of Electoral Reform,
which drew from Horace Walpole an agitated lament of
the waning eighteenth century: 'We have lost our grandeur!
I hope our liberty is not to follow it!' But neither Dundas's
India Bill, which was introduced and dropped in April, nor
Pitt's fluctuating speech, was the signal for renewed activity
in the Opposition. Indeed the most energetic of the Coalition's enemies were to be found outside Parliament. Both
Fox and North were easy subjects for the caricaturists, and
a combination of the two was irresistible. From the first
day of the Coalition a series of cartoons began portraying
the ignoble association of the Fox and the Badger. There
were also double-headed statues, hackney coachmen squab-
bling on the box, thieves sharing plunder, and always the
Fox outwitting Boreas. The cartoon of the eighteenth
century was a powerful and savage weapon, and these
incessant attacks had their effect on both statesmen.

The first shock to the new alliance came in an unexpected
way. The Prince of Wales was now growing up, and it was
necessary to provide him with an 'establishment'. There
was nothing in the matter to cause undue anxiety to
Ministers, although the amount of His Royal Highness's
income might occasion some difficulty, for Florizel's views
on the standard of living necessary for the First Gentleman
of Europe were altogether princely, and his Whig friends
felt some embarrassment in announcing the formidable
estimate of £100,000. But it had to be done, and the Duke
reflected uncomfortably on the best manner of putting it
to Parliament. Reflection produced the ingenious solution
that only £50,000 need be asked of Parliament, if the King
could be persuaded to grant the remaining £50,000 from
the Civil List, with a possible arrangement for repayment
from the Sinking Fund 'in case Your Majesty should judge

it expedient to call upon your Parliament for the whole of
their assistance on the present important occasion'. This
suggestion was conveyed to the King with the alarming
news that the Prince's debts to tradesmen now amounted
to over £29,000. The King did not keep them waiting, nor
did his answer leave them in doubt. At 'm. 59 pt. 10 a.m.'
next morning he informed the Duke that he could not 'find
words expressive enough of my utter indignation and
astonishment at the letter I have just received', complaining bitterly that under the new proposal 'I am to be saddled
with the whole Odium of this measure, and the expense at
the same time ultimately to fall entirely on me who am not
from my numerous progeny in a situation to bear it', and
accusing his Minister of neglecting King and Country 'to
gratify the passions of an ill-advised Young Man'. It was
useless for the Duke to protest his loyalty and to offer to
go back to the original plan. The King repeated 'every
sillable of my letter', and assured Lord North that 'the
people shall know how well founded the principles of
Oeconomy are in those who have so loudly preached it up'.
After a day of agitated correspondence he went back on the
whole proposal, changed his mind, and finally announced
that rather than allow a 'shameful squandering of Public
Money' he would give the Prince £50,000 from the Civil
List, which, with the revenue of the Duchy of Cornwall,
would 'make his income twenty-seven thousand pounds
more than the late King thought expedient to grant me in
a similar situation'. At the same time he sent for Lord
Temple and stopped the Duke of Richmond from going to
France.

It was a real crisis. The Prince urged his friends to resign
and 'had a fever with vexation'. For a day it seemed that
they had gone too far to avoid resignation, but the situation
was saved by the King himself, who at the last moment felt
a doubt whether his grounds of quarrel were entirely well
chosen. He decided to retreat, and 'in an agony of tears,
kissed the Duke, confessed he had gone too far, and begged

the Duke to rescue him'. The Ministers, no less anxious than the King to get out of the difficulty, responded to this appeal, and Charles Fox was sent to persuade the Prince to put himself in the King's hands. The task needed all his eloquence and charm, but he ultimately succeeded. The Prince accepted the King's allowance, and Parliament was asked only to pay his debts. 'But the Prince', says Walpole, 'declared he would never forgive Lord Temple.'

After this encounter it was perhaps not surprising that the King should firmly refuse any new peerages. '*No peerages, no marks of real support*,' wrote Fitzpatrick, 'but civility enough.' And they anxiously debated whether the royal civility might indicate a frame of mind less hostile than the refusal of peerages would suggest. But it was difficult to avoid the conclusion that the King was waiting with all the practised experience of his twenty-three years on the throne to overthrow his ministers on the first possible opportunity. 'The King', wrote Fox, 'continues to behave with every degree of civility and sometimes even with cordiality; *cependant il faut voir.*'

Leaders of the Opposition were also making discreet inquiries. Lord Thurlow, tirelessly intriguing, was seeing the King 'as if his audience had had no particular view, and had been in a manner casual', and he was trying on His Majesty's behalf to sound Pitt on the question of modifying his declared view 'on the subject of Parliamentary reform, and of the influence of the Crown, especially the latter'. It was hinted that 'the King has gone through the worst' when the new ministers took office, and 'a change was not so necessary to the King', but it was not difficult for Pitt to meet this rather ingenuous manœuvre by a firm refusal to make terms of any kind. 'I reminded him', he wrote in a letter which his opponents a few years later would joyfully have quoted, 'how much I was personally pledged to Parliamentary reform on the principles I have publicly explained, which I should support on every seasonable occasion.'

Tempers wore a little thin during the summer, and Fox

was acrimonious at the refusal of General Conway to 'oblige him' with promotions in the Army. Requests for patronage from him were unusual, as his Aunt, Lady Sarah Napier, found when she tried to advance the careers of her husband and the consistently unsuccessful Mr. O'Brien. Conway's share in the transaction brought him a lecture from Horace Walpole: 'I have a high opinion of Mr. Fox, and believe that by frankness you may become real friends, which would be greatly advantageous to the country. There is no competition in my mind where you are concerned: but Fox is the minister with whom I most wish you united—indeed, to all the rest I am indifferent or adverse: but, besides his superior abilities, he has a liberality of acting that is to my taste; it is like my father's plainness, and has none of the paltry little finesse of a statesman.'

But neither superior abilities nor paltry finesse could extort from the French any improvement in the terms of peace. The negotiations were accompanied by a series of acid comments from the King, such as 'for every difficulty in concluding Peace the Country has alone to blame itself', and 'I am not surprised at France not putting the last strokes to the Definitive Treaty as soon as we may wish, as our having totally disarmed in addition to the extreme anxiety shown for Peace . . . certainly makes Her feel that she can have no reason to apprehend any Evil from so shifting a position.' Finally, on the 7th of September, when the Peace, in which it was not easy to find any appreciable improvement on Lord Shelburne's terms, was proclaimed, His Majesty was 'glad it is on a day I am not in town, as I think this compleats the Downfall of the lustre of this Empire: but when Religion and Public Spirit are quite absorbed by Vice and Dissipation, what had now occurred is but the natural consequence; one comfort I have, that I have alone tried to support the Dignity of my Crown and feel I am innocent of the Evils that have occurred, though deeply wounded that it should have happened during my Reign.'

In November the crisis in Ireland developed alarmingly. The Volunteers were still under arms, intimidating the new Irish Legislature, and politicians were beginning to reflect anxiously on the possibility of buying off these formidable patriots with new concessions. It was a question of principle, and on such questions Fox was always at his best. Observing morosely that 'this Country is reduced low enough, God knows, but depend upon it we shall be tired if, year after year, we are to hear of granting something new, or acquiescing in something new, for the sake of pleasing Ireland', he wrote to Lord Northington a memorable letter urging no surrender to threats:

'If they are treated as they ought to be, if you show *firmness*, and that firmness is seconded by the aristocracy and Parliament, I look to their dissolution as a certain and not very distant event. If otherwise, I reckon their government, or rather their anarchy, as firmly established, as such a thing is capable of being, and your Government certainly as completely annihilated. If you ask me what I mean by firmness, I have no scruple in saying, that I mean it in the strictest sense, and understand by it a determination not to be swayed in any the slightest degree by the Volunteers, nor even to attend to any petition that may come from them. This sounds violent, but I am clear it is right, for if they can pretend with any plausibility that they have carried any one point, it will be a motive for their continuing in their present state.'

Lord Northington, who had shown signs of vacillation, responded to this appeal, but hinted that his difficulties with the Volunteers were increased by 'the influence of a *secret hand* attempting to undermine Government here; I mean a secret hand from a high quarter'. He deplored, also, the quality of his assistants. It was, he said, the unfortunate habit of ministers to make Ireland 'the first step in politics', and to send there 'gentlemen taken wild from Brooks's to make their dénouement in public life'.

From these depressing subjects they turned hopefully to

India, 'our India business', as Fox called it, 'on which all depends', and on the 18th of November the India Bill was introduced. Sweeping reforms were expected by a House which had for years listened to stories of misgovernment, and the expectations of the House were not disappointed. The main purpose of the Bill was to remove the government from the Court of Directors and the Court of Proprietors and vest it in a Board of seven members, who were to be answerable to Parliament. The first members of the Board were named in the Bill. They were persons of recognized qualifications headed by Lord Fitzwilliam, a close friend of Fox. They were to hold office for five years, and vacancies thereafter were to be filled by the King.

By modern standards there is nothing remarkable about the Bill, which anticipated the present practice of creating a statutory body to relieve an overburdened legislature. But to the Parliament of 1783 it was both remarkable and disconcerting. The displacement of the Court of Directors and Court of Proprietors was an interference with property which could hardly pass unchallenged; and it was evident that the new Board appointed by the Coalition would exercise during its term of office a patronage which might go far to counterbalance the patronage of the Court. This was the real ground for alarm in the Opposition. The Coalition might be turned out, but it would retain Indian patronage and the influence in elections, which went with patronage, as long as the members of the new Board remained. No doubt Burke and Fox appreciated this aspect of their scheme, and intended their Bill to be at once a genuine reform and a point in the party game.

But whatever their motives, it was a dangerous venture for a Government whose existence nothing but success could justify. The Company was the most powerful trading corporation in the country, and other corporations would rally to its support. The enemies of the Bill would be strong and determined, while its friends, according to Burke, would be 'all the people, and all the names and descriptions that,

relieved by this Bill, will bless the labours of this parliament'.
'There is', he concluded in a memorable peroration, 'not a
tongue, a nation, or a religion in India, which will not bless
the presiding care and manly beneficence of this House, and
of him who proposes to you this great work.' It was an inspiring picture, but the enemies were in Westminster with their
votes and their money, and the applauding tongues, nations,
and religions of India were remote and voteless.

Fox introduced his Bill in a speech of two hours and a
quarter. 'The die', wrote Fitzpatrick, 'is cast, and Administration is to stand or fall upon the issue of the question.' The first reading was two days later, and Fitzpatrick
again reported progress to his brother: 'We appear to be
strong in the House of Commons, though I think it is difficult to foresee the event of the business.' The forecast of
Boreas was even less confident. 'Influence of the Crown',
wrote that experienced statesman, 'and influence of party
against Crown and people are two of the many topics which
will be urged against your plan. The latter of the two objections will not be sounded so high and loudly in the House of
Commons, but it may be one of the most fatal objections to
your measure.'

The cartoonists increased their efforts, and Sayer produced his famous Carlo Khan, in which Lord North, as a
docile and rather bewildered elephant, triumphantly ridden
by Carlo Khan, the Man of the People, as an oriental poten-
tate, is escorted down Leadenhall Street by Burke as an
Indian herald. It was among the cleverest of its kind, and
its success was immediate.

The second reading was on the 27th of November, and it
was preceded by petitions against the Bill from the East
India Company and the Common Council of the City of
London. The protest of John Company was expected, but
opposition from the City was alarming. Fox spoke long
and showed a knowledge of Indian finance, which, as usual,
aroused the astonishment of members who still found it
difficult to believe that he was capable of serious and

CARLO KHAN

From a cartoon by SAYER *in the author's possession*

prolonged work, and on the second day Burke made one of the greatest of his orations. Towards the end, knowing that the scheme would be attacked as a measure of Coalition patronage, he turned to the mover of the Bill:

'He has put to hazard his ease, his security, his interest, his power, even his darling popularity, for the benefit of a people whom he has never seen. This is the road that all heroes have trod before him. He is traduced and abused for his supposed motives. He will remember that obloquy is a necessary ingredient in the composition of all true glory; he will remember that it is not only in the Roman customs, but it is in the nature and constitution of things, that calumny and abuse are essential parts of triumph. These thoughts will support a mind which only exists for honour, under the burthen of temporary reproach. He is doing, indeed, a great good; such as rarely falls to the lot, and almost as rarely coincides with the desires, of any man. Let him use his time. Let him give the whole length of the reins to his benevolence. He is now on a great eminence, where the eyes of mankind are turned to him. He may live long, he may do much; but here is the summit. He never can exceed what he does this day.' The House divided at half-past four in the morning with a majority of 114 for the Bill.

Meanwhile the enemy was preparing. Mr. Atkinson, a member of the Court of Proprietors, and Mr. Jenkinson, active as a King's Friend, were in frequent consultation with Mr. John Robinson, who was now retiring from the Treasury. They were convinced that no one but the King could now prevent the passing of the Bill, and, once the Bill was passed, the Coalition would be firmly established. But how could the King be persuaded to act? He had contemplated a breach with his Government on the Prince's allowance, and he had thought better of it in floods of tears at the last moment. The India Bill filled him with that voluble indignation which any liberal proposal might be expected to arouse in him, and he quite appreciated the alarming possibilities of patronage under Lord Fitzwilliam's new Board. He disliked the Bill intensely, but was it safe to refuse the royal assent? If he refused it, and was afterwards defeated in Parliament, would he not be driven to use that draft message of abdication, which he had kept handy since the Whigs had taken office? On this point the experienced Robinson was invaluable. He was able to demonstrate from his vast knowledge of the less attractive side of political life that if the King dismissed his Government and a new Government, sympathetic to royal prejudices, were formed, the new administration would beyond question win the election, if Parliament were dissolved and the election were 'managed' in the manner which the King and Mr. Robinson so well understood. Robinson's opinion carried much weight with the King, and Lord Thurlow and Lord Temple were able to suggest a form of intervention which should produce the desired effect with the least possible danger to the King himself. On the day of the second reading Lord Thurlow left with the King a note of their proposals signed 'Nugent Temple'. It would be dangerous, they suggested, to refuse the royal assent, and it would be dangerous to give it, but suppose the King allowed a hint of his feelings to be conveyed to some of the Peers 'whose duty to His Majesty would excite them to appear', then there would be every chance of the Bill being thrown out in the House of Lords, and it was probable that the Ministers would soon follow their Bill. 'Everything', wrote Atkinson to Robinson on the 3rd of December, 'stands prepared for the blow if a certain person has courage to strike it.' The King meditated anxiously on Lord Temple's suggestion, and the more he meditated the more he liked it. Before the Bill reached the House of Lords he had made up his mind, and without giving the slightest hint to his Ministers that he objected to their measure or wished to see it altered, he gave his authority to Lord Temple to inform peers that 'he should deem those who should vote for the bill not only not his friends but his enemies'.

On the 9th of December the Bill was presented to the House of Lords, and rumours of royal activity were already abroad. The Duke of Portland, instead of approaching the King, bickered with Lord Temple about the advice offered, which, Lord Temple declared, would remain undisclosed and 'lodged in the breast of His Majesty'. The wrangle only strengthened the opposition, and on the second reading defeat became certain. 'The bishops waver,' wrote Fitzpatrick dramatically, 'and *the Thanes fly from us*.' Two days later the Bill was rejected by nineteen votes, the Prince of Wales voting for the minority.

On the same day the Commons discussed the rumours of royal intervention, and passed a belated resolution declaring it a breach of privilege for any one to 'repeat any opinion or pretended opinion of His Majesty upon any bill or other proceeding depending in either House of Parliament', with much denunciation of secret influence, backstairs intrigue, and plotting cabals.

The King's answer to the resolution was prompt. At midnight on the 18th of December the Ministers were dismissed, and Fox and North were directed to surrender their seals by the hands of their Under-Secretaries, as a personal interview would be distasteful to the King.

Once more Boreas, if we may believe a contemporary account, supplied a touch of comedy on leaving office. He was in bed when the King's messenger arrived and insisted on seeing him, and after some discussion he admitted the messenger, with the remark that 'if you see Lord North you will see Lady North too'. He then handed over the key of the cupboard, in which he had put the seal, and turned over to sleep again. It was his last speech as a minister.

CHAPTER VI

1783–1784

Mɪɴɪsᴛᴇʀs had been dismissed but they were far from accepting defeat. The mood of the more active members of the Coalition combined indignation with confidence. 'We are beat in the Lords', wrote Fox, 'by such treachery on the part of the King, and such measures on the part of his *friends* in the House of Lords, as one could not expect either from him or them. . . . However we are so strong that nobody can undertake without madness; and, if they do, I think we shall destroy them almost as soon as they are formed.' Fitzpatrick wrote to his brother that they expected a dissolution, but were 'sanguine enough to hope for a majority in the new Parliament', and a few days later he assured the lady who temporarily held his affections that 'it is supposed the old ministry *must* be reinstated, but I suppose there will be a long struggle first'.

They had every cause for indignation, for they were entitled to expect that the King would inform them of his objection to their Bill, and give them at least a chance of amending it, before he intrigued against them in the House of Lords. But their grounds for confidence in the future are less evident. They had no one of Mr. Robinson's experience to forecast for them the result of an election in each constituency, but some of Robinson's information was available to them, and they must have known that many of their seats were in danger. But, in spite of danger signals from the constituencies, they began their opposition in the confident belief that no one would dare to form a Government against them; that such a Government, if formed, could not exist for a moment against the solid Coalition majority; and that the return of the Coalition to office was then inevitable.

Their confidence remained unshaken when Parliament met on the next day, the 19th of December, and Lord

North took his seat with Fox on the front Opposition bench. No one seemed to know what would happen until a young lawyer, Mr. Pepper Arden, rose in his place to move a new writ for the borough of Appleby 'in the room of the Right Honourable William Pitt, who, since his election has accepted the office of First Lord of the Treasury and Chancellor of the Exchequer'. So the King had turned to Pitt and not Shelburne, and the Opposition roared with laughter at the news that the Angry Boy would try to make a Government. Dundas, on behalf of the new administration, asked the House to sit on the next day, a Saturday, to proceed with the third reading of the Land Tax Bill. Fox flatly refused, and warned the House that Parliament was on the eve of a dissolution, which would leave the country exposed to 'dreadful calamities'. He was 'struck with astonishment that there could be found in the Kingdom a subject daring enough to advise his Sovereign to so desperate a measure', and, without questioning the prerogative of the Crown in dissolving Parliament, he claimed 'the undoubted right of that House to call ministers to account for any wanton or imprudent exercise of that prerogative'. 'No one', he thundered, 'could say that such a prerogative ought to be exercised merely to suit the convenience of an ambitious young man.'

During the week-end more became known of the new Government. Thurlow was inevitably Lord Chancellor; Lord Temple was to be Secretary of State and Leader in the Upper House; Lord Gower, a valuable acquisition, was to be President of the Council; and the Duke of Richmond, Fox's uncle, who had not forgiven the party for passing him over for the Duke of Portland, was to be Master General of the Ordnance. But it became apparent when the House met on the 22nd of December that the new Prime Minister's difficulties were not ended. Mr. Grenville announced that his kinsman, Lord Temple, had resigned because he did not wish to shelter himself in office from any inquiry which the House might contemplate. It was true that he had resigned, and the news had given Pitt a sleepless night. But Lord

Temple's withdrawal could hardly be attributed to the lofty motives suggested by Mr. Grenville. His Lordship thought that some 'mark of the King's approbation', to be precise a Dukedom, was due to him, and he resigned without ceremony when it was not forthcoming. After hearing Mr. Grenville the House went into Committee, and Erskine moved an address to the King calling upon him not to dissolve Parliament. The resolution was passed without division, although Mr. Bankes assured the House that dissolution was not proposed and that Mr. Pitt would resign if Parliament were dissolved against his opinion. It was a day for the Opposition. 'The confusion of the enemy', wrote Fox, 'is beyond all description, and the triumph of our friends proportionate. I own I am one of those who rather am sorry that the thing was not brought to a decision by a dissolution, because the blame will now be laid on Temple's cowardice, and not upon the real impracticability of the attempt.'

But the Prime Minister did not mean to allow a dissolution. He had refused to form a Government when Shelburne went out, because he was not sure that he could count on winning the election if Parliament were dissolved. But this time he had good grounds for confidence. Mr. Robinson had again been at work, and he had ready an analysis of the House of Commons seat by seat. He showed first the division of votes which Pitt might expect on taking office. They were 149 pro, 104 hopeful, 54 doubtful, and 231 against. The next columns foretold the result of a general election as 253 pro, 116 hopeful, 66 doubtful, and 123 against. Scotland, under the drastic management of Dundas, and the English close boroughs were expected to account for most of the change, and the analysis included a 'wild wide calculation' of the probable cost of 'managing' 137 of the seats. It would need £193,000, besides promises of patronage; but Robinson had no doubt of the result if his methods were applied. Meanwhile time was on the side of the new Government. Members of the North section of the Coalition, whose seats depended on Government patronage, would realize

that unless they quickly came to terms with the new order
they would certainly lose their seats, and members who
depended on the Chatham interest were in the same dilemma.
Unless Fox could drive out the Government it was certain
that coalitionists whose seats were not safe would begin to
cross over. Delay would also allow the East India Company
to diffuse propaganda over the country and to make other,
less public, arrangements against the Coalition. And Pitt
had, besides, a personal reason for prolonging the life of
Parliament. He intended to make it absolutely certain that
after the election he would be Prime Minister. He had seen
that appointment offered to Lord Gower and Lord Weymouth, he had seen Lord Shelburne passed over, and he did
not propose to be passed over himself. His claim would be
unassailable if he could hold out for a few months against a
hostile majority. Neither on private nor public grounds did
he want an immediate election.

The House met again on Christmas Eve to hear the King's
assurance, in answer to their resolution, that there would be
no dissolution during the recess. They adjourned until the
12th of January with an intimation from Fox that he
contemplated 'some pointed resolution after the holidays in
order to secure the House against a dissolution'. The Whigs
were still cheerful. Fox wrote to Lord Northington vehemently urging him not to resign the Lord Lieutenancy until
he knew 'the event of the 12th of January' of which he had
'no doubt but it will be the most decisive victory on our side
that has ever happened in Parliament'. Mrs. Crewe, who
usually reflected the opinion of the advanced section of her
party, was heard to opine that 'Mr. Pitt may do what he
likes during the holidays; but depend upon it, it will be
only a mince-pie administration'. And Mr. Gibbon in less
homely metaphor committed himself to the opinion that
'Billy's painted galley must soon sink under Charles' black
collier'.

Fox returned from his Christmas holiday more than
ever convinced that a 'pointed resolution' would not only

prevent a dissolution but would demolish both Pitt's
Government and the King's power. The Whig leaders, after
discussions by day and night at Burlington House, were now
resolved to fight. But Burlington House was not the only
scene of activity during the recess. From Leadenhall Street
the Committee of Proprietors were sounding the alarm to
corporate bodies throughout the country. 'Our property
and charter are forcibly invaded' was their message. 'Look
to your own.' There were perceptible signs of response to this
appeal, and the Prime Minister had other causes for increasing confidence. He had secured a peerage for his cousin,
Thomas Pitt, and he had refused to accept for himself the
Clerkship of the Pells of the Exchequer which had just
become vacant. He had given it to Barré in exchange for
that veteran's pension, which would now cease to be a public
charge. This evidence of the King's favour and his own high
principles had its effect on wavering coalitionists.

On the 12th of January, the day of the 'pointed resolution', it was decided that resolutions should be moved by
Fox declaring it a high crime and misdemeanour to issue
money for the public service without the sanction of an
Appropriation Act, and postponing the second reading of
the Mutiny Bill, and that Lord Surrey, selected for the duty
by Sheridan's exclamation at Burlington House, 'Saddle
white Surrey for the field to-morrow!' should move resolutions calling for the appointment of 'an Administration
which had the confidence of that House and the public' and
condemning the manner in which 'the sacred name of the
King had been unconstitutionally used'. It was the Prime
Minister's first meeting with the House, and he rose to
deliver a message from the King. But Fox would have none
of it until the resolutions had been passed, and Pitt had to
give way. The debate took its now customary course. Fox
made play with 'secret influence, backstairs intrigue, the
dark junto' and the 'inordinate ambition' of the Prime
Minister; and Pitt vehemently repudiated any influence or
intrigue so far as concerned his own actions. The resolutions

were carried, but the majority showed an alarming fall from the great days of the India Bill, and it was disconcerting to observe signs of approval among the country gentlemen when Mr. Powys spoke of a possible union of parties, suggesting that 'it would immortalize the individual who could effect a reconciliation and produce a union between the late Secretary and the present Chancellor of the Exchequer'. Reconciliation, as Fox saw, would mean compromise, with the King undefeated and the Court strongly represented in the Cabinet. The debate ended in an anticlimax when Pitt was at last allowed to deliver his message from the King. It proved to be only an intimation that some Hessian troops returning from America must be landed temporarily in England until the ports of the Weser were unfrozen.

The 'pointed resolution' was less encouraging than they had hoped, although it made an immediate dissolution difficult; and the Duchess of Devonshire, in the style of her more oracular Whig friends, warned her mother gravely that 'if Mr. Pitt succeeds, he will have brought about an event which he himself, as well as every Englishman, will repent ever after—for if he and the King conquer the House of Commons, he will destroy the consequence of that House and make the Government quite absolute'.

Pitt's next move was to introduce his own India Bill. It was in many respects not unlike Fox's ill-fated measure, but it left the Charter of the Company in being and it vested the appointment of the new Board of Control in the King. It had, of course, no chance of even a hearing and it was rejected on second reading on the 16th of January by a majority which had fallen ominously to eight. Fox at once gave notice that he would again bring in his own Bill, and tempers rose when he called upon Pitt to disclose to the House his intention as to dissolution. The Prime Minister sat unmoved while the Opposition bellowed disapproval and Fox accused him of 'sulky silence'. They proceeded, in no improved temper, to pass Lord Charles Spencer's resolution demanding the removal of ministers, and Fox's speech in that debate may be quoted as an example of his Parliamentary style at that time:

'I readily agree with an honourable member who has asserted that the failure of any bill proposed by ministers[1] is no cause for their dismission from office. This is a sound doctrine; let it be applied to the dissolution of the late ministry. A bill received the sanction of one branch of the legislature, and was submitted to the consideration of the other.

'Everything seemed to promise at first a favourable reception in the other House: there was only one method, a method as new as it was unexpected, as secret as it was infamous, by which it could be overthrown. This dark design was accomplished by a member of the present administration, but who has since, for reasons best known to himself, resigned his charges. It was not therefore the failure of the India Bill in the other House which ejected the late ministry from office, but the move by which that failure was accomplished; which being new and extraordinary, this House has condemned. . . .

'To confound personal and political confidence is a common error. That His Majesty may repose a personal confidence in his present ministers, separately and individually, I have no doubt; but that he should repose a confidence in their political character, under the opprobrium which rested on them, is too gross an idea to be admitted or entertained. What language does such a supposition hold out to every member in the House? It is not saying to him, spend not your time in politics; cease to study the constitution of your country, or to rise to eminence in the senate; study rather the arts of ductility and secret intrigue; these are much better calculated to give you distinction in the state, by rendering you the object of royal regard. I venerate the character of the young man who holds the reins of government at present; I admire his virtues and respect his ability;

[1] The reference was to Pitt's India Bill, which had just been rejected.

but if he would conciliate the favour of such a monarch, he must sacrifice every ingenuous quality in his nature; he must substitute cunning instead of wisdom, complaisance instead of honesty, and meanness instead of zeal, fortitude and magnanimity. He, therefore, who maintains that the present ministry enjoy the confidence of the Crown, affronts the dignity and wisdom of majesty, and even fights on his stumps in defence of a reprobated administration.'

Unfortunately the reprobated administration was growing stronger every day. Addresses and resolutions voting horror on the Coalition were arriving from all parts of the country. The City of London led the way with an address to the King, thanking him for his intervention in terms very different from the cantankerous protests which he had heard so often in the days of Wilkes and the American War; and other cities—York, which was regarded as a Cavendish stronghold, Exeter, and Edinburgh—were declaring for Pitt. In the House the signs were no less plain. Not only was the Coalition majority falling, but there were indications of unrest among the country gentlemen who had followed North. At present it took the form of a vague insistence on the possibility of an agreement between parties, but it was manifest that this demand for a reconciliation was only the first step towards a desertion, if no compromise were reached; and on the 20th of January Fox found it necessary to demolish the rumour that negotiations for a compromise were in progress. But members thought otherwise, and sixty of them met at St. Albans Tavern, irrespective of party, and agreed upon an address to the Duke of Portland and the Prime Minister, entreating them to open negotiations in order that 'the united efforts of those in whose integrity, abilities, and constitutional principles we have reason to confide' might be made available 'to rescue the country from its present disastrous state'. It was an unwelcome and embarrassing communication to both leaders. Pitt had not the least intention of taking office as anything but Prime Minister, and he could hardly expect that in a coalition the Duke of Portland, Fox, and North would all stand aside for him. Fox, to whom the resolution was really addressed, found the answer no easier. He was convinced that a coalition with Pitt would mean defeat, since the Cabinet, as part of the terms of compromise, would necessarily abandon the struggle with the King, and he now regarded that struggle as the political issue which must dominate all others. But that was precisely the issue which his rebellious followers were unwilling to face. Their demand for a new coalition made it manifest that they would compromise on the constitutional issue. With such doubtful support, it would be safer to put the responsibility for a breakdown on Pitt, so the Duke began with a suggestion that, as a preliminary to negotiations for union, Mr. Pitt should resign from the office which he held in defiance of resolutions of the House. This, of course, was rejected, and on the 2nd of February Mr. Thomas Grosvenor, chairman of the enthusiasts of St. Albans Tavern, moved a resolution calling for 'a firm, efficient, extended, united administration'. Fox supported the resolution, and dealt with 'the punctilio', which, he declared, was not between persons, but was on the question of principle 'between the House and the servants or servant of the Crown'. Let the Prime Minister solve that question of principle by resigning as a preliminary to negotiations, and no personal difficulties would stand in the way of the resolution. The resolution was carried without a division, and it was at once followed by a resolution by Coke of Norfolk protesting against 'the continuance of the present ministers in their offices'. The debate was acrimonious, and Pitt's refusal to resign was absolute. He was defending the fortress of the constitution, and he would never 'consent to march out of it, with a halter round my neck, change my armour, and meanly beg to be re-admitted as a volunteer in the army of the enemy!'

But the St. Albans group were not discouraged. They went on with their lobbying and their resolutions. On the 11th of February Lord North most gallantly offered to withdraw any claim to office, if his presence was an obstacle to

union, and the King sent the unconvincing message to the
Duke of Portland that it was 'His Majesty's earnest desire
that his Grace should have a personal conference with Mr.
Pitt for the purpose of forming a new administration on a
wide basis, and on fair and equal terms'. Such a command
calls for unconditional obedience, but the Duke saw difficulties
in the proposed meeting. He told Lord Sydney, the intermediary, that he could not confer with Pitt until 'he shall
have signified to the House in some way or other his inclination to comply with their wishes', and he reminded the King
that the leader of the majority in the House was entitled to
expect a personal interview rather than a message through an
intermediary. On the next day, the 16th of February, he
had private news from the Government side, and passed it
on to Fox. The King's confidence in a joint administration
would depend on Lord Thurlow, the Duke of Richmond,
Lord Gower, and Pitt being in the Cabinet, 'as they were
the determined supporters of the King against the encroaching spirit of the Commons'. They could not, according to
the Duke's informant, expect even a 'virtual resignation' of
the Government, but 'if the House was rash, or wicked
enough, to refuse or postpone the supplies to-morrow, one
consequence of which, he asserted, would be your being
execrated, and probably torn to pieces by the people, *they*
would immediately resign, but rather with the determination
of commencing an immediate action and opposition; which,
being countenanced by the King, would effectually defeat
every measure attempted to be brought forward in the House
of Lords, and by that means render our Administration
as inefficient as theirs was by our influence in the House
of Commons'. It was an unpromising outlook, and Sir
Gilbert Elliot gives us a glimpse of Fox's anxiety at that
time to ascertain how far his party would support him.
'Fox,' he wrote on the 26th of February, 'in speaking to his
company to-night, reminded us that it would be necessary for
us to make up our minds fairly upon the question of how far
we would go in the contest; for, if the cause of the House of

Commons was to be given up by a want of unanimity among ourselves, it would be proper to think of some means to surrender our claims in the manner the least disgraceful, and the least fatal to the House; but, if we thought it right, at all events, to resist the attack, we must determine on the necessary measures. The question of ultimately refusing supplies, and passing the Mutiny Bill for a third time, were those which we must most seriously consider. Some gentlemen spoke after him, and I was sorry to observe a sort of boggle about the extreme, but the only decisive measure of refusing supplies.'

The same 'sort of boggle' was becoming noticeable elsewhere, and in his own constituency Fox had to face a hostile meeting. Mr. Jenkinson mingles exaltation with horror in his description of the affair. 'I am assured', he wrote to Robinson, 'that Mr. Fox was defeated to-day in Westminster Hall by 5 to 1. Others make the parties more even. It is clear however that Mr. Fox was forced to leave the Hall and to leave the other party in possession of it, and that he afterwards harangued the mob from one of the windows of the King's Arms Tavern. He was then drawn in his chariot by a low mob of about 100 to Devonshire House, but what will astonish you is that Col. Stanhope, Mr. Hanger, and Mr. O'Byrne were on the coach box, and that Mr. George North, Mr. Adam and a third person stood as footmen behind. How disgraceful!'

Neither leader was entirely fortunate in his public appearance during those days of tension. When Pitt returned triumphantly after receiving the freedom of the City at the Grocers' Hall, the procession of his supporters was attacked in St. James's Street by an opposition force armed with chair-poles. The Prime Minister had to take refuge in White's Club, and it was suggested that some of 'Brooks's hellish sprites' had been seen in the crowd encouraging the attack. Recriminations became so bitter that Fox found it necessary to reveal his convincing alibi in Mrs. Armistead's bed.

Any possibility of agreement was finally destroyed by the

Prime Minister's terse announcement to the House that 'the King, notwithstanding their recommendations, had not thought proper to dismiss his Ministers, and they had not resigned'. This was designedly provocative, but Fox dared not risk his precarious majority on the direct refusal of supplies, which was the only suitable answer to such a challenge. He proposed a postponement of supplies for three days to give members leisure to reflect on the whole position. This was carried by a majority of twelve.

The 'independents' were still, as Pitt contemptuously described them, 'indefatigable for Coalition, but as ineffectual as ever', but their numbers were growing, as distracted country gentlemen sought a way out of the confusion of loyalties to their leader and their King. On the 20th of February Mr. Powys moved another resolution calling upon the King, 'in his royal wisdom', to establish 'an united and efficient administration'. It was carried by a majority of 20, and an address was accordingly presented by the whole House. The King was as anxious as the party leaders to put the blame for failure on some one else, and his answer to the address was a model of royal wisdom. His object, he said, was to secure a 'firm, efficient, extended, united administration, entitled to the confidence of my people', and he had made 'very recent endeavours' to unite on a fair and equal footing 'those whose joint efforts appear to me most capable of producing that happy effect'. But they had been unsuccessful, and, while he was still anxious to do everything possible to achieve his object, he did not see how it could be advanced by the 'dismission of those at present in my service', against whom, he observed, no charge or complaint had been made. It was an awkward position for Fox, for the independents were under the impression that the initial difficulty would be overcome if the King would appeal personally to the Duke of Portland, and they were much annoyed to find, after pressing Pitt to ask for this concession, that the Opposition still insisted on the resignation—it was now only 'virtual resignation'—of the Government. On the 1st of March the royal answer was debated, and Fox needed all his ingenuity to persuade his followers to reaffirm the demand for resignation. There was wrangling on the meaning of 'fair and equal'. No one could object to 'fair', but what did 'equal' mean? Pitt was unwilling to suggest a definition. He would not accept 'equitable' in place of 'equal', but suggested that his idea of the meaning would best be explained in personal conference. The motion was carried by 12. Once more the address was carried to St. James's, and once more the royal answer was returned in almost the same terms as before. On the next day the House postponed the Mutiny Bill. It was not a deed of daring, for the existing Act had nearly three weeks to run before it expired, but the majority fell to 9.

Fox made his final effort on the 8th of March, when the galleries were packed with spectators who sat for six hours to hear him. Unfortunately they were too closely packed, and there was no room for a friend brought by Sir James Lowther, who arrived half an hour before the debate. Sir James had his own way of dealing with such a situation. If his friends could not sit in the gallery, nobody else should sit there. He formally 'espied' strangers, and the Speaker was forced to clear the galleries. The results of Sir James's intervention were that the debate began with tempers already exacerbated, and no report comes down to us of one of Fox's greatest efforts in oratory. He carried his motion, but only by one vote, and it was manifest that the game was now in Pitt's hands. Fox evidently thought so; for his speeches ceased from that day, and his example was followed by Burke and Sheridan, who had been his principal supporters in the struggle. Dissolution was obviously impending, and members were growing more interested in their constituencies than in the proceedings of the dying Parliament. Outside Parliament preliminary skirmishes had already begun. The Duchess of Devonshire reported to her mother a remarkable scene at the Opera when the Duchess of Rutland bellowed 'Damn Fox' and was answered with a

shriek of 'Damn Pitt' from Lady Maria Waldegrave. Some
half-hearted attempts were still made to corner the Prime
Minister on the use of public moneys without an appropriation by Parliament, but he refused to commit himself, strong
in the certainty that there would soon be no Parliament to
call him to account, and confident that he had nothing to
fear from the next. On the 24th of March a speech from the
throne informed the faithful Commons that His Majesty had
decided 'to return as speedily as possible to the sense of his
people by convoking a new Parliament'. A mild flutter of
excitement was provided by a gang of burglars who on
the same night broke into the Lord Chancellor's house and
stole the Great Seal. It was suggested that the theft was
a last effort by Fox to make dissolution impossible. But
a Great Seal was hastily improvised and the election
began.

The first results of contested seats were declared at the
beginning of April, and they showed that Fox's Martyrs, as
they were called, would suffer all, and more than all the
losses, that Mr. Robinson had foreseen. Mr. Robinson could
estimate the results of an election in December, but he could
not foresee that electoral opinion would experience one of
those emotional disturbances which are among the mysteries
of British politics; nor could he foresee the immense activity
of the East India Company among property owners throughout the country. The election showed that the country was
deeply moved, and it revealed also the existence of political
forces which had hardly been considered by the managers
of elections in the past.

Sheridan, Burke, and Lord North kept their seats, but
the Martyrs included Coke of Norfolk, Lord John Cavendish, Erskine, Foljambe, George Byng, Conway, Gilbert
Elliot, Sir George Savile, Sir Charles Bunbury, Charles
Townshend, and Thomas Grenville, to name only a few.
Traditional loyalties and family influence were alike dis-
regarded. Even in Yorkshire the great Whig Houses, Bol-
ton, Castle Howard and Wentworth could not hold their

own against an almost unknown candidate, the young Mr. Wilberforce, who was believed to be among the few personal friends of the Prime Minister.

But the eyes of the world were fixed upon Westminster, where Charles Fox was making his fight against the Court. Robinson had estimated that Westminster would be 'very open: two good men would run hard if not turn out the present members'. The two Government candidates were Lord Hood and Sir Cecil Wray. Hood was a naval hero of the war, who might be expected to appeal to voters. But Wray had been brought in by Fox at the last election and he was now turning against his colleague. He was suspected, too, of supporting a proposed tax on servant girls and wishing as a measure of economy to abolish Greenwich Hospital. But he was, nevertheless, regarded as a strong candidate, who might well be expected to keep his seat.

Fox's election address had the merits of terseness:

'To the worthy and independent electors of the city and liberty of Westminster.

Gentlemen,

His Majesty's ministers having thought fit, in contradiction to their own declarations, in defiance of the sense of the House of Commons, and without any public pretence whatever, to subject the nation to all the inconveniences which must infallibly attend a dissolution of parliament at the present moment, I humbly beg leave, once more, to solicit your votes and interest, to represent this great and respectable city.

To secure to the people of this country the weight which belongs to them in the scale of the constitution has ever been the principle of my political conduct.

Conscious that in every situation, (whether in or out of office) I have invariably adhered to this system, I cannot but flatter myself that you will again give your sanction to those principles which first recommended me to your

notice, and which induced you, at two subsequent periods,
to honour me with your suffrages.

I have the honour to be,

GENTLEMEN,

Your most obliged and

grateful humble servant,

C. J. Fox.

St. James' Street,
24th March 1784.'

A hotly contested election in the eighteenth century was
a long orgy of noise, drunkenness, corruption, bullying, and
general rowdiness. Hogarth's famous cartoon shows an
election at its worst, and it is not an unfair caricature. As
the Westminster election surpassed all others in public
interest, it surpassed all others no less in its rowdiness
and noise. Charges of lying, bribery, fraud, and violence
were made and returned. Bands and processions perpetually
marched and countermarched. They came into collision,
and fought daily with sticks and fists, and when 'a gang
of fellows, headed by naval officers, and carrying His
Majesty's colours', as the Foxites described them, came to
support the Government, they were met in pitched battle
by a force which consisted, according to the Government
agents, of 'Irish chairmen and pick-pockets (the friends of
a certain candidate)'. In one of the encounters a constable,
who had harmed no man, was killed, and each party strove
energetically to fix the blame on the 'banditti of ruffians'
attached to the other side.

But in one respect the proceedings rose to a higher plane.
The election songs and lampoons were certainly above the
usual level. Many of them displayed the scurrilous vul-
garity which was considered suitable to the occasion, but
some of the songs which, contemporary report assures us,
were actually sung at political dinners, and some of the
'impromptu epigrams' were admirable. In this Fox had
the best of it, for Fitzpatrick and Sheridan, each fighting

as if the seat were his own, were daily at his side to celebrate their champion with:

> Pray how did *Charley* speak last night?
> Was he all burning, strong and bright,
> > As Tully or the Greek?
> The next time, friend, you would ask this,
> Know that the shorter method is,
> > To ask—Did Charley *speak*?

or, to emphasize Sir Cecil Wray's treachery in deserting the man who had brought him in, with:

> That Fox is an impostor, thus,
> Sir Cecil, you may prove is true,
> He grossly has imposed on us,
> By having spoken well of you.

and

> To Fox, Sir Cecil says, small praise is due,
> By G-d, Sir Cecil, what you say is true;
> For 'tis to *him* that we're obliged for YOU.

Sheridan is said to have written the jingle which greeted the enthusiastic efforts of Lord Mountmorres for the Government candidates:

> Mountmorres, Mountmorres,
> Whom nobody for is,
> > And for whom we none of us care,
> From Dublin you came,
> It had been much the same,
> > If your Lordship had stayed where you were.

And Sheridan may have had a hand in the burlesque of a play-bill headed 'A Farce' in which 'Mr. King' is cast for the part of 'Old Obstinate', and a 'House that George built' with Lord Nugent as 'the *Rat* that ate the malt', Fox as 'the Cat that killed the *Rat*', Lord Thurlow as 'the *Bull* with the crumpled horn', Dundas as 'the *Scot* by all forsworn', and Wilkes, on this occasion miraculously aligned with the Court, as 'the *Patriot* covered with scorn', who was to be wakened by Conscience in the guise of 'the *Cock* that crowed in the morn'.

A typical Foxite song was the swinging 'Liberty Hall':

> Of old our forefathers corruption withstood;
> The charter of freedom they bought with their blood;
> Shall we, their descendants, degenerate fall?
> He that does, may he die, out of Liberty Hall.

> Long life to the King, he's assured of our aid,
> If—honour and wisdom his councils pervade;
> Nor frowns, nor neglect can true patriots appal,
> For they're the main pillars of Liberty Hall.

> The course we'll maintain, the great fabrick support,
> In spite of the schemes and intrigues of the Court,
> Then firmly united we'll stand one and all,
> By the Man of the People, in Liberty Hall.

Supporters of simpler taste were invited to chant to the tune of the National Anthem,

> Time-servers, wond'ring, shall
> View us determined all,
>   Spite of the Court:
> Spite of their wily tricks,
> And back-stair politics,
> Fox is the man we fix
>   On to support.

or to declaim in 'The Champion of Liberty':

> He's loyal, he's noble, he's chosen by me,
> My rights to protect and my sons to keep free.

Of course Fox's own weaknesses were not forgotten by the other side in such songs as 'The Fox and the Geese':

> One uniform dress had this whimsical fellow,
> 'Twas a coat of plain blue and a waistcoat of yellow;
> For he gambled among such an infamous pack,
> They left him no more than the coat on his back.

> Of principles tho' (which don't cost quite so dear)
> He had changes and suits for each day of the year,
> Thus he shifted his principles, shifted his speeches,
> But ne'er shifted his coat, nor his waistcoat and breeches.

or in 'The General Toast':

> Here's to the patriot of every degree,
> Who a friend to cheats, gamblers and rooks is,
> And thinks that no country can flourishing be
> Till governed by statesmen from Brookes's.

Even the misdeeds of the first Lord Holland were exhumed in a catechism beginning, 'Whose councils put Admiral Byng to death? Mr. H. Fox.'

The Poll opened on the 1st of April when Fox was escorted to the hustings by a procession led by marrow-bones and cleavers with bands and banners, followed by 'Honest Sam House', a sporting publican, who by a remarkable coincidence was landlord of the Intrepid Fox.

On the first two days Fox was at the head of the poll, but on the third day Hood led with 2,185 votes, Wray had polled 1,975, and Fox 1,923. He was not dismayed. 'Plenty of bad news from all quarters,' he wrote to a friend, 'but I think I feel that misfortunes, when they come thick, have the effect rather of rousing my spirits than sinking them.' On the next two days the lead was increased, but he still had hopes. But on the fifth day, when he was 209 behind Wray his mood changed, and his main anxiety was to determine how soon he could retire from the contest without disappointing his still hopeful friends. 'I have serious thoughts,' he wrote, 'if I am beaten here, of not coming back into Parliament at all.' His friends, no doubt, were not greatly impressed by such serious thoughts produced in the overcharged atmosphere of the hustings. But they might have taken his exclamation of impatience more seriously if they had known what he was saying to Mrs. Armistead in the series of notes which kept her informed of the day's fortunes. It was not only a lover's passion which made him protest that every day spent on the hustings away from her was abhorrent to him. It was becoming an effort to him to maintain his interest in the daily affairs of politics when he thought of Mrs. Armistead and his books and the peaceful house near Chertsey, St. Ann's Hill, which he wanted to make his home, if he could by any means find £2,000 to buy it.

But as long as the poll was open he must appear on the hustings and appear at his best. So from the hustings he harangued and from house to house he canvassed daily, answering an opponent who professed to 'admire your abilities, but damn your principles' with a genial 'My friend, I applaud your sincerity, but damn your manners', and extinguishing a heckler, who offered him a halter, with a quick refusal to deprive him of it, 'as I presume it must be a family relic'.

Until the eleventh day, when he was 318 votes behind, he lost ground. Thenceforward he began to gain, and on the twenty-second day he passed Wray and kept his lead. The turn of fortune was attributed to the energetic canvassing of the beautiful Duchess of Devonshire and her sister, Lady Duncannon. Such intervention by ladies was unusual, and it aroused much comment. The Duchess was reputed to have canvassed in the most unusual way, to have conversed with a cobbler, even to have kissed a butcher. The Government agents were furious and turned on her all the worst scurrility that an election can produce, but she was unmoved by insults, and continued her visits to the increasing enthusiasm of the Whigs:

> Arrayed in matchless beauty, Devon's fair
> In Fox's favour takes a zealous part.
> But, oh! Where'er the pilferer comes—beware!
> She supplicates a vote and steals a heart.

In vain did the Government agents bring Tory ladies to canvass on their side. They could make no way against the Duchess, and Foxite songsters advised them to go home:

> Get out, you female Tory,
> Tho' Courts prevail, I'll not turn tail,
> The Duchess was here before ye.

Every day the friends of Charles Fox gathered to support him. The Prince of Wales appeared with a badge of laurel and a fox's brush, escorted by a guard of prizefighters;

Perdita Robinson drove about asking for votes; and the carriages of Whig ladies were constantly in line on his side of the hustings.

> The gentle Beauchamp, and the fair Carlisle,
> Around their favoured FOX expecting wait;
> And Derby's lips suspends the ready smile,
> To ask 'the Poll?' and 'what is Charles's fate?'

At last on the fortieth day, the 17th of May, the Poll was closed. Hood had polled 6,694 votes, Fox 6,234, and Wray 5,998. Sir Cecil Wray demanded a scrutiny, and the High Bailiff refused to declare Fox elected until the scrutiny had been made. Perhaps Charles Fox would not have been sorry if the High Bailiff could also have postponed the next stage of the proceedings, for the ceremony of chairing a winner was exhausting. But the chair was waiting for him as he left the hustings, and the procession set forth amid the blaring of trumpets, the crashing of bands, and resounding cheers.

Heralds on Horseback.
Twenty-four *Marrow-bones and Cleavers.*
The Arms of Westminster.
Thirty Freemen of Westminster.
Martial Music.
Committees of the Seven Parishes with white wands, following their respective banners, and attended by numberless Gentlemen of the Several Districts.
Squadron of Gentlemen on Horseback in the Blue and Buff uniform.
Trumpets.
Flag.   The RIGHTS of the COMMONS.
Grand Band of Music.
Flag.   THE MAN OF THE PEOPLE.
Marshals on Foot.
TRIUMPHAL CHAIR,
Decorated with laurels, in which was seated
The Right Hon. CHARLES JAMES FOX
Trumpets.
Flag.   The WHIG CAUSE.
Second Squadron of Horse.
Liberty Boys of Newport Market.

Mr. FOX's Carriage *crowned with Laurels.*
Banner.   *Sacred to Female Patriotism!*
Blue standard, inscribed,
INDEPENDENCE!
State Carriages of their Graces
The Duchesses of PORTLAND and DEVONSHIRE,
*drawn by six horses, superbly caparisoned, with six running foot-
men attendant on each.*
Gentlemen's servants, closing the Procession, two and two,
etc. etc.

On the shoulders of his panting and perspiring supporters
the victorious candidate was slowly born round Covent
Garden to Charing Cross, down Whitehall and back to
Charing Cross, by Pall Mall and St. James's Street to Piccadilly, round Berkeley Square into Devonshire House court-
yard. As they went through Berkeley Street they were
saluted from the wall of Devonshire House by the Whig
Ladies and the Prince of Wales, who had, to quote an ecstatic
reporter of the scene 'ascended some unaccommodating steps
to the wall, with two illustrious Duchesses, in order to salute
the triumphant sons of Freedom on their march'. He had,
in fact, attended a review on Ascot Heath that morning with
the King, and he had galloped back to London in time to
put on the Foxite badge of laurel and fox's brush and take
his part in the triumph. There were speeches at Devonshire House, but even then the day was not ended, for the
procession returned to dine at Willis's Rooms, where more
speeches were made, new songs 'full of applicable points'
were sung, and the night, to quote the same reporter, 'was
spent with unusual exhilaration'.

On the next day it was the Prince's turn to celebrate the
victory, and he did so with a Morning Fête of unexampled
splendour at Carlton House. After a breakfast in marquees
decorated with devices 'equally expressive of the political
principles and the gallantry of *his Highness*', the Company
danced in the garden, pleasurably conscious that the sounds
of their rejoicings were audible in the Mall, where the King
was passing in state to open the new Parliament. No doubt

the King, as his coach passed Carlton House, felt that mortification and resentment which his son intended him to feel, but his annoyance may have been tempered by more consoling reflections. He could well afford to let the Whigs cheer for Westminster, when they had been so overwhelmingly defeated in the rest of the country, and he could meditate with satisfaction on the change in his own position. Only a few years ago, during the American war, a royal procession had been a depressing experience. He had been received without enthusiasm, and an irreverent satirist had been able to put into his mouth an unkind, but hardly exaggerated, description of the scene:

> No acclamations burst upon the air.
> The vulgar stared, and I returned the stare.

But now it was all changed. He was the Father of his loving People. He might safely tear up the message of abdication, which he had so long kept ready for use. It would not be wanted again. The country had decided for the sceptre of George III against the tongue of Fox.

The Whig leaders dined with the Prince that evening in their buff and blue, and, after the Prince had entertained them by singing several songs in his best style, they all went on to Mrs. Crewe's ball. At supper Captain Morris was made to sing his celebrated 'Baby and Nurse' and several 'droll songs applicable to the times', which 'the fair circle chorused with the most heart-felt spirit'. The supreme moment of enthusiasm was reached when the Prince proposed the toast 'Here's buff and blue and Mrs. Crewe!' to which the delighted hostess replied, with much presence of mind, 'Here's buff and blue and all of you!'

CHAPTER VII

1784–1785

W HEN the cheering for Westminster died down, the Whigs had leisure to reflect upon the election and upon their immediate future. Some hundred and sixty seats had been lost by the Coalition, and Pitt had a majority which could not be assailed by any probable combination of groups or interests. The history of the party since the glorious days when North had fallen with Yorktown had been eventful. Beginning with a majority, which might have insured a long life of security, they had split almost at once on the death of Rockingham, and now, after the adventures of Coalition and India Bill, their disaster and the King's triumph were complete. As they reviewed the events of the last two years they could hardly avoid the conclusion that Fox, who had chiefly contributed to their original glory, had contributed no less to their later eclipse. There had been doubts of his wisdom in resigning when Shelburne became Prime Minister. He had good grounds to distrust Shelburne as a King's man in a Whig Cabinet. But was it wise to resign so promptly? If he had remained in office, might he not have rallied the true Whigs and defeated the Shelburne party, or might he not at any rate have waited for a better moment for resigning on some issue which would have kept his party united? There had been many doubts about the wisdom of the Coalition, and there had been the gravest apprehensions about the India Bill. If the Coalition could, as Fitzpatrick said, be justified only by success, was it wise to jeopardize its success by an India Bill which must inevitably unite and concentrate the strongest forces of opposition? So calamitous a record would be fatal to any ordinary leader. Bad fortune would tell against him almost as heavily as bad judgement, and he would be expected to make way for a successor whose name was less closely associated with defeat. But Charles Fox was not an ordinary leader, and his ascendancy over his followers was such that no thought of criticism arose. His hold over them was three-fold. They felt daily his influence as the greatest debater in Parliament; they accepted him as a political thinker, who had given them a purpose and a cause worth many sacrifices; and they adored him as a friend with an unquestioning devotion which left no room for doubts.

It is difficult to-day to appreciate Fox's immense power over the House of Commons. We hear of him from time to time making a great speech; the parliamentary reporter descends sometimes from his aloofness to hint at the enthusiasm which such a speech aroused; contemporary letters and diaries refer to his speeches among the outstanding events of the day; and an occasional report survives which in the view of his friends will convey, when read aloud, some idea of Fox in action. But none of these things convey the impression of his power over the House. For such a description we must turn to the diary of a visitor from abroad. Herr Moritz, a young German pastor, who was in London in 1782, when Fox was in office, has left a vivid impression of the House under the spell of its favourite orator:

'Fox was sitting to the right of the Speaker not far from the table on which the gilt sceptre lay. He now took his place so near that he could reach it with his hand, and thus placed, he gave it many a violent and hearty thump, either to aid, or to show the energy with which he spoke. . . . It is impossible for me to describe with what fire and persuasive eloquence he spoke, and how the Speaker in the chair incessantly nodded approbation from beneath his solemn wig; and innumerable voices incessantly called out, hear him! hear him! and when there was the least sign that he intended to leave off speaking, they no less vociferously exclaimed, go on; and so he continued to speak in this manner for nearly two hours.'

He describes Fox as 'a short, fat and gross man, with a swarthy complexion; and in general he is badly dressed. There certainly is something Jewish in his looks. But on

the whole he is not an ill-made nor an ill-looking man: and
there are many strong marks of sagacity and fire in his
eyes.'

A few days later the observant German was in the crowd
during a by-election for Westminster, and was himself in-
fected with the general enthusiasm when 'the people took
it into their heads to hear him speak, and everyone called
Fox! Fox! I know not why I seemed to catch some of the
spirit of the place and time; and I also bawled Fox! Fox!
and he was obliged to come forward and speak; for no other
reason that I could find, but that the people wished to hear
him speak.'

As a political thinker his reputation stood even higher
with his followers than as a debater. The 'principles of Mr.
Fox' were treated with more respect than was accorded
to the political wisdom of Burke, who, as Fox was always
ready to admit, was the master from whom he had learnt
'more than from all the men with whom he had ever conversed'. Burke's wisdom might be profound, an inspiration to statesmen for all time, but Fox possessed that
peculiar quality which inspires both confidence and obedience, the quality which makes a leader, who towers above
his fellows. To that quality of leadership was added an
unswerving constancy to his declared principles. He might
make mistakes in judgement, he might be outwitted in
manœuvre, he might lead his party to disaster, but his
followers knew that in triumph and in adversity they might
count upon his loyalty to his friends and upon his greater
loyalty to his principles. Later generations, reviewing his
life as a whole, can judge how much that constancy has
meant to his country. If in the panic of revolution and
war no statesman of Fox's eminence had continued to proclaim his faith in liberty and justice and his hatred of
tyranny and oppression, the claims of democracy might
have been drawn from constitutional into revolutionary
methods, and the reforms of the next century might not
have been achieved without bloodshed.

And above all he held them by the ties of friendship. From his early days, when his Eton contemporaries were content to lose their money in guaranteeing his debts, down to those years near the end of his life, when his political fortunes were at their lowest, and the Chancellor growled to the King that the Opposition was now reduced to forty, 'but they would all hang for Fox', he inspired among his friends and followers a personal affection which made party loyalty a matter of minor significance. It was not only that he was the best of companions in every company, a scholar at The Club, a sportsman at Newmarket, a gambler at Brooks's, and a brilliant conversationalist at Devonshire House. Other men of his time had all these advantages, but none of them had also the cheerful simplicity of character and the unfailing kindness which made his friendship a thing to be cherished through life and commemorated after death, as some of his friends commemorated it, with inscriptions on their tombstones, proclaiming that, whatever else their lives might have held, they had 'lived the friend of Fox'. 'Perhaps no human being', wrote Gibbon near this time, 'was ever more perfectly exempt from the taint of malevolence, vanity, or falsehood.' For any one, who had known such friendship, or had known even the jovial look which the leader would give to his followers in the House, disagreement or desertion on any grounds except an essential matter of principle was unthinkable.

The discovery of startling contrasts is always attractive, and it was already a habit of his contemporaries to compare him with that other phenomenon of the age, the new Prime Minister, also a genius by general admission, but so different a genius from Charles Fox. It was conspicuously a contrast of opposites. From the nursery days when Lady Holland had found him 'brought up so strictly and so proper in his behaviour', the training of Pitt had been implacably directed by himself no less than by his parents to the making of a Prime Minister. At the age of eight he had announced that he was 'glad I am not the eldest son; I want to speak in the

House of Commons like Papa', and before he was ten he had
begun under the formidable direction of his father a course
of public speaking. At Cambridge there was the same relentless pursuit of knowledge, so different from the curriculum
of Charles Fox with its interludes of Paris and gambling;
and when he left Cambridge the virtuous young man had
gone to earn his living with the strictest economy in Lincoln's Inn, where his début and manner of life were conspicuously unlike the sensational appearance of Charles Fox
in the world of London. No one would support Lord Holland's theory of education against that of the Earl of Chatham, especially when the latter system triumphantly produced a Prime Minister victorious at the age of twenty-five,
but observers could not help noticing that the subject of the
Chatham method had certain defects, which were certainly
absent from his rival. It was perhaps due to his unremit-
ting attention to work and his apparent disregard of all
other interests that Pitt gave to his contemporaries an
impression of intolerant superiority, of inhuman frigidity,
of dignity on its defence, which were markedly in contrast
with the universal geniality of Charles Fox. Sir Nathaniel
Wraxall has left a description of Pitt taking his place in
the House: 'From the instant that Pitt entered the doorway of the House of Commons, he advanced up the floor
with a quick and firm step, his head erect and thrown back,
looking neither to the right nor to the left, nor favouring
with a nod or a glance any of the individuals seated on
either side, among whom many who possessed £5,000 a year
would have been gratified even by so slight a mark of attention.' And when he reached the Treasury Bench his manner
was, according to the same authority, 'cold, stiff and without
suavity or amenity. He seemed never to invite approach,
or to encourage acquaintance, though when addressed he
could be polite, communicative, and occasionally gracious.'
Very different were the appearance and manner of Charles
Fox in his faded buff and blue, as he advanced with an
energetic waddling movement up the floor of the House,

M

casting cheerful glances on his friends on both sides and occasionally pausing for a little conversation. He was able, as every public man must be able, to elude the advances of intrusive bores, but he was none the less, whether in or out of office, the most accessible and sympathetic of statesmen, and followers never had to complain of any coldness or aloofness in his manner.

The contrast was no less remarkable when they rose to speak. Each of them was a supreme artist in his own manner but it was again a contrast of opposites. Fox, with his harsh, thrilling voice and rapid delivery, poured out his arguments in an impetuous torrent of urgency, while Pitt presented his case with faultless precision and complete self-possession. Each of them suffered from the faults of his manner. To listen to Fox was, as Pitt said, to be 'under the wand of the magician', but the headlong flood of Fox was apt to carry the speaker and his followers into difficulties which might have been avoided by prudent reflection, while the perfect order and smoothness of Pitt's discourse, 'never', as Fox said, 'at a loss for *the* word, and I am never at a loss for *a* word', sometimes gave an impression of disingenuous evasion. 'Mr. Pitt', said Porson, 'conceives his sentences before he utters them. Mr. Fox throws himself into the middle of his, and leaves it to God Almighty to get him out again.'

So striking a contrast in character, manner, and appearance could hardly have been obtained if the new leaders had been chosen for histrionic purposes by a dramatic author. And the stage was indeed set for a new scene with new roles. The soldiers and sailors were no longer to be seen. Lord North with his blue ribbon, Lord Shelburne with his intriguing subtlety, even the King himself, were now in the background, while the two new champions held the stage in their duel for supremacy.

It was a moment calling for a hero, for the country was faced with something more than war's aftermath of debt and reconstruction. The immediate and urgent task was nothing less than the rebuilding of the British Empire. At home the machinery of state was creaking ominously. With a floating debt of fourteen millions to be funded our methods of taxation were failing. The tea tax, for example, was an important source of revenue, and it was known that thirteen million pounds of tea were drunk every year, but duty was collected on only five and a half. It was the same with other taxes. When duties were raised to increase revenue, the result was only to encourage the great maritime industry of smuggling. In regard to loans the position was no better. The robbery and corruption which accompanied Government borrowing under the old system had become a notorious scandal, which could no longer be tolerated. Debts must now be funded, and there must be a complete reform of finance to the detriment of many interests snugly lodged in the fabric of incompetence and corruption. Hardly less urgent and no less difficult was the case, supported by growing forces in the country, for electoral reform, which also must affect many lives and fortunes long dependent in the old system.

British territories overseas were also calling for reform. The old commercial system which made a colony a dependency with trading rights reserved to Britain, had been obsolete at the end of the Seven Years War. Failure to recognize that delay had brought the War of Independence and the loss of America. Politicians contemplating the remains of the Empire had learnt their lesson, and, even if the War had taught them nothing, the clamour of colonists, who had observed the results of American resistance, made it clear that delay would be dangerous. The old mercantile system of trading restrictions must go, and a new British Empire must be created, based on a new philosophy of self-government and liberty. The case of Ireland was urgent, for a new crisis was impending; and crisis could not long be averted in India unless an acceptable system of government could be devised where two India Bills had failed. The opportunity and the difficulties were immense.

It would be impossible to renew the machinery of government and rebuild the British Empire without a lasting peace in which it could be done. Britain was no longer at war, but new relations with foreign countries must be developed with a new basis of international trade before the country could regain security. Here again delay might be disastrous.

For this task the Prime Minister depended on a majority elected by interests of surprising diversity. He had been supported in the election by the Court interest, apprehensive of Parliamentary encroachment, and by the Yorkshire freeholders and reformers asserting the rights of the people, by high churchmen rallying to the Crown and by dissenters demanding toleration; and his ranks included veterans of intrigue like Thurlow and Jenkinson, avowed democrats like Sawbridge and Wilkes, and such an impressionable idealist as Wilberforce. There was no sign of disunion among them and no group of bargainers willing to make terms with either side; but it was a majority which might be dissipated by blunders in leadership or by sufficiently adroit manœuvres of the Opposition. The debating strength of the Government was not impressive. Dundas and Grenville were not attractive speakers and Wilberforce was a beginner; none of them could compete against the unsurpassed brilliance on the Whig benches. In the Lords the position was no better, for Lord Camden as a rule maintained silence, Lord Carmarthen was said to carry 'more of polish than of weight', and the Lord Chancellor left his colleagues in a state of nervous uncertainty whether he would at any time publicly support or attack them. For the present the burden would be borne by the Prime Minister alone.

But Parliament meeting in May showed no excessive haste in proceeding to the high task of regeneration. The High Bailiff of Westminster, instead of making a return, had informed the Crown Office that he had granted a scrutiny in the Westminster Election. Charles Fox was excluded from Parliament as member for Westminster, but he had got himself returned *ex abundante cautela* for Orkney, and, as member for Orkney, he rose, before a Speaker had been chosen, to protest that the House was not complete. The Scrutiny debates began, and for days they held the first place in Parliamentary time and thought. On the 24th of May, Mr. Lee moved that the High Bailiff make an immediate return, and Sir Lloyd Kenyon, the Master of the Rolls, in a moment unfortunate for his future peace of mind, thought it material to the question to remind the House that Fox had been under age when he sat for Midhurst over fifteen years ago. The motion was lost by 233 votes to 136.

On the next day Fox, determined to make the most of his case, presented a petition for his return, and on the 8th of June Welbore Ellis moved for an immediate return by the High Bailiff. It was the occasion of one of Fox's best debating speeches, in which he challenged the House with a provocative sentence, and returned to the same words again and again until he had roused the attention of every member to hear his main argument. The speech is well reported in *oratio recta*, and it is worth examining by students in the technique of public speaking. Beginning with a diffident complaint that Government speakers might in fairness have stated their case and allowed him to speak last, he checked himself with the observation, 'But, Sir, I have no reason to expect indulgence, nor do I know that I shall meet with bare justice in this House'. This sentence produced, as might be expected, a murmur of protest. He made full use of it to repeat the offending statement with greater emphasis, inviting any member who complained of it to move that it be taken down by the clerk. He then began to justify it by a reference to Grenville's Act, which had removed from Parliament the jurisdiction to try election petitions. 'Mr. Grenville's Bill', as he called it, was passed because the House of Commons had been 'a mass of men capable of political dislike and personal aversion; capable of too much attachment and too much animosity; capable of being biased by weak and by wicked motives; liable to be governed by ministerial influence, by caprice, and by corruption'. He complained that he was to be deprived of the benefits of that Act, and 'thrown entirely upon the mercy, or if you please upon the wisdom, of the House. Unless, then, men are to suppose that human nature is totally altered with a few months—unless we can be so grossly credulous as to imagine that the present is purged of all the frailties of former Parliaments—unless I am to surrender my understanding, and blind myself to the extraordinary conduct of this House, in this extraordinary business for the last fortnight—I may say, and say with truth, that I expect no indulgence, nor do I know that I shall meet with bare justice in this House.' He then turned on some of the members to whom he might 'upon every principle of equity, fairness, and reason, object as judges to decide upon my cause', Lord Mulgrave, 'who from the fullness of his prejudice to me, and predilection for my opponents, asserts things in direct defiance of the evidence which has been given at your bar', Lord Mahon, 'who has relinquished his right as an elector of Westminster, that his voting may not disqualify him from being a judge upon the committee to decide this contest', and 'a person of sober demeanour', the Master of the Rolls. 'This demure gentleman, Sir, this great lawyer, this judge of law, and equity, and constitution, enlightens this subject, instructs and delights his hearers, by reviving this necessary intelligence, that when I had the honour of first sitting in this House for Midhurst, I was not full twenty-one years of age; and all this he does for the honourable purpose of justifying the High Bailiff of Westminster in defrauding the electors of their representative in this House, by robbing me of the honour of asserting and confirming their right by sitting as their representative.' Finally he proceeded to his arguments, confident that after such an opening every word would not only be heard but would be considered. The point, which he wanted to bring home, was that the High Bailiff had no power to grant a scrutiny, which could not begin until after the day on which the writ was returnable. Having established his point, he touched upon the cost of a scrutiny, which he put at £18,000, and lamented that, as he had no means, 'the misfortune of my being obnoxious to bad men in high authority should extend beyond myself' to friends who would provide the cost.

Now was surely the moment for the young Prime Minister to endear himself to the House by a few words of welcome to its most distinguished member and some indication that he would support any means of avoiding the delay and expense of a scrutiny. But youthful inexperience and perhaps a natural lack of human sympathy combined in Pitt to lose the opportunity. He answered sharply, and was reproved by Sheridan for 'severity of epithet, redundancy of egotism, and pomp of panegyric'. The Government won by a reduced majority, and Pitt had reason to regret his blunder in the following January, when the scrutiny was still drearily under way with no apparent prospect of conclusion. His majority on the question fell to nine, and on the 3rd of March, when the question was renewed, he was defeated. The members for Westminster were returned on the next day after a marked humiliation to the Prime Minister.

They began more serious business in June with the Budget, in which Pitt laid the foundations of solvency by funding nearly half the floating debt and imposing a long list of new taxes. It had not yet become the habit of an Opposition automatically to oppose, and Fox received the Budget with applause, tinged only with a slight doubt whether the tax on ribbons would produce as much as the Chancellor hoped. But Fox was far from acquiescing when Pitt produced the first of his great measures, the India Bill, at the beginning of July. It was in fact no less revolutionary by contemporary standards than the hapless measure which had destroyed the Coalition. But it was revolutionary in the British manner. Forms were preserved, if powers were curtailed. The charter, and with it the monopoly, of the Company remained, but the Government of India passed, as Clive had intended that it should pass, to the British

Government; and it is a sign of the waning of the eighteenth century that the proposal could no longer be demolished in the name of Property. The possibilities of patronage under the new scheme were less apparent than under Fox's Bill, but they were none the less sufficient to enable Dundas for nearly twenty years to maintain his influence in Scotland by the judicious distribution of Indian appointments. The Whigs surpassed themselves in denunciation. Fox pointed out that the new India Board would be as much a Fourth Estate as the Board of coalitionists under his Bill; Sheridan was sarcastic about the wire-pulling of the Company; and Burke apologized to Newgate for accidentally comparing its residents with Warren Hastings and those 'who have left whole provinces without a habitation, and have exterminated the natives throughout the fairest portions of the globe'. But recrimination was useless. It was a question of confidence, and it could not be denied that the new Ministry commanded confidence in matters in which virtuous coalitionists aroused only suspicion.

It was a strenuous session for the Ministry, but it had few attractions for Charles Fox. He was moving into his new house, St. Ann's Hill, and every day of that summer which parted him from Mrs. Armistead, the nightingales in the garden, and the peace of his country home was counted as lost to him. 'With respect to my inclination', he wrote, when the Duke of Portland ventured to remonstrate at his absence, 'I know it ought to give way, but yet, if anyone else had done all I have for the last eight months, and was as completely tired out with it, body and mind, as I am, I believe he would think he had some right to consult it. I cannot express to you how fatigued I was with the last day's attendance, and how totally unequal I feel myself in point of spirits to acquit myself as I ought to do, either for the good of the party or for my own reputation. However I must submit to your judgement and to theirs, if you persist in your opinion. But I am sure you will not repent it, if you will so far trust me as to believe that I know

CHARLES JAMES FOX. *Undated*

From a sketch by LADY DI BEAUCLERK *in the possession of* MRS. HENRY LASCELLES

the House of Commons as well, and myself something better, than those who differ from me.'

It was true that he needed rest after the feverish activity of the last two years, but his letter indicates something more than temporary depression of mind and body. He was beginning to seize a little too eagerly on any pretext which would remove him from the daily round of parliamentary life.

While Charles Fox dallied at St. Ann's Hill, another exalted supporter of his party was also forgetting his politics and his career for the lady of his choice. The affairs of the Prince of Wales commanded that publicity which is inseparable from the life of royalty. His youthful passion for Perdita Robinson had on the whole increased his popularity with the general public. A ballad writer had even given it an air of romantic nationalism:

> My Brother Frederick abroad may roam
> While British beauty keeps my heart at home.

And now that the affair with Perdita was over (Charles Fox had taken a hand in negotiating the financial side of the parting), the general public and the ballad writers were no less interested in Maria Fitzherbert. She provided indeed even more interesting gossip, for the lady was a Roman Catholic, and rumour declared that the Prince was deeply smitten. In this respect rumour did not exaggerate, for the Prince was in the habit of calling upon the Duchess of Devonshire and Mrs. Armistead and demonstrating the intensity of his passion by rolling on the ground, beating his forehead, and bursting into tears. He even declared that he would sell his jewels and plate, much of which had probably not been paid for, in order that he might marry her and withdraw to America. Once more the ballad writer was kind, and made Florizel a model of devoted altruism:

> This lass so neat, with smiles so sweet,
> Has won my right good will,
> I'd crowns resign to call thee mine,
> Sweet lass of Richmond Hill.

But Fox's longing for a rest was not shared by all members of the party. A group of them, which included Fitzpatrick, George Ellis, Lord John Townshend, and Dr. Lawrence were anxious to strike a blow, and they found in the *Rolliad*, which they wrote in collaboration, a weapon of precision against the complacency of ministers. That remarkable work, which appeared in a series of parts, takes for its hero Mr. John Rolle, one of the members for Devonshire, who had made himself conspicuous in his efforts to cough down Burke and in his support of the High Bailiff on the question of scrutiny. The *Rolliad* proper is a review of an imaginary epic on the origin and history of the Rolle family. The reviewers begin with a dedication to Sir Lloyd Kenyon, Master of the Rolls, to whom Pitt had confided the task of defending the scrutiny. 'I am myself', Rolle is made to say in explanation of the dedication, 'but *a simple Rolle*; Sir Lloyd is a Master of Rolls.' We are then shown in the language of the Heralds' College the descent of Mr. Rolle from the ancient Rollo and the wife of a Saxon drummer until we reach the living representative of the family:

> Great Rollo's heir, whose cough, whose laugh, whose groan,
> Th'Antaeus Edmund has so oft o'erthrown:
> Whose cry of 'Question!' silenc'd Charles' sense;
> That cry more powerful than Pitt's eloquence . . .

The satirists are at their best in the extracts from the imaginary epic, and Ellis's well-known contributions on Pitt are perhaps the best of all:

> Above the rest, majestically great,
> Behold the infant Atlas of the state,
> The matchless miracle of modern days
> In whom Britannia to the world displays
> A sight to make surrounding nations stare,
> A Kingdom trusted to a schoolboy's care.
>
> .   .   .   .
>
> Pert without fire, without experience sage,
> Young with more art than Shelburne gleaned from age,
> Too proud from pilfered greatness to descend,
> Too humble not to call Dundas his friend,

> In solemn dignity and sullen state,
> This new Octavius rises to debate!
> Mild and more mild he sees each placid row
> Of country gentlemen with rapture glow;
> He sees convuls'd with sympathetic throbs,
> Apprentice Peers and deputy Nabobs!
> Nor Rum Contractors think his speech too long,
> While words like treacle trickle from his tongue!
> O Soul congenial to the Souls of Rolles!
> Whether you tax the luxury of coals,
> Or vote some necessary millions more
> To feed an Indian friend's exhausted store. . . .

Sir Nathaniel Wraxall has said that he could never read
the words 'solemn dignity and sullen state' without seeing
Pitt before his eyes. Much scorn is directed to the Prime
Minister's youth, and concern is expressed at the uncushioned
hardness of the Treasury Bench:

> Alas! that flesh, so late by pedants scar'd
> Sore from the rod should suffer seats so hard.

But youth alone does not provide material for many witti-
cisms, and, apart from his youth, they could find nothing
better to attack in the Prime Minister that his supposed
observance of the Seventh Commandment: To this rather
surprising ground for criticism they return again and again;
nor are they alone in their prejudice, for the Reverend Mr.
Wolcott writing as Peter Pindar makes endless fun of the
Prime Minister's chastity.

In the House we are shown the Speaker in his chair
unable to escape from the dullest of bores:

> There Cornewall sits, and, O unhappy fate!
> Must sit for ever through the long debate;
>   .   .   .   .
> Painful pre-eminence! He hears, 't is true,
> Fox, North, and Burke, but hears Sir Joseph too.

Sir Joseph was Sir Joseph Mawbey, an old member, who
was said to be interested in the breed of pigs and their food,
('He is indeed a knowing man——in grain.').

The leading members of the Government could expect no mercy, and Dundas was among the least popular of them:

> Alike the advocate of *North* and Wit,
> The friend of *Shelburne* and the guide of Pitt,
> His ready tongue, with sophistries at will,
> Can say, unsay, and be consistent still;
> This day can censure, and the next retract,
> In speech extol, and stigmatize in act;
> Turn and return; whole hours at Hastings bawl,
> Defend, praise, thank, affront him, and recall.
> By opposition he his King shall court,
> And damn the People's cause by his support.

Grenville's top-heavy appearance is emphasized:

> A youth, who boasts no common share of head;
> What plenteous stores of knowledge may contain,
> The spacious tenement of Grenville's brain!

The formidable Lord Chancellor was an obvious target:

> The rugged *Thurlow*, who with sullen scowl,
> In surly mood, at friend and foe will growl;
> Of proud prerogative the stern support,
> Defends the entrance of great *George's* court
> 'Gainst factious Whigs, lest they who stole the seal,
> The sacred diadem itself should steal.

The Duke of Richmond had a reputation for economy in the entertainment of his guests, and he is assumed to have extinguished his kitchen fire:

> Whether there go'st, while summer suns prevail,
> T'enjoy the freshness of thy kitchen's gale,
> Where, unpolluted by luxurious heat,
> Its large expanse affords a cool retreat.

Mr. Jenkinson and Mr. Atkinson, whose joint labours had so successfully prepared the way for the general election, appear as the masters of the Prime Minister:

> Shall *Chatham's* off-spring basely beg support,
> Now from the India, now St. James's Court;
>
> .　　.　　.　　.　　.　　.　　.　　.　　.
>
> And prove a pupil of St. Omer's school,
> Of either *Kinson*, *At* or *Jen* the tool?

And Mr. Atkinson is again noticed as the ally of Major
Scott, the zealous but disastrous agent of Warren Hastings:

> The minor *Kinson* and the Major *Scott*.
>
> .   .   .   .
>
> And reams on reams of tracts, that without pain,
> Incessant spring from Scott's prolific brain.

Lord Sackville is reminded of the part which, as Lord
George Germaine, he had played in the loss of the American
colonies:

> His grateful countrymen, with joyful eyes,
> From *Sackville's* ashes see this Phoenix rise.
> Perhaps with all his master's talents blest,
> To save the East as he subdu'd the West.

And the veteran Selwyn, still clinging to his reputation as
a wit, is not forgotten:

> A plenteous magazine of retail wit,
> Vamp'd up at leisure for some future hit;
> Cut for suppos'd occasions, like the trade,
> Where old new things for every shape are made!

The *Rolliad* with its successors, *Probationary Odes* and
Political Miscellanies, appeared in parts for a year and
achieved much success.

The autumn was not eventful. Loyal subjects were
alarmed in September by the news that His Majesty had
narrowly escaped injury in collision with a cart horse. A
month later two statesmen, who, each in his manner, had
saved the King from his enemies, entered upon their reward, Lord Shelburne as the Marquis of Lansdowne and
Lord Temple as the Marquis of Buckingham. And in
December died Dr. Johnson, among the best of Fox's
friends, and Fox had the honour of selection as a pall-
bearer at the funeral.

Play still had its attractions for him in spite of the delights
of St. Ann's Hill and Mrs. Armistead. But his play was now
occasional, and he was no longer a regular loser. At the end
of that year creditors again became aggressive, and he had
to seek temporary refuge with a friend in Sackville Street.

But fortune was sometimes kind. It must have been at about this time that some ladies who were calling upon Mrs. Armistead were startled by the sudden appearance of Mr. Fox, who danced rapidly into the room to a chant of 'Great run! Great run! Finest thing you ever saw! Pay the Jews! Pay 'em all! Great run!' and disappeared with undiminished velocity.

Once more, when the session opened, the affairs of the country had to give way to the more attractive theme of the Westminster Scrutiny, which was discussed intermittently, until, on the 3rd of March, Pitt's majority deserted him. For two nights a mob turned out in the old tradition of Wilkes, with the new attraction of rioting on the side of the Prince, to demand illumination in honour of Mr. Fox and break unilluminated windows. 'Our new generation', remarked Walpole, who had been roused in the night to obey the command of the mob, 'are rather bacchanalian and not averse to being rioters under the Princeps Juventutis'.

It was a busy session in which the House ranged over the probable intentions of the Emperor Francis towards the Dutch, the most suitable part of the Empire for the establishment of a convict settlement, the qualifications of the Duke of Richmond to design fortifications, and two of Pitt's great measures of reconstruction, electoral reform and the commercial agreement with Ireland.

Electoral reform provided his first disappointment. The demand for it was manifest and the case unanswerable. He proposed to disfranchise thirty-six rotten boroughs, with compensation to owners, and to distribute the seventy-two seats so obtained to populous cities. As other boroughs decayed they would be extinguished in the same way. It was a simple plan, and, with the simple logic of youth, Pitt persuaded himself that so obvious a reform would appeal to the House, as it had appealed to him. He had Fox's support, and Dundas worked hard in a cause which was not his own. But it was too much for private interests and

for that body of politicians and middlemen to whom the
traffic in boroughs was an essential part of public life. Lord
North spoke against it, and both parties were divided. A
defeat by seventy-four votes taught the young Prime
Minister something of the realities of public life and perhaps weakened his early zeal as a reformer.

Commercial relations with Ireland brought even greater
disillusionment. Ireland had won liberty from the American
War, and the Irish were learning, as other soldiers of freedom have learnt, that political liberty does not of itself
destroy poverty. Trade was falling, the movement of arms
was becoming a menace, and a tariff war with England
seemed probable. A student of Adam Smith, Pitt believed
that both countries would profit by unrestricted trade, and
his proposals for a commercial Union with Ireland were
inspired by the economics of his master and by his own
vision of a new Empire. Trade between the two countries
was to be free for all time, and when the Irish revenue rose
above a fixed sum the surplus was to be contributed 'towards the support of the naval force of the Empire'. The
proposals had a difficult passage in the Irish Parliament,
where the naval contribution was attacked as an attempt
to force on Ireland the political subjection which America
had resisted. But Grattan carried the day, risking his
political future. They had still to pass the British Parliament, and there the storm broke. The traders and indus-
trialists of the North were not students of Adam Smith,
and they were unimpressed by the advantages of free trade.
Petitions against the Bill poured in, and Horace Walpole
heard rumours of the Prime Minister being burnt in effigy.
It would be too much to suggest that a parliamentary Opposition should come to the rescue of a harassed Government.
The Opposition was entitled to oppose, and no one could
criticize Fox, whose reading did not include the *Wealth of
Nations*, for putting the case of the Manchester traders. He
put it with effect, and wrote gleefully of his triumph in
Manchester:

'Our reception in Manchester was the finest thing imaginable, and handsome in all respects. All the principal people came to meet us, and attended us into the town, with buff and blue cockades, and a procession as fine, and not unlike that upon my chairing in Westminster. We dined with 150 people; and Mr. Walker (one of their principal men, who was in London last year on their business), before he gave me as a toast, made them a speech, in which he told them, they knew how prejudiced he had been for Pitt and against the India Bill; but that in the course of his business in town, he had occasion to know both Pitt and me, and found how much he had been mistaken in both . . . and all this in the town of Manchester which used to be reckoned the worst place for us in the whole country.'

But he went far beyond economic doctrine, and appealed to all the racial animosity which had flamed up since the war. 'I will not barter', he declaimed, 'English commerce for Irish slavery; that is not the price I would pay, nor is this the thing I would purchase.' He may have been misled on questions of free trade, but he well knew what he was saying in that peroration, and the speech is among those which bring no credit to his memory. The scheme was mutilated to appease the traders, and in its mutilated form it was contemptuously rejected by the Irish Parliament. Another chance of a settlement with Ireland was lost.

September brought its round of visits and partridge shooting, with much anxious discussion of foreign affairs in the Whig houses, for the outlook in Europe was obscure and a new war was not an impossible development from the Austrian Emperor's recent claims upon the Scheldt. There were also rumours of Pitt's tentative moves for a commercial agreement with France, which was directly opposed to Fox's favourite plan of a League of Northern Nations to balance the power of the Bourbons. He was convinced that any approach to France would do harm by increasing the difficulties of a northern agreement, and would gain nothing to compensate for the loss, because Bourbon France, as he

firmly believed, was not to be trusted. We find him in
November gloomily warning Fitzpatrick of 'France rivet-
ing the Dutch still more to her, preserving the Emperor and
King of Prussia, and gaining ground even with Russia,
without losing her influence with the Porte . . . all these
things appear to me circumstances of alarm beyond any
that have ever existed, and I question much whether France
has not gained much more since the peace than during the
war. In short, unless some of these things can be undone,
there seems to be little left for England but to join the train
and become one of the followers of the House of Bourbon,
which would be almost as dangerous as it would be disgraceful. I am sure this was Shelburne's system. I have
been persuaded by Sir James Harris that it was not Pitt's
but there are several circumstances that look like it, and
indeed it may be a doubt whether the German League leaves
him the choice of any other. The worst of all is that I am
far from sure whether the country in general would not like
a good understanding with France (from the vain hopes of
a durable peace) better than anything. I am sure that any
Minister who can like it must not only be insensible to the
interests of his country but to any feelings of personal pride:
for, depend upon it, whenever you are in such a situation the
French will make you feel it enough.' A few weeks later
he was again lecturing Fitzpatrick on the best means of
arousing public opinion on foreign affairs, and rather
pedantically defining his views on the political value of the
eighteenth-century press:

'I cannot think as you do of the insignificancy of newspapers, though I think that others over-rate their importance. I am clear too that *paragraphs* alone will not do.
Subjects of importance must be first treated gravely in
letters or pamphlets, or best of all perhaps, in a series of
letters, and afterwards the paragraphs do very well as an
accompaniment. It is not till a subject has been so much
discussed as to become almost threadbare, that *paragraphs*
which consist principally in allusions, can be generally

N

understood. Secret Influence, Indian Government, and now Irish Propositions, are all fit subjects therefore for paragraphs; but foreign politics must be first treated in some serious and plain way, and must be much explained to the public, before any paragraphs alluding to them can be understood by one in a thousand.'

Autumn brought a new anxiety. Mrs. Fitzherbert was again in England, and it was rumoured that she was now willing to marry the Prince. A year ago the affair had, as it seemed, ended on a note of melodrama not unmixed with farce. The Prince, after declaring his feelings by rolling on the ground, sobbing, and tearing his hair, had reached such a pitch of dramatic emotion as to attempt suicide. The royal bosom had been pierced, or, perhaps more accurately, scratched with a carving knife, and Mrs. Fitzherbert had been escorted by the Duchess of Devonshire to see with her own eyes that gaping wound. The interview was highly emotional, and the wounded lover pressed a ring on to her finger. The significance of this informal ceremony was never tested, for the lady realized her imprudence as soon as she left Carlton House, and she at once sought refuge from the royal frenzy by leaving the country for a year. Now she had returned, and Fox felt bound to utter a solemn warning. He reminded the Prince that marriage with a Roman Catholic would exclude him from the succession, if his marriage was a real one; but under the Royal Marriages Act the marriage would not be a real one, and it was unlikely that Parliament would respond to any suggestion that the secret marriage should be legalized. 'This appears so clear to me, that if I were Mrs. Fitzherbert's father or brother, I would advise her not by any means to agree to it, and to prefer any species of connexion with you to one leading to so much misery and mischief.'

The Prince's answer arrived in a few hours, and its terms were such as to allay all anxiety:

'My dear Charles,—Your letter of last night afforded me more true satisfaction than I can find words to express, as it is an additional proof to me, wh I assure you I did not want, of yr having yt true regard and affection for me wh it is not only ye wish, but ye ambition of my life to merit. Make yourself easy, my dear friend; believe me, the world will now soon be convinced yt there not only is, but never was, any grounds for those reports, wh of late years have been so malevolently circulated.'

He then changed the subject, a little abruptly, to abuse Eden, who had infuriated his party by accepting from Pitt the post of diplomatic agent to negotiate a commercial agreement with France. Four days later the Prince, without a word to Charles Fox, was secretly married to Mrs. Fitzherbert.

CHAPTER VIII

1786–1787

Apart from the temporary interest aroused by the robbery of the French mail in Pall Mall, the new year brought little to distract attention from politics, and the session began with an incident from which the discerning might have discovered a theme which was to become familiar to the point of tedium.

On the first day of the session Major Scott, the agent of Warren Hastings, invited Burke either to proceed with his charges or withdraw them. Major Scott has often and rightly been blamed for his mishandling of his principal's affairs, and it has even been suggested that the impeachment was due to his question on that day. It is fair to him to record that the challenge was offered on the instructions of Hastings himself, and preparations for impeachment were already in hand. Probably the only result of the Major's question was to accelerate the charges.

It is not surprising that Warren Hastings should have decided to test his position. He had landed in England conscious that he had enemies, conscious that he had committed acts which Parliament could not be expected to approve, but confident that his public services as the Chatham of the East would be recognized. He knew well enough that Francis wanted to ruin him, and that Burke, inspired by Francis, was moving the Whigs against him. But the Whigs were not the Government, and he saw no reason to expect enmity from the Government. He had been received enthusiastically at India House, graciously by the King, and, although Pitt displayed more than his usual frostiness, the Lord Chancellor, who described the Government as a Hastings Administration, was talking about a peerage. Apart from Francis and Burke the Whigs were tepid, and it seemed not a bad moment for forcing the issue.

But he had not sufficiently appraised the spiteful industry

of Francis and the energetic exaltation of Burke. We know from Junius what concentration of malice the mind of Francis could contain, and for the last five years that mind had been preoccupied above all things with the feud with Hastings. In Burke, the champion of oppressed India, he had found an ally more than ready to believe the worst. Perhaps if Fox had been less frequently occupied with Mrs. Armistead and St. Ann's Hill, he might have seen more of Francis and guessed something of the spite which lay behind the charges, for Fox could judge men, and it is unlikely that he would have followed Burke in presenting Junius to the House as the man who 'has had no other reward and no other distinction but that inward sunshine of the soul which a good conscience can always bestow on itself'. Burke indeed feared that Fox viewed the affair 'not as a point he means to exert strength to carry', and he apparently found it prudent to conceal from his leaders certain aspects of the case until it was too late to protest against them. 'If', he wrote to Francis, 'the matter is planned and settled without them, only taking care they are well instructed, there are many things which they could never permit in consultation, which in debate they must support or disgrace themselves for ever.'

It was to be a Hastings Session, but in the intervals, while Francis and Burke were preparing their twenty-two charges, the House considered matters which were perhaps even more important than the terms of Mr. Hastings's contracts for draught and carriage bullocks. Pitt again introduced the Duke of Richmond's scheme for fortifying Plymouth and Portsmouth, and he was again defeated. Fox opposed the scheme on the grounds that it was useless to fortify Plymouth and Portsmouth alone, when no defence was proposed for other parts of the coasts. He took occasion to disclaim motives of party by pointing out that defeat seemed to make no difference to the Government. Had not Pitt already been defeated on the Duke of Richmond's fortifications, the Irish propositions, the Westminster scrutiny and the cotton duty, and successive defeats did not 'take an atom from his consequence'. 'The fact is,' he went on, 'he is a minister who thrives by defeat, and flourishes by disappointment. The country gentlemen oppose him upon one occasion, only to give him more strength upon another; he is beaten by them upon one subject, only to be assisted by them in a succeeding one: if he falls by the landed interest to-day, he is sure to rise by them to-morrow with added energy and recruited vigour.' The jibe, unfortunately for the Opposition, exactly represented the truth.

The Prime Minister fared better when he introduced that scheme for the sinking fund, which was accepted by our ancestors as the masterpiece of political wisdom. But a later generation has supported Fox, who made no pretence to economic science, against the student of Adam Smith. Fox criticized the fallacy of borrowing money in time of war to provide the annual contributions to the sinking fund, and he argued with such force that Wraxall, a confirmed supporter of the Government, was 'persuaded, if he had been placed at the head of the Treasury and the Exchequer, he would have made as able a First Minister as his rival'.

Meanwhile Burke was demanding more and more papers on the affair of Hastings and hoping that the Prime Minister would soon commit himself to something beyond the neutral declaration that he was 'neither a determined friend or foe of Mr. Hastings'. At the end of April Hastings himself made a move by petitioning to be heard on the charges, and on the 1st of May the House was packed to see him kneeling at the bar. He believed that a plain statement from him would dispose of the whole business, and he may also have hoped that his appearance alone would have answered some of the charges, for Macaulay's description is borne out by the portraits. There are the 'brow pensive, but not gloomy' and 'face pale and worn, but serene' which should convince observers that he 'looked like a great man and not like a bad man'. But his statement, whether great or bad, was immensely long and his voice was not equal to the strain. It was read in official monotone by relays of parliamentary clerks, while members withdrew in dismay. On the second day the reading was finished and Hastings withdrew. His appearance had been a failure.

The House had now to consider the charges and decide whether they justified impeachment. On the 1st of June Burke began with the Rohilla charge, which was to the effect that, in 1773, Hastings had, in defiance of his instructions, agreed with the Nabob of Oude that, in return for a payment to the Company, troops should be provided 'for thoroughly extirpating the nation of the Rohillas'. It was a carefully chosen charge, for the Rohilla war had been censured by Parliament and disavowed by the Court of Directors, and it was difficult to imagine that Parliament could now decide that Hastings had no charge to answer. But Dundas in such matters could manœuvre with subtlety. He did not defend the Rohilla war, but he pointed out that Parliament after the war had passed an Act reappointing Hastings as Governor-General, and that Act must be taken as a condonation of the offences then known to Parliament. Dundas was assumed to be reflecting the view of Pitt on the whole question of impeachment, and the majority voted with him, in spite of Fox's passionate appeal to 'the laws of nature, not the statutes to be found in those books before us, or in any books, but those laws which are to be found in Europe, Africa, and Asia—that are to be found amongst all mankind—those principles of equity and humanity implanted in our hearts'.

The Hastings party triumphed. It seemed clear that they could count on Pitt, and the Whigs had no wish to move with the certainty of defeat each of the twenty-two charges in turn. But there was an element of technicality in the decision on the Rohilla charge. Pitt had not spoken, and it was just possible that his vote had been secured only by the argument of condonation, which would appeal to the barrister of Lincoln's Inn. They agreed that the next charge, which had been allotted to Fox, should be moved before they finally decided to throw up the case.

Accordingly the Benares charge was moved by Charles Fox on the 1st of June. It was known that Government members had received the usual note from the Treasury instructing them to attend, and it was assumed that Pitt would lead them against the motion. Perhaps for this reason, the reporters have left us very little of Fox's speech, which was said to be at his highest level. It was not a simple charge. It alleged that Cheyt Singh was Rajah of Benares, subject only to payment of a yearly tribute; that Hastings had unlawfully called upon him to provide money and cavalry; that Hastings had imposed a fine of £500,000 when Cheyt Singh objected to these demands; that Hastings had plundered the fortress of Bidgigur. The speech ended with an indication that on the Benares charge he would ask a decision on the whole case. 'I must acknowledge that there was something like a colour for the vote to which we came respecting the Rohilla war. The extreme distance of the time at which it happened, the little information the House had of it till lately, the alleged important services of Mr. Hastings since that period (although I maintain that they were neither meritorious nor in truth services)—all these, with other causes and justifications might then be urged. But there are none such on the present occasion. The facts are all of them undeniable; they are atrocious, and they are important; so much so that upon the vote of this night, in my judgement, the fate of Bengal depends.' Francis seconded with able animosity, and Pitt rose to make his declaration. It began much as was expected. Cheyt Singh was not independent; he was a vassal; and as a vassal he could be called upon for help in time of danger; and if he refused help, he could properly be fined. In all these things Hastings was right—but there remained the amount of the fine. It was too high; it was exorbitant; and for that reason alone the Prime Minister would vote in support of the Benares charge. The House gasped with astonishment; Grenville and Mulgrave rose from the Treasury bench to oppose their leader; Major Scott expressed his horror; Dundas said nothing whatever but voted with Pitt. The charge was adopted by a majority of 119. Impeachment was now certain.

'The hum and buzz of political insects', as Lord Rosebery has described it, rose at once in speculation on Pitt's motive. Why had he suddenly thrown Hastings to the wolves? Had Dundas secretly talked him over because Hastings at large and unaccused might be dangerous to the Dundas influence on the India Board? Or was Pitt himself afraid that Hastings with a peerage and the friendship of Thurlow and the King might become a competitor? Or was it an astute device to keep the Opposition busy with Hastings while highly controversial measures were hurried through unobserved? In fact there is no mystery to be revealed. Pitt would, no doubt, have been wrong in allowing Hastings to be impeached only for imposing too large a fine if he had been guilty of no other offences. But ministers do not invariably read State papers as soon as they arrive, and there is no reason to doubt the explanation of Dundas that after the Rohilla debate Pitt for the first time examined the other charges, and decided that in some of them the defence was not one on which he could risk his Government. He accordingly supported the charge but reduced it as far as he could in favour of Hastings. The remaining charges were adjourned to the next session.

The finances of Charles Fox had apparently recovered, for we hear of him in May buying a picture from a dealer for 200 guineas. He was still enthusiastically improving St. Ann's Hill, and full of anxiety at the prospects of his hay crop, which he would discuss with every agriculturist, whether landowner or labourer, whom he might meet in his daily walk. But if his own debts threatened no immediate crisis, he had cause for anxiety in those of the Prince of Wales. Carlton House had been equipped with a magnificence which had won praise from Horace Walpole, although the building was not of the school of Strawberry Hill Gothic. But bills had not been paid, and the Prince had been living in a manner far beyond the £50,000 a year which the Coalition had secured for him in 1783. A year ago matters had become serious. He had appealed to the King without success, and only the adroit diplomacy of Sir James Harris had dissuaded him from the project of living abroad incognito as the Earl of Chester. Now the position was positively desperate, and when the Civil List was discussed Charles Fox announced his intention of bringing the question of the Prince's allowance before the House. But the response was not encouraging. Pitt was 'not instructed to make any communication to the House respecting the branches of the royal family', and only one member, a city alderman, showed any interest in Florizel's income. The debts were now enormous, probably well over £200,000, and there were increasing difficulties in finding money for daily expenses.' A list of the debts was sent to the King, all carefully explained except one awkward item of £25,000 which he was 'obliged in honour not to tell from whom he got it'. But the experiment was a failure, for His Majesty only suggested that he should lay by £10,000 a year 'to pay my debts at a time when, with the strictest economy, my expenses are twice my income'.

There were urgent and agitated conferences during the spring. The Prince distractedly sought help from each of his friends in turn. He even negotiated a timely loan from the Duke of Orleans, who was in England in April and ready to play or drink with the best of them at Brooks's. But it was of no avail. His English friends were unwilling, and in many cases unable, to pay the bills, and Fox could only tell him that Parliament in its present mood was unlikely to be sympathetic. So in June the Prince decided to break up his establishment and set aside a yearly sum variously reported as £40,000 and £10,000 to pay his debts. A few weeks later he was able to show that his filial piety was not conquered by adversity, for on the 21st of August a woman of obvious insanity tried to murder the King with a carving knife, so flexible that it failed to penetrate the royal waistcoat. The King showed that composure which he invariably maintained

in moments of personal danger, and the Prince gained credit
by hastening to London with loyal congratulations.

When the House rose, Charles Fox withdrew with Mrs.
Armistead to Cheltenham, where, if we may believe the surprising story of his friend Hare, he was 'entirely occupied
with taming a young rabbit'. Nothing happened while he
was so occupied to call him to London. Frederick the Great
died, but his end 'accelerated by eel pies and polenta' produced no European crisis. As Lord Hawkesbury, Mr. Jenkinson, the 'Jenky' of the *Rolliad*, received his reward for
many years' service to the Court, choosing for his new motto
'Palma non sine pulvere', which the wits of Brooks's ren-
dered as 'The reward of my dirty work'. For merits which
were less apparent the sporting Duke of Queensberry, 'that
polished sin-worn fragment of the Court', also received an
English peerage.

The King's speech opening Parliament in January 1787
announced that a commercial treaty had been signed with
France. It was the result of skilful negotiation by Mr. Eden,
who had gone over from the Whigs, and he earned his
reward from his new party. The difficulties of negotiation
would have been greater if French finances had been in a
state to allow ministers to forgo revenue while they bargained. But French finances were in a parlous state, and
Calonne gloomily confided to Eden that he would need eight
years to save France from ruin. Fox made it clear that he
would examine the treaty with suspicion. 'I spoke pretty
strongly against French connexions and France, and Pitt
made as bad a speech in answer as could be wished. There
was no debate and no division; so that I was time enough to
go to dinner at Derby's, where everybody seemed to think I
had done right. I know the French well enough to know that,
though they are very civil, and such of them as hear me may
say I speak well upon those subjects, yet that they will make
it the fashion in some way to run me down.' This was not
factious opposition. Many of his most experienced contemporaries shared the view that the Bourbons and their family

allies could not be trusted, and that attempts to reach agreement with them would not only be useless but might do positive harm by alarming other governments which might have been friendly. When that experienced diplomat, Sir James Harris, discussed with the Prince of Wales the plan of living abroad, he disposed of France as a suitable asylum with 'As for France I hope never to see a Prince of Wales there on any other purpose than that which carried the Black Prince; or even to hear of his being at Calais, but to fix the British standard on its walls'. Our Ambassador, in Paris, the Duke of Dorset, was no less suspicious of the French. 'The spirit of intrigue which Versailles is endowed with', he wrote in 1786, 'is more dangerous to the balance of power than all the mighty armies of Louis XIV; and if we do not watch him close, we shall be in a most unpleasant situation.' Statesmen at the beginning of the twentieth century, who were convinced of the malignant intention of Imperial Germany, might have objected in the same way that a treaty with Germany would not save the country from aggression and might strain the delicate structure of the *entente cordiale*.

But before debating the treaty, the House considered another of the charges against Hastings. It was the Begum charge and it had been allotted to Sheridan. The subject had aspects—captive princesses, corrupt judges, the treasure of kings, the gorgeous East—which appealed to the dramatist in Sheridan, and he devoted to it one of the most profound efforts of his life. The result was acknowledged to be the greatest display of eloquence ever known in the House of Commons. 'All I have ever heard,' said Fox, 'all I have ever read, when compared with it dwindle to nothing and vanish like vapour.' Only a few echoes of that memorable oration, which held the House for nearly six hours, have come down to us, and they are worth reading for comparison with the method of Fox. Here is an analysis of the mind of Hastings:

'We see nothing solid or penetrating, nothing noble or

magnanimous, nothing open, direct, liberal, manly or
superior, in his measures or his mind. All is dark, insidious,
and insincere. Wherever he has option in the choice of his
objects, or his instruments, he instinctively settles on the
worst. His course is one invariable deviation from rectitude.
And the only trace or vestige of system discernible in the
whole of a dozen years' administration is that of 'acting without any'. The serpent may as well abandon the characteristic obliquity of his motion for the direct flight of an arrow
as he can excuse his purposes with honesty and fairness. It
is all shuffling, twisting, cold and little. There is nothing in
him open or upright, simple or unmixed. . . . His crimes are
the only great thing about him, and those are contrasted by
the littleness of his motives. He is at once a tyrant, a trick-
ster, a visionary, and a deceiver. He affects to be a con-
queror and lawgiver, an Alexander and a Caesar; but he is
no more than a Dionysius and a Scapin. His very writings,
though here he wants not for admirers, discover the same
intrinsic poverty of intellect, are marked with the same
mixture of bitterness and pride. . . . He reasons in bombast,
prevaricates in metaphor, and quibbles in heroics. So that
in composition he hurts the mind's taste, as much as in conduct he offends any feeling of the heart.'

The dramatic passage on the treatment of Indian princes
might almost have been spoken by a character from the
School for Scandal:

'It was in this manner that nations have been extirpated
for a sum of money, whole tracts of country laid waste by fire
and sword to furnish investments; revolutions occasioned
by an affidavit, an army employed in executing an arrest;
towns besieged on a note of hand; a prince expelled for the
balance of an account, statesmen occupied in doing the
business of a tipstaff, generals made auctioneers, a truncheon
contrasted with the implements of a counting-house; and
the British Government exhibited in every part of Hindu-
stan holding a bloody sceptre in one hand and picking
pockets with the other.'

Sujah-ul-Dowlah is congratulated for leaving his son without wealth and therefore safe from extortion:

'He clothed him with poverty as with a shield, and armed him with necessity as with a sword.'

On the profanation of the zenana he professed himself unable to describe 'the confusion, the uproar, the screaming of females, the barbarity of the troops, and the trepidation of the neighbourhood'. The people of Oude on that occasion are 'compared to a flight of birds. With fluttering trepidation they crowded together in the air on discovering the felon kite, who, having darted at one bird and missed his aim, singled out a new victim and sprang on his prey with redoubled vigour of wing and keener lightning in his eye.'[1]

For the first time in parliamentary history the House adjourned because members felt themselves unable to go on with the debate under the emotion of Sheridan's eloquence. Pitt supported the charge when the debate was resumed and it was carried by a majority of 107.

The discussion of the French treaty was carried on with intermittent acrimony for a fortnight. Charles Fox has been much criticized for his opposition. It consisted of an uncompromising statement of his view that France was 'the natural foe of Great Britain'. The 'amiable character of King Louis', the 'assurances of friendship' from the Court of Versailles, the friendly intentions of Vergennes and

[1] When reading reports of the Begum speech it is useful to recall that eighteen years later Sheridan, according to Creevey, met Hastings as a guest of the Prince of Wales, and 'lost no time in attempting to cajole old Hastings, begging him to believe that any part he had ever taken against him was purely political, and that none had a greater respect for him than himself, &c., &c.; upon which old Hastings said with great gravity that it would be a great consolation to him in his declining days if Mr. Sheridan would make that sentence more public; but Sheridan was obliged to mutter and get out of such an engagement as well as he could'. Major Scott is responsible for the story that a translation of the great speech was read to the Princesses of Oude, but they were 'so exceedingly callous as not to betray the slightest emotion of gratitude, though they expressed great remarks of astonishment on the occasion'.

Rayneval were a snare. The benevolent King Louis thought
only of exalting the name of France, and he had professed
friendship no less fervently immediately before he joined the
rebels in the last war. France had now 'little reason to part
with anything', and was planning 'by entering into a commercial treaty with us to tie our hands and prevent us from
engaging in any alliances with other powers'.

In speaking of France as the 'natural foe of Great Britain'
he was careful to explain that he did not mean that France
'is and must remain the unalterable enemy of England'. As
his letters and speeches after the fall of the Bastille make
clear, he had in mind only the established policy of Bourbon
France. Holding that view he was probably unwise in using
such words as 'natural foe' even with the qualification which
he added; and, in the modern view of foreign affairs, Pitt
was right in his attempt to overcome a long-standing enmity
by an understanding on the basis of trade. Whether Fox
may have been right in doubting the possibility of good
faith in a Bourbon must remain conjectural, for Calonne fell
from office a few weeks after the debate, and his fall brought
the end of Bourbon France a stage nearer. Pitt's handling of
the matter convinced Rigby, who had little affection for him,
that 'Fox and Sheridan and all of them put together are
nothing to him'.

Rigby's 'all of them' had been reinforced by a notable
recruit. In the debate on the French Treaty Mr. Charles
Grey at the age of twenty-two made his maiden speech in a
manner worthy of the career which was to make him the
Prime Minister of the Reform Bill. He had been adopted by
Devonshire House, and his success put him in the first rank
of the Whigs. Another member had recently come in on the
Government side. He was the son of Lord Chatham's doctor, and, with Pitt's support, he might expect promotion.
But nothing in the speech or manner of Mr. Henry Addington
suggested that unkind promotion would lift him to the
position of Prime Minister.

CHAPTER IX

1787-1789

WITH the spring of 1787 the Prince's debts and the Prince's income were again before Parliament. It was an unwelcome subject to Fox's party. Political alliances are seldom without their drawbacks, and many of the Whigs doubted whether the advantages in this reign or the next of the Prince's favour outweighed the too frequent embarrassments of their association with him. The scheme of retrenchment, announced in the summer of last year with the shutting of Carlton House and the general cutting down of establishment, had not solved the problem. It had provoked unseemly levity from the *Morning Post* and the cartoonists, but it had not relieved the pressure of creditors, nor had it enabled Mr. Weltje, the Prince's caterer, to meet current expenses. And now crisis was again imminent. The Son of England was not secure from bailiffs nor from the threat of 'Papa's Bench'.

The support which might have been found among country members of either party for the state and dignity of royalty was sadly discouraged by the incessant scandals of the Prince's life. Apart from the rumour of a secret marriage, the affair of Mrs. Fitzherbert might not have aroused much criticism. But the cartoonists and the *Morning Post*, revelling in a licence unknown to modern newspapers, were never tired of commenting on the Prince's proceedings at Brighton, his friendship with Captain Hanger and others even less reputable, his desperate attempts to raise money, and the general lack of dignity in his amusements. His arrival in Brighton is announced in the *Morning Post* with a report that he had 'frightened away a number of old maids who used constantly to frequent that place', and he is described as having 'amused himself for some time in attempting to shoot doves with single balls . . . but lowered the tops of several chimneys in the Hon. Mr. Wyndham's house'.

The scheme of economy was not accompanied by any toning down of the princely manner, and we have a lurid description of his arrival at a ball in those days of retrenchment and reform: 'Lo! at twelve o'clock in reeled H.R.H. as pale as ashes, with glazed eyes set in his head, and in short almost stupefied. The Duchess of Cumberland made him sit down by her, and kept him tolerably peaceable till they went down to supper, when he was most gloriously drunk and riotous indeed. He posted himself in the doorway, flung his arms round the Duchess of Ancaster's neck, and kissed her with a great smack, threatened to pull Lord Galloway's wig off and knock out his false teeth, till some of his companions called for his carriage.' No wonder the Duke of Portland was unwilling to make Florizel's debts a major issue in the Whig programme, and Sir Gilbert Elliot, after sounding his friends, wrote that 'several of *our country gentlemen* are against him'.

But they were pledged to do something, and it fell to a City member, Alderman Newnham, to make the first move by asking the Prime Minister what steps were proposed to rescue the Prince from his very distressing situation. Pitt gave his usual answer that he had no commands from His Majesty on the subject, and the alderman gave the usual notice of motion. So far matters had proceeded according to expectation, but when the debate began a week later a new aspect of the affair, unwelcome to both parties, was disclosed. Mr. Rolle, the victim of the *Rolliad,* inspired by zeal for the established Church and for personal vengeance, indicated that the proposition was one which 'tends immediately to affect our constitution, both in Church and State'. There was no doubt what he meant. Hints of the Prince's secret marriage had appeared in newspapers and cartoons for over a year. Nobody knew whether the rumours were true, but every one knew that such a marriage without the King's consent would be invalid under the Royal Marriage Act, although it might be argued that going through the form of marriage with a Roman Catholic was enough to exclude the Prince from the succession under the Act of

Settlement. It was not an issue which either Pitt or the Whigs wished to face, but Rolle was insistent, and, in the absence of Fox, Sheridan declared that the Prince wished 'every part of his conduct to be laid open without ambiguity or concealment'.

Fox was in his place two days later, and he took occasion to refer to the rumour as a 'calumny, destitute of all foundation, impossible ever to have happened, and propagated with the sole view of depreciating the Prince's character in the estimation of the country'. But Rolle was unmoved. He agreed that the marriage might be legally impossible, but was it only in the eyes of the law that no marriage had taken place? Fox at once denied the marriage in fact as well as in law. Did he speak from direct authority, asked Rolle. Yes, he had direct authority for what he said. Pitt expressed the relief of the House at the declaration which they had just heard, and sat down murmuring a remarkably apt quotation from *Othello*.[1] On the next day Fox was accosted at Brooks's by a member of the Club, who made him a formal statement: 'I see by the papers, Mr. Fox, you have denied the fact of the marriage of the Prince with Mrs. Fitzherbert. You have been misinformed. I was present at that marriage.'

No contemporary of Charles Fox, whether friend or enemy, and no one who had the opportunity of meeting his contemporaries, has ever suggested that he did not entirely believe every word of his declaration. There is some suggestion in a letter of Mr. Eden[2] that he may have misunderstood some statement by the Prince as authorizing a complete denial. But the Prince, who had every grounds for defending his honour, never ventured to suggest that Fox had any hint of the marriage, and it may be assumed that the First Gentleman in Europe, who four days before his marriage had assured his 'dear friend' that 'there not only is, but never was, any ground for these reports', had allowed

[1] 'Villain, be sure thou prove my love a whore.'

[2] 'Mrs. Fitzherbert's connections are abusing Fox, I hear, loudly, for having said more in the Commons than he had authority for.'

his dear friend to remain secure in that assurance after the marriage.

But even with the certainty that no one questioned his honour, the dilemma of Charles Fox was appalling. What was he to do? He had misled the House by an untrue statement, and members who voted for payment of the debts would do so on the faith of his statement. Should he then withdraw his statement? The results of a withdrawal might be serious—a crisis in Parliament, perhaps a change in the succession to the Throne. His solution of the problem does not do him credit, but the method is not unknown to harassed statesmen. He did nothing at all, and prudently abstained from any further part in the discussions.

The Prince was in a condition bordering upon panic. The whole structure of his world was threatened. If the truth came out, he might lose the throne, and he would certainly lose any hope of inducing Parliament to pay his debts; and without a grant from Parliament the immediate prospect was awful. On the other hand if he did nothing, how could he explain matters to Mrs. Fitzherbert? His first efforts to soothe that lady's feelings were not convincing. 'Only conceive, Maria,' he began, 'what Fox did yesterday: he went down to the House, and denied that you and I were man and wife.' But she did not seem disposed to treat the matter as ended, and the Prince turned distractedly to Grey. Would he say something in Parliament 'for the satisfaction of Mrs. Fitzherbert, which might take off the effect of Fox's declaration'. Grey did not see how anything could be said without 'calling in question Mr. Fox's veracity', and the Prince 'dreadfully agitated' confessed the truth. On this Grey expressly told him 'how prejudicial a continuance of the discussion must be to him', and positively refused to do what he desired. The Prince put an end to the conversation abruptly by saying: 'Well, if nobody else will, Sheridan must.' And Sheridan, confident in his dialectical powers as a dramatic author, agreed to do his best.

Meanwhile Pitt had intervened. The Prince had a case

for an increased allowance, and it would be damaging to the King and to the Government if letters were published revealing the Roman firmness of George III to his heir. There were conferences with the Prince, tactful representations to the King, explanations, promises, and finally, on a 'well-grounded expectation that the Prince will avoid contracting any new debts in future', the King increased his allowance by £10,000 a year from the Civil List, and Parliament voted £20,000 for the new work at Carlton House and £161,000 for the other debts. On the 4th of May the alderman, informed of the negotiations, withdrew his motion, and Sheridan had the opportunity for his promised intervention. It was less easy than the Begum speech, but he did his best: 'But whilst His Royal Highness's feelings had no doubt been considered on this occasion, he must take the liberty of saying, however some might think it a subordinate consideration, that there was another person entitled in every delicate and honourable mind to the same attention; one whom he would not otherwise venture to describe or allude to, but by saying it was a name which malice or ignorance alone could attempt to injure, and whose conduct and character claimed and were entitled to the truest respect.' With this rather indefinite testimonial Mrs. Fitzherbert had to rest content, while the Prince enthusiastically ordered building to be resumed on the Great Dome of his Pavilion at Brighton.

He had got his money, but he had lost the best of his friends, for Fox and most of the Whig leaders from that moment refused to speak to him. The Prince's tastes in his better moments were above the level of George Hanger and the Singing Captain, and, disregarding rebuffs, he tried again and again to recapture his injured friend. In September Fox went to Holkham for the partridge shooting, which was always one of the great events of his year. The Prince at once wrote proposing a visit, but received from Coke of Norfolk the bleak reply that 'Holkham is open *to strangers* on Tuesdays'. Undeterred by this gigantic snub the Prince

arrived, but found that Fox had that morning returned to
Mrs. Armistead, who was ill. But the Prince was in a Whig
house, and he made the most of his visit. Twice during
dinner that night he called for 'the health of the best man in
England—Mr. Fox'. But, in spite of these advances, Mr.
Fox refused to meet him for a year, and it would have been
better for the reputation of Fox and his party if the refusal
had been maintained longer.

While the finances of the Prince were being set in order,
it is pleasant to find that those of Charles Fox also obtained
relief. Since he left office it is not clear how he had contrived
to live, but it is certain that his existence had been largely
one of credit, and his debts were growing uncomfortably.
In August he informed Fitzpatrick that he had 'seen Coutts
who is very handsomely willing to lend me £5,000, but says
he should lend it with much more pleasure, and would even
go farther, if either by means of you or your brother there
were hopes of exonerating me altogether. I have therefore
desired Macartney to state the things to Ossory, but I am
sure you will agree with me that the chance of success will be
greater in proportion as the assistance asked is less, and
therefore I should be very glad to deduct this £600 from the
sum I have mentioned.' He ends his letter with the lofty
sentiment that he does not consider 'any difference of opinion
about such *rascal counters*, of any consequence'. The transaction was negotiated successfully, for in the memorandum
book of Mr. Thomas Coutts the sum of £5,000 is entered as
advanced to Mr. Fox, with a note, presumably by the
magnanimous Mr. Coutts himself, 'never to be pressed or
any interest ever asked for'. Another advance of £5,000
appears in the following June, with the memorandum, 'N.B.
Never to be demanded.' There is no record of repayment,
and on the opposite page some one has entered his view of
the business in the words, 'Worth nothing.'

The chief event of the autumn was Sir Gilbert Elliot's
motion, an offshoot of the Hastings case, for the impeachment of Sir Elijah Impey. He did it well and was much

applauded by his leaders. In a letter to Lady Elliot he describes the moment when Fox, 'who is not apt to praise to any one's face', began after dinner to '*open* a little' with enthusiastic congratulations on the speech, 'and went on with passages of it just as if he had spoken it himself'. Sir Gilbert's success brought him frequently into the society of his leaders, and his impressions were duly posted to his wife. 'Fox', he wrote, 'drinks what I should call a great deal, though he is not reckoned to do so by his companions, Sheridan excessively, and Grey more than any of them: but it is a much more gentlemanlike way than our Scotch drunkards, and is always accompanied by clever lively conversation on subjects of importance. Pitt, I am told, drinks as much as anybody, generally more than any of his company, and that he is a pleasant convivial man at table.'

The dominant event of 1788 was to be the impeachment, although for a moment it seemed that it would give place in general interest to the great fight between Humphries and Dan Mendoza. But in February the gossip of the ring dwindled, and the world talked increasingly of Westminster Hall and the articles of charge. At last came the 13th of February when the boxes and galleries were packed to see the procession of Lords Spiritual and Temporal take their places for the trial. The Hall was draped in scarlet. Mrs. Fitzherbert sat in the Royal box, the Queen and the Princesses in the Duke of Newcastle's gallery. The Royal Dukes walked at the end of the procession behind the Lord Chancellor. Spectators observed with some surprise that Charles Fox was sufficiently impressed by the solemnity of the occasion to appear, like the other managers, in Court dress with a sword. The accused looked tired and ill, according to Sir Gilbert Elliot, 'as if he could not live a week'. But Sir Gilbert, like his friends, felt little pity for the prisoner. 'The clearness of his guilt', he wrote to Lady Elliot, 'and the atrociousness of his crimes can leave no hesitation in anybody's mind, who thinks as I do about him, what one's duty is.'

ST. ANNE'S HILL.

ST. ANN'S HILL

On the next day Burke opened the case with one of the greatest orations in his career. For four days he spoke, ending with his final appeal to the Court: 'I impeach, therefore, Warren Hastings in the name of our Holy Religion, which he has degraded. I impeach him in the name of the English Constitution, which he has violated and broken. I impeach him in the name of the Indian Millions, whom he has sacrificed to Injustice. I impeach him in the name, and by the best rights of Human Nature, which he has stabbed to the heart. And I conjure this High and Sacred Court to let not those pleadings be heard in vain.' He was heard with profound emotion, and Mrs. Sheridan collapsed in a swoon.

On the 22nd of February, before a hall 'this day crowded to a degree beyond anything we had hitherto witnessed', Charles Fox moved the Benares charge. Ladies rose at six to reach Westminster Hall at nine, and 'waited there shivering, without either fires or beaux to warm them, till eleven, when the managers made their appearance'. They were rewarded for their patience, for he spoke, according to Sir Gilbert Elliot, 'with all his own ability'. The report gives little idea of the speech except in a passage where he celebrates the unity of Tory and Whig for the purpose of the impeachment:

'For surely it is grand and edifying indeed, to display the collective vigour of national humanity, paramount over all! to vaunt the dignifying because useful, instance of two political parties uniting, unexpectedly, in the point of reciprocal disinterestedness!—finely foregoing every fair purpose of allowable self-gratification!—sheathing those arms they both had wielded so ably, to mutual annoyance; and attacking to a different array, what they deemed, whether right or wrong was to be proved, the Common Enemy to Truth and Feeling.'

There was truth in this flourish of rhetoric. Certainly much might be said against the impeachment. It was not a satisfactory method of trial in such a case; the charges were sometimes presented unfairly; the attack was due in part to personal enmity. No doubt the impeachment and its managers were open to criticism; but behind the impeachment was a new spirit in public life which was calling for something better than the corruption and cruelty of the old world. The spirit which moved in the impeachment was the spirit which had responded to Burke's measures against public dishonesty and was in that year to respond to Wilberforce's appeal for the slaves. Fox had cause for pride as he stood up to speak in the managers' box.

His friends were elated at his success for another reason. They hoped against all probability that he was about to marry an heiress with a fortune big enough to satisfy every creditor and maintain him in solvency. He was showing unusual warmth and perseverance in his attentions and the lady seemed to respond. His friends encouraged these hopeful symptoms with enthusiasm. Whig ladies competed to entertain her, and, when she appeared in the gallery of Westminster Hall, it was observed that Fitzpatrick secured a seat next to her and entertained her with his best epigrams until Fox could leave the managers' box and take the place of his friend. But after a few weeks the affair languished, and the lady was seen no more.

The climax of public interest was reached on the 3rd of June when Sheridan opened the Begum charge. Fifty guineas were offered for a seat, and once more ladies were 'mobbing it' in Palace Yard at six in the morning waiting for doors to open at nine. The struggle when doors were opened was severe with many losses of caps and shoes. 'Several ladies', wrote Elliot, 'went in barefoot; others, after losing their own, got the stray shoes of other people, and went in with one red and one yellow shoe.' The speech was great, but it did not touch the supreme success of its original version in Parliament. Once more emotion was general, and Mrs. Siddons swooned from sensibility. But it was the last of the great days. Thenceforward public interest in Mr. Hastings and his impeachment dwindled, and when sittings were resumed in November the Duchess of Devonshire found Sheridan 'heartily tired of the Hastings trial, and fearful of Burke's impetuosity says he wishes Hastings would run away and Burke after him'.

The impeachment was accompanied by a remarkable comedy in Parliament. The Government was at issue with the East India Company on the maintenance of an army in India, and events turned to provide the spectacle of Fox rising to defend the threatened rights of John Company, while Pitt explained that no abandonment of principle was intended. It was a scene of comedy, but it was a moment of crisis, for Pitt's majority fell to 59, and for a moment it seemed that once more a Government might fall on a question of India.

The cause of oppressed races was popular at that moment, and on the 9th of May Parliament was asked to consider an abuse of power far exceeding anything which Burke in his least restrained moment could allege against Warren Hastings. The agitation against the slave-trade was gaining ground. Slavery in England had been declared illegal; and Granville Sharp, that crusading fantastic, who had induced Lord Mansfield to declare its illegality, was hard at work with a group of enthusiasts denouncing the horrors of the Trade. They had a devoted ally in Wilberforce, and Wilberforce was himself the friend and ally of Pitt. They learnt what that friendship might mean when Wilberforce became ill and they heard from the Prime Minister the promise that 'he considered himself pledged to Mr. Wilberforce that the cause should not sustain any injury from his indisposition'. He was now redeeming his promise by a motion that the House should consider the circumstances of the slave-trade during the next session when the results of an inquiry by the Trade Committee of the Privy Council would be available. With a divided Cabinet and a hostile King, Pitt could not pledge his Government; but Fox had no such difficulty, and at once committed himself to the view that the Trade 'ought not to be regulated but destroyed'. Pitt's resolution was carried amid alarm from the members in the West Indian interest, one of whom observed that news of the agitation had already reached the plantations, where insubordinate slaves were heard to murmur: 'Mr. Wilberforce for negro: Mr. Fox for negro: the Parliament for negro: God Almighty for negro.'

The immediate result of the debate was the visit of a private member, Sir William Dolben, to a slave-ship in the Thames. What he saw appalled him, and he at once introduced a Bill to provide some measure of tolerable existence for slaves during the Middle Passage, as the voyage on the slave-ship was called. It was, as might be expected, opposed by Thurlow, who knew that the King was with him, but Pitt made it clear that his promise to Wilberforce would be kept. 'If it fails', he wrote to Grenville, 'I have made up my mind after very full reflection.to bring it in immediately in the House of Commons . . . and to summon all the strength we can in the House of Lords. If it fails there, the opposers of it and myself cannot continue members of the same government, and I mean to state this distinctly to the Cabinet before the House meets to-morrow.' The Bill was passed by a majority of 35. It was not a very helpful contribution to the welfare of African slaves, but it was evidence of a new spirit in political thought.

As the session ended the hopes of the Opposition received a much needed stimulant. Lord Hood, the senior member for Westminster, was given office, and in the election which followed his appointment, he was decisively beaten by Lord John Townshend. The behaviour of Westminster was in its worst tradition. Once more Lord Hood's sailors encountered the Irish chairmen. On this occasion the battle was in Bond Street, 'as formidable as any contest can be without gunpowder and bayonets', and one of the Royal Household who ventured into the crowd had to withdraw with a broken head. The winners trumpeted victory, although they had little cause to hope that the free and independent of Westminster represented the mind of electors elsewhere.

At the beginning of August Charles Fox started for

Switzerland with Mrs. Armistead. One of his greatest pleasures was to observe the reaction of his friends to his own
favourite works of art. He would make one of them read a
poem and watch him intently to see the effect of his favourite passages, rejoicing when it produced a delight as great
as his own. He now meant to introduce Mrs. Armistead to
all the beauty that he had found in his travels in Italy.
Nothing was to disturb the perfection of that idyllic journey.
They would need no newspapers nor would they seek out
English friends. They would be out of reach of politics.

There was nothing to keep him in England. France, it
was rumoured, had some thought of war, but it might safely
be assumed that the French were sufficiently occupied with
the desperate crisis of their finances to make it unlikely that
they would face a new war. The King was taking a cure
at Cheltenham, suffering, it was believed, from the effect of
a series of bilious attacks. It was noticed that the incoherence of his conversation had increased, and there was something more than his usual habit of rambling soliloquy in the
long conversation which he was observed to carry on with
an oak-tree in Windsor Park. It was even said that he had
absent-mindedly shaken hands with the oak-tree. But no
one doubted that Cheltenham would restore his customary
toughness of mind and body. The Prince was playing
cricket, and shooting at Brighton; and, even when blame-
lessly occupied in partridge-shooting, he incurred the criticism of the *Morning Post*, which pretended to be unable to
distinguish by the dress of the sportsmen 'which the fashionable tribe most resemble, a set of grooms or a company of
smugglers'. There was no cloud on the political horizon,
and Fox might go on his travels without anxiety.

But in a few weeks the outlook had indeed changed. The
King came back from Cheltenham in the middle of October,
and it was manifest that his health was worse. He was
walking with a stick and he said that he felt weaker every
hour. In a few days more alarming symptoms appeared.
The King's mind was affected. He held a levée on the 24th

of October 'to stop further lies and fall of the stocks', and
there was no longer any doubt. He was insane.

He was taken to Windsor and the royal doctors were summoned. The diagnosis was not reassuring. He was getting
worse every day, and it was rumoured in the Household
that he was dying.

In an instant the world of politics turned from torpor
to feverish activity. Every one hurried to London, and the
Duke of Portland sent messengers to search northern Italy
for Fox, whose movements were unknown. When the Prince
of Wales had seen the doctors, he sent for Lord Loughborough, and announced that he wished to be advised by
the leaders of the Opposition. Lord Loughborough, buoyant with pleasant visions of the Woolsack, hastened to summon his colleagues. But, as the King's condition became
worse and the hopes of courtiers fell, it became clear that
the Prince might expect a reinforcement of his counsellors,
and Lord Loughborough's hopes of the Woolsack receded.
Some of the Government's supporters were believed to be
meditating a transfer of allegiance, and the Lord Chancellor
himself was tentatively negotiating the terms on which he
might retain his high office in yet another Government. It
is not clear who was responsible for the favourable reception of Lord Thurlow's overtures. The Opposition leaders
in the absence of Fox were not united. The Duke of Portland had still to be 'reconciled' to the Prince, and the claims
of Burke, Grey, and Sheridan were in conflict. But before
Fox returned Lord Thurlow had established a claim to the
Woolsack which could not be ignored.

Fox was caught at Bologna. He had not looked at a newspaper since he left England, except once to read racing news
from Newmarket. But a rumour had reached him that his
young nephew, Lord Holland, to whom he had always been
devoted, was dying. He felt sure, when the Duke's messenger
arrived, that the worst had happened, and his joy was wonderful when he heard that not only was his nephew in good
health, but he himself, instead of moving unwillingly to the

House of Lords, might now remain a commoner and once more look to office. The messenger, without a moment's rest, was sent posting back to order horses in advance along the road, and Fox began his racing journey of nine days to London. At Lyons he heard that the King was dead, and Mrs. Armistead, who was feeling the strain of the journey, was left to follow at leisure. As Fox raced northwards, rocking and quivering as his coach lurched over the French roads, he had leisure not only for mental bets on the day's mileage, but for repeated estimates of the position at home. The new king would, of course, dismiss Pitt and send for the Whigs, and the new Government might surely count on a transfer of allegiance by at least enough members to provide a safe majority in the Commons. And it would be a Government with no untrustworthy colleagues. Fitzpatrick, Spencer, Fitzwilliam, Sheridan, Burke, Grey, they would all have office in that model administration. Once before in his ardent youth he had made that journey from Lyons after an expedition with Fitzpatrick in search of patterns for waistcoats, when the conversation during the whole journey had been devoted to clothes. He had made many mistakes since those days, and he had much to regret. But he had shown his quality, and now he would come into his kingdom.

In Paris he heard later news. It would be a Regency and not a new reign. But he might count on a change of government under the Prince's Regency. He was now feeling the strain of his hurried journey, for he was no longer the indefatigable youth who could drink and play for three nights on end and dominate the House with an unprepared speech on the fourth. He became ill as he travelled through France. He was probably poisoned by one of his hurried meals, and refused to delay his journey until he could recover from the effects. When he reached England his condition was serious, and he was visibly unfit for work of any kind. He found much to alarm him. The Prince, whose behaviour while the King was at Windsor had been admirable, had offered a less favourable impression of filial piety since his father's removal to Kew. He was in close alliance with the Duke of York, and there were rumours of indiscreet conversation on the prospects of the King's recovery and too frequent appearances at Brooks's, where members gave a topical interest to their game by referring to a court card as the Lunatic. Even worse was the intrigue with Thurlow, to which the party was now committed. He profoundly disliked the Lord Chancellor; he hated throwing over Loughborough; and he believed that a new Government, of which Thurlow was a member, would risk and deserve failure. 'I have swallowed the pill,' he wrote dejectedly to Sheridan, 'a most bitter one it was; and have written to Lord Loughborough, whose answer of course must be assent. . . . Pray tell me what is to be done; I am convinced, after all, the negotiations will not succeed, and am not sure that I am sorry for it. I do not remember ever feeling so uneasy about any political thing I ever did in my life.'

It was hardly the note of a leader, but he was not in a fit state to lead or take decisions. His friends were horrified at his appearance. The Duchess of Devonshire described him as 'grown very thin and liked peoples talking to him to avoid thinking which puzzled him', and Wraxall recorded a fortnight later that 'his body seemed to be emaciated, his countenance sallow and sickly, his eyes swollen, while his stockings hung upon his legs, and he rather dragged himself along than walked'. He withdrew to St. Ann's Hill, where, after an interview with the Prince, he collapsed, and for ten days 'almost thought he was dying'.

He was able with the support of laudanum to return to the House on the 4th of December for the report of the royal doctors, who had been examined by the Privy Council. Their opinions were hopeful but ambiguous, and the House met again two days later to discuss a Regency. Another report of physicians was presented, reinforced now by the opinion of a new authority, the Rev. Dr. Willis, who looked forward to complete recovery within three months. Pitt moved for a committee to examine precedents, and Fox retorted that no search for precedent was necessary: 'There is here among us an heir-apparent, of full age and capacity to take upon him the royal authority. In my opinion the Prince of Wales possesses as clear a right to assume the reins of Government, and to exercise the sovereign power during his Majesty's incapacity, as he would have in case of a natural demise.' It was the legal view propounded at Carlton House by Lord Loughborough, but it was hardly the view to be proclaimed by Whig statesmen permeated with the spirit of the Glorious Revolution, and Pitt murmured to his neighbour that he would now 'unwhig the gentleman for ever'. He instantly asserted the right of Parliament. 'The assertion of such a right, either in the Prince of Wales or in any other individual, is little less than treason to the constitution. Under the actual circumstances, unless by decision of the two remaining branches of the Legislature, the heir-apparent possesses no more strict right to assume the Government than any other subject of the realm.' It was a scene of high comedy, in which the dignity of Parliament was defended by Pitt, who had entered office by an unconstitutional flouting of the House of Commons, and the sacred right of the royal family was upheld by Fox, whose life had been passed in conflict with the Crown. It was an occasion for sardonic amusement, but the moment was too grave for laughter. Pitt was fighting for delay in the hope that Willis might be right and the King might soon recover, and Fox, believing that no early recovery was possible, had fallen into the trap and himself provided an issue on which discussion might drag on indefinitely. It was not an issue on which his party felt enthusiasm. 'I suppose', remarked Sheridan sourly as they drove away after the debate, 'he has some little right, has he not?' He tried to modify the claim, but it was too late, and on the next day the rights of the Prince were discussed in the House of Lords, where Thurlow, with enviable ingenuity, delivered a discourse to which neither party could

object. On the 15th of December the Prince, through the
Duke of York, withdrew in the House of Lords all claim of
right. The Chancellor again spoke, but he had now seen
the latest bulletins of Dr. Willis, and they had convinced
him that the King would recover. In floods of tears he proclaimed his resolution to stand by his beloved sovereign,
ending with a tearful reference to 'the numerous favours
which he has conferred on me, which whenever I forget may
God forget me!' This pious invocation was too much for
members of the Lower House who knew something of Lord
Thurlow's proceedings during the last month. Wilkes remarked audibly 'God forget you! He'll see you damned
first', while Burke opined that oblivion was 'the best thing
that can happen to you', and from Pitt was heard an ejacula-
tion of 'Oh, the rascal!' One member felt profound relief.
'Charles Fox', wrote the Duchess of Devonshire, 'is very
happy that he has declared against us.'

Fox was still confident of success. 'We shall have several
hard fights in the House of Commons this week and next,'
he wrote, 'in some of which I feel we shall be beat; but
whether we are or not, I think it certain that in about a
fortnight we shall come in. If we carry our questions, we
shall come in in a more creditable and triumphant way, but
at any rate the Prince must be Regent, and of consequence
the Ministry must be changed. The manner in which the
Prince has behaved through the whole, has been the most
steady, the most friendly, and the handsomest that can be
conceived. You know when he sets his mind to a thing he
can do it well, and in this instance he has done it most
thoroughly. . . . In short, with regard to Princes, everything
is easy and pleasant, much beyond what I could form any
idea of. In regard to other things I am rather afraid they
will get some cry against the Prince for grasping, as they
call it, at too much power; but I am sure I cannot in conscience advise him to give up anything that is really necessary to his Government, or indeed to claim anything else
as Regent, but the full power of a King to which he is

certainly entitled. The King himself (notwithstanding the reports which you may possibly hear) is certainly worse, and perfectly mad. I believe the chance of his recovery is very small indeed, but I do not think there is any possibility of his dying.'

Dr. Willis might be hopeful, but a Regency seemed probable; and Pitt, who was contemplating an early return to his practice in Lincoln's Inn, had to decline an embarrassing offer of £100,000 as a testimonial from the City of London to provide for him out of office.

The Regency debates proceeded without haste. On the 10th of December Pitt carried his resolutions declaring the right of the two Houses to provide a means of Government. Fox, still very ill, made according to Grenville 'one of the best speeches I ever heard from him'. Armed with the resolution Pitt wrote to the Prince, setting out his views on the powers and duties of a Regent, and the Prince rallied his friends to advise him on the form and manner of his reply to 'such restrictions as no Dictator could possibly, I think, ever have been bare-faced enough to have brought forward'. Many were the drafts and many the consultations in the framing of the Prince's letter, which had to combine the fire of Burke, the legal wisdom of Loughborough, the polish of Sheridan, and the principles of Fox. The credit of the final document goes chiefly to Sheridan. It was a fine piece of writing, but it was acknowledged only by an expression of regret that Ministers 'still feel themselves bound to adhere to those principles in the propositions to be offered to the consideration of Parliament'. The debate continued, interrupted only by the death of the Speaker and the election of Grenville in his place. Once more the doctors were called upon for an opinion, and Fox has been much criticized for his insistence in questioning the favourable reports of Dr. Willis. No doubt Dr. Willis was right in his diagnosis, but the testimony of an eye-witness,[1] who was in attendance

---

[1] *The Diaries of Robert Fulke Greville*, edited by F. McKno Bladen (1930), pp. 172 and 187.

as equerry, makes it clear that the official announcements were sometimes misleading. The King's condition showed extraordinary fluctuations. Sometimes he was violent and in a strait waistcoat, sometimes only eccentric to a degree not greatly exceeding his usual eccentricity, and there were tragic intervals when he understood what had happened, and the equerry heard him praying piteously 'that God would be pleased either to restore him to his senses, or permit that he might die directly'. If the action of Parliament was to depend on the bulletins, Fox had good reason for his questions.

He was questioning his own doctors no less insistently; for his illness continued despite his efforts to ignore it, and before the end of February he had become so weak that he was forced to acknowledge defeat and withdraw for a cure at Bath, exhorting his friends a little acidly from that retreat that 'if it were possible to cure that habitual spirit of despondency and fear that characterises the Whig party, it would be a good thing, but I suppose that is impossible'. He may have been not sorry to remove himself from Parliament during the Regency debates, for any subject connected with the Prince exposed him to an uncomfortable encounter with Mr. Rolle and the secret marriage. When the matter was raised in Fox's absence Grey floundered into a denial, which was not in keeping with his later character.

On the 12th of February the Regency Bill with its restrictions on the Prince's powers—no power over the Household, no power to grant peerages, only limited powers over offices and pensions—passed the House of Commons, where Pitt, to the indignation of the Duchess of Devonshire, affected 'almost republican sentiment all at once'. A week later, when it was in Committee of the House of Lords, it was announced that further discussion might be postponed, as the King was now convalescent. For some days Pitt had hesitated, but he decided at last to trust Dr. Willis. On the 23rd of February complete recovery was proclaimed, and the crisis of the Regency was over. Two days later an unfortunate deputation from the Irish Parliament, starting before the news of the King's recovery, arrived to offer unconditional Regency to the Prince. He received them with the exquisite courtesy of which he was a master.

Public rejoicings began, and in a few days the mob of London was at its old amusement of calling upon householders to illuminate their windows or have them broken. The illumination, whether spontaneous or compulsory, exceeded all previous displays, and traffic was blocked in the streets for hours.

The climax of rejoicing came on the 25th of April, when the King drove in state to St. Paul's. The enthusiasm was unbounded. He had overcome the assaults of disease and the machinations of his enemies, and 'happy and glorious' he was restored to his affectionately bellowing people.

> A theme for poetry divine,
> A theme to ennoble even mine
> In memorable eighty-nine.

CHAPTER X

1789–1792

MEMORABLE 'eighty-nine was to offer themes more stirring than King George's temporary recovery from insanity.
In the early spring, while London was celebrating the King's
return and Brooks's was competing with White's in loyal
ball-giving, the people of France were electing representatives for a States General, summoned as a last hope against
imminent bankruptcy. On the 7th of May the members
assembled at Versailles in a procession which has become
famous, the nobles in cloth-of-gold with white-plumed hats,
the higher clergy in red with velvet cloaks, the parish priests
and Tiers État in unrelieved black; and the French Revolution began. It was a portent in history, but such portents
are seldom recognized at the moment of their appearance,
and in London the eighteenth century held its pleasant
course with no apparent sense of impending change. Burke
was censured by the House of Commons for declaring in the
impeachment that 'Mr. Hastings had murdered Nuncomar
by the hands of Sir Elijah Impey'; Fox represented to the
Government how profoundly the retailers of Westminster
disliked a Shop Tax; the Bishops successfully defended the
Test Act as a necessary safeguard to the Church of England;
the Duke of York fought a duel with Colonel Lennox, in
which the Colonel's bullet passed through the Prince's curls;
and Wilberforce, renewing his motion for abolition with
support from Fox and Pitt, found the Trade developing
unexpected powers of resistance.

In the early summer the King withdrew to Weymouth
for sea air, and loyal bathing women displayed a 'God Save
the King' across their wide bosoms; Mr. Addington, whose
qualification for high office was not easily discernible, was
elected Speaker on Grenville's return to the Ministry; and
at Carlton House Charles Fox discussed with the Prince
drafts of a letter, which would necessarily be a long one,

since it was intended to explain and justify stage by stage
the Prince's conduct during the King's illness. Events in
Versailles were now moving quickly. King Louis had quarrelled with his Estates, and defiant members had met in a
tennis court to swear that they would not separate until they
had established a constitution.

It was a hot summer, and on the 13th of July King George
began his bathing at Weymouth. 'He had', says Miss Burney, 'no sooner popped his royal head under the water, than
a band of music, concealed in a neighbouring machine,
struck up "God Save Great George our King".' In Paris the
temperature rose higher than at Weymouth, and it combined with an acute shortage of food to produce intermittent rioting, which the authorities seemed unable to control.
Orators were haranguing crowds of hungry citizens reinforced by robbers and vagrants from the provinces, and the
disturbances became more alarming when it was announced
that M. Necker had been dismissed. A few days later London heard the news that the rioters, described according to
taste as the populace of Paris or as a mob of the *canaille*,
had stormed the Bastille.

To Charles Fox it was a matter for unqualified rejoicing.
'How much the greatest event it is that has ever happened
in the world! and how much the best!' he wrote to Fitzpatrick at the end of the month, and he begged his friend,
who thought of going to Paris, to tell the Duke of Orleans
and Lauzun 'that all my prepossessions against French
connexions for this country will be at an end, and indeed
most part of the European system of politics will be altered,
if this Revolution has the consequences that I expect'. This
was not an unusual view. Successive ministers had found
in France of the Bourbons a constant menace to peace and
a source of constant intrigue. They were naturally relieved
by the thought that France had become, as Pitt remarked,
'an object of compassion even to a rival'. For the present
at any rate that danger was removed. It was also in no way
surprising that Fox should express delight at the news that

the French had rebelled against their king, and were, as it was believed, devising a constitution on the English model. No Whig worthy of the name could withhold his generous applause on such an occasion, and, if Fox's letter had been made public, his views would have caused no surprise.

But liberal enthusiasm waned a little as the summer wore on and refugees began to arrive with stories of general insurrection, castle-burning in the provinces, and murders *à la lanterne* in the streets of Paris. In August the Assembly declared the Rights of Man in the best tradition of Philadelphia, and English Whigs, hearing the familiar refrain that 'all men, being born free, should have equal rights', glowed with enthusiastic recollection of their great days of opposition in the American war. A few weeks later the Gardes du Corps, inspired by the ladies of the Court and 'Richard, ô mon Roi, l'univers t'abandonne', mounted the white cockade; and the next day brought the march of hungry women to Versailles, the murderous invasion of the palace, and the shameful journey of the King and Queen to Paris. This was hardly the building of a constitution on the English plan, and Burke began to elaborate the distinction between true and false liberty and to warn his correspondent M. Dupont of impending dangers: 'You have made a revolution, but not a reformation. You may have subverted monarchy, but not recovered freedom.'

The 4th of November was the anniversary of the Glorious Revolution of 1688, and the Revolution Society held its customary meeting and dinner. The speaker or preacher for the occasion was Dr. Price, an eminent but rather tedious divine, who could not resist the temptation to discourse on events in France. In a passage which became famous from quotation, he congratulated himself on having lived to see salvation: 'I have lived to see the rights of man better understood than ever; and nations panting for liberty which seemed to have lost the idea of it. I have lived to see thirty millions of people, indignant and resolute, spurning at slavery, and demanding liberty with an irresistible voice.

Their King led in triumph, and an arbitrary monarch surrendering himself to his subjects.' The Society then adopted
an address of congratulation to the National Assembly of
France. It was the first public declaration of sympathy
from England, and it began a long exchange of compliments
between English reformers and Jacobin clubs all over
France.

But the Whigs did not all share the enthusiasm of Dr.
Price. The session of 1790 began in January, and on the
6th of February the Army Estimates were discussed. Fox,
supporting a reduction in the Army, pointed out that he
did so on the grounds of economy, and not on the traditional
grounds that a standing army was a danger to the constitution, because the example of a neighbouring country had
proved, and it was now universally known throughout
Europe, 'that a man by becoming a soldier did not cease
to be a citizen'. When the debate was resumed, Burke
delivered the first of his great orations on the French
Revolution. His theme, which was soon to be familiar to
the House, was the danger to England of revolutionary con-
tagion from France. In the past we had been in danger of
'being entangled by the example of France in a net of relentless despotism'. Now we were in no less danger of
'being led through an admiration of successful fraud and
violence to an admiration of the excesses of an irrational,
unprincipled, proscribing, confiscating, plundering, fero-
cious, bloody, and tyrannical democracy'. The recent
declaration of the Assembly was 'a sort of institute and
digest of anarchy, called the rights of man, in such a pedan-
tic abuse of elementary principles as would have disgraced
boys at school'; the soldiers of France had become 'not
citizens but base hireling mutineers, and mercenary sordid
deserters'; and property was being destroyed by a 'furious
licentious populace . . . whose savage war-whoop was *à l'Aris-
tocrate* by which senseless, bloody cry, they animated one
another to rapine and murder'. With the utmost gentle-
ness, with repeated compliments, with protestations of

unbounded affection, he elaborated his objection to Fox's casual remark that France had shown that a soldier 'did not cease to be a citizen'. Fox, with a leader's eye to party unity, answered with care. The compliments and protestations of friendship were returned in the manner of which he was a master. Had he not 'learnt more from his right honourable friend than from all the men with whom he had ever conversed'? What he had said did not 'warrant the idea that he was a friend of democracy'. He was 'the enemy of all absolute forms of government, whether an absolute monarchy, an absolute aristocracy, or an absolute democracy'. He would never 'support any cabal or scheme formed in order to introduce any dangerous innovation into our excellent constitution', but he was not 'an enemy to every species of innovation'. As to France, he was horrified by the 'scenes of bloodshed and cruelty', but he thought that the excesses of the people in their attempt to shake off the yoke of despotism might be 'spoken of with some degree of compassion', and he was persuaded that their present state was 'preferable to their former condition'. He ended with a solemn assurance that he would not 'on any occasion act in a manner incompatible with the principles which he had so repeatedly professed, and which he held in common with his right honourable friend'. This pronouncement in the best parliamentary manner was eagerly accepted by Burke, who protested that 'the separation of a limb from his body could scarcely give him more pain than the circumstance of differing from him, violently and publicly, in opinion'. The affair would have ended, temporarily perhaps, in an atmosphere of political goodwill, if Sheridan, who had fidgeted impatiently during Burke's speech, had not felt moved to utter his complete dissent from Burke. It was in the Sheridan manner. Had Burke 'found his doctrine among the stones of the Bastille, or had he collected them from the baggage of Marshal Broglie?' And he ended with the definite suggestion that Burke was now the 'advocate of despotism'. Burke was up in an instant. In a few bitter sentences he complained of misrepresentation, and declared that henceforth he and Sheridan were separated in politics. The danger of disruption in the party was manifest.

Fox at once busied himself with the task of conciliation before the breach could widen. Sheridan was made to express contrition, and Burke and Sheridan were brought together at Burlington House. Sheridan again apologized, and for a moment it seemed that reconciliation was in sight; but Burke caught up some fancied reservation in Sheridan's apology, and the conciliators could do no more. It was a difficult position for the leader. He knew that if the dispute developed to the stage of resignations neither Burke nor Sheridan would go alone; but one or other would go unless he could keep the party so balanced that both of them on opposite wings would feel at home in it. It would not be easy with such energetic controversialists, but it would in some degree help him that the middle course on the whole was his own course. He had exactly defined his views when he answered Burke. He was an enemy of oppression and a friend of liberty. These, with a passionate hatred of war and injustice, were the principles which in the main controlled his political life. Always an aristocrat, he was, as he said, no friend of democracy. Doctrines of equality, levelling, and the rights of man had faint attraction for him, and revolutionary fervour aroused in him no response. But he was convinced that the Revolution in France was essentially a struggle for liberty against tyranny, and that all the destruction and violence which alarmed his friends were but unfortunate incidents in that emancipation. With these views a middle course between Burke and Sheridan was natural for Fox. Pitt, also, was not anxious to commit himself, and opined that 'the present convulsions of France must sooner or later terminate in general harmony and regular order; and though such a situation might make her more formidable, it might also make her less obnoxious as a neighbour'.

A debate which followed showed how profoundly the

mind and judgement of Burke was affected by the French
Revolution. On the 2nd of March Fox revived Beaufoy's
motion for the repeal of the Test and Corporation Acts.
The cause of religious toleration had always commanded his
support since the days of his earlier indiscretion, when he
had recorded the comfortable opinion that religion was 'best
understood when least talked of'; and his speech reviewing the origin and the effects of the Tests was in his best
manner. It was not easy to defend a law which made the
Anglican Sacrament a necessary formality for appointment
to official positions. The profanation of the Sacrament, the
automatic inclusion of candidates who were willing to sink
their religious opinions, or the absence of opinions, for the
sake of office, and the exclusion of the better candidates
who were honest enough to stand by their faith, were obvious results of it. The bishops, by a majority, had advised
Pitt that for the sake of the Church of England the Test
should be retained; but they had not expounded this remarkable doctrine in the House of Lords. To Burke one consideration was decisive. If the resolution had been moved ten
years ago, he admitted that he would have supported it.
But to-day things were very different. Many of the dissenters were 'men of factious and dangerous principles'.
They would get no help from him. In his reply Charles Fox
could only repeat his now familiar compliments to the mentor who had formed his political education and 'governed
his principles', but he could not resist a word of self-con-
gratulation that, starting with the same principles, he had
'retained his opinion upon the subject ten years longer than
his right honourable friend'.

In May Parliament turned to the Budget, and Pitt was
able to assure the House, with pardonable complacency,
that 'the country at this moment is in a state of prosperity
far greater than at any period, even the most flourishing,
before the late war'. It was pleasant to compare such opulence, the result of financial probity, with the bankruptcy
of spendthrift France, where loans failed, taxes were not

paid, and Church property was being nationalized to be made the doubtful security of a new currency.

It was not an eventful session. Mr. Flood moved for Parliamentary reform, and was opposed by Windham, a convert to the views of Burke, on the grounds that no prudent householder would repair his house in the hurricane season. Fox remarked that he could imagine no moment when the householder might feel more urgently called upon to repair his house than the hurricane season, that he had not altered his views on parliamentary reform, but he believed his views were not those of the majority 'within or without doors' and he regarded parliamentary reform as a 'sleeping question'. Burke spoke against reform, and it needed all Fox's nimbleness in debate to avoid entanglement.

The Session ended with a revival of interest in foreign affairs. Spanish ships of war had arrested an English ship in Nootka Sound and hoisted the Spanish flag at the trading settlement of Nootka. The dispute arose on the Spanish claim to trading rights on the west coast of America, and for a moment war seemed probable. The Government ordered a 'hot press' for the Navy, and made ready for war with full approval of Fox.

In June came the general election, and Fox, with an eye to economy, hoped that he had escaped a contest in Westminster. 'Mr. Fox', announced *The Times* sarcastically, 'to do him justice, continues *to give his advice gratis*, but is determined, he says, never to break through the little fortune he had acquired with so much industry, integrity and economy.' But the enthusiasts of parliamentary reform doubted, with some reason, whether he could be accepted as being entirely devoted to their interests. Horne Tooke, whom he had encountered in his early days as Parson Horne, stood against him as champion of the cause. The interloper was of course defeated; but he petitioned against the election, and, on losing the petition, refused to pay his opponent's costs, for which he was ultimately sued. Such changes as the general election produced were, on the whole, favourable to the Government.

The summer brought stories from France to increase the anxiety of Burke. The Assembly had received an impromptu deputation from all nations of the earth led by Anarcharsis Clootz, 'the orator of mankind'; and a few weeks later came the Festival of Federation on the Champ de Mars, when the Bishop of Autun celebrated the mass in a setting which even he, most cynical of ecclesiastics, found remarkable, and the King, amid a tempest of enthusiasm, swore to maintain the new constitution.

> Que l'aristocratie
> Crève de jalousie
>   Au Champ de Mars;
> Mais que l'on chante d'aise
> Le bon roi Louis seize
>   Au Champ de Mars.

Another song of the occasion, inspired by the rain which had delayed the preparations, was to achieve a sinister reputation as the war-cry of militant revolution:

> Ah! ça ira, ça ira, ça ira
> En dépit d'z'aristocrat et d'la pluie:
> Ah! ça ira, ça ira, ça ira,
> Nous nous mouillerons, mais ça finira.

It was a rapturous day for Paris, but King Louis could not rejoice with his subjects. The new civil constitution of the clergy had been brought to him for signature, and he was enduring that agony of indecision which was to end in surrender. In England it was believed among reformers that the French Revolution had now been successfully accomplished, and the 14th of July was enthusiastically celebrated in London by a dinner at which an authentic stone taken from the Bastille itself was brought in on a dish and placed upon the table amid acclamation. From these proceedings Fox could only remain aloof. He knew that Burke was about to express his views in a pamphlet which would certainly not command approval from Sheridan and Grey;

and he knew that Sheridan and Grey were uttering sentiments which would cause the utmost pain to Burke. There was no question of reconciling the divergent sections, nor was it possible to restrain the ardour of either of them. He could only wait for the next crisis, and hope that when it came he would find means to emerge from it with an undivided party. Meanwhile he could take his ease at St. Ann's Hill. 'A few days ago', wrote Storer in August, 'I made a visit at St. Ann's Hill, and found our blue and buff chief surrounded by the arts, lolling in the shade. Mrs. Armistead was with him; a harper was playing soft music; books of botany lying about; and astronomy in the shape of Sir Harry Englefield, assisted in the group. I received a commission from him to get a plant from Mrs. Ellis; and thus you see, like Solomon, he is to seek wisdom in the search of herbs and flowers.'

This pleasant detachment could not be shared by the Prime Minister, who spent the summer in repeated alarms of war. No diplomacy would have settled the affair of Nootka Sound, if France had been prepared to fight. It seemed, for a time, that the party of the *noblesse* favoured intervention on behalf of their Spanish allies as a diversion of energy from revolution at home. Then Mirabeau, convinced, it was rumoured, by one thousand louis d'or from the Spanish ambassador, proclaimed himself a respecter of alliances and national obligations, pending the arrival of a new age when an enlightened Europe would no longer need diplomacy. At a later stage, convinced by arguments and considerations known only to Pitt and his agents, he revised his opinion, and declared against intervention. In any case the French navy was of uncertain discipline and value, and Spanish admirals were reluctant to bring their crews into close association with the sailors of Liberty and their new songs:

> Ennemis de la tyrannie,
> Paraissez tous, armez vos bras,
> Du fond de l'Europe avilie,
> Marchez avec nous aux combats.

The dockyards of England were hard at work, and the fleet was stronger than it had been since the great days of Chatham.

In November appeared Burke's long-awaited *Reflections,* and it aroused the universal excitement which its incomparable writing deserved. Most of its readers, whose minds were already filled with terrifying stories of murder and riot, responded easily to Burke's appeal, although to eighteenth-century taste the famous rhapsody on the Queen of France seemed to lack restraint and dignity, and was indeed described by Francis, who gave Burke his candid opinion before publication, as 'pure foppery'. The King was delighted. It was, he said, a book 'which should be read by every gentleman', and Miss Burney, with no less enthusiasm, described it as 'the noblest, deepest, most animated and exalted work that I think I have ever read'. But other, less emotional, critics were doubtful. References to the 'hooves of the swinish multitude' and the 'Government of five hundred country attorneys and obscure curates' might be dismissed as the exuberance of Burke's style in controversy. But was it true that the French before the Revolution 'had the elements of a constitution very nearly as good as could be wished?' And did he really think that parliamentary representation in England had been 'found perfectly adequate to all the purposes for which a representation of the people can be desired or devised?' It was a challenging and provocative book, destined to arouse passions very different from the noble ideals of its author, and to harden political enmities beyond hope of repair. A copy was sent to Fox, with the author's compliments, but no record survives of the manner in which Fox conveyed his appreciation.

When Parliament met on the 26th of November the House of Commons missed the familiar spectacle of the Prime Minister supported by his two lieutenants Grenville and Dundas, for Grenville had been promoted to strengthen the debating forces of Government in the House of Lords,

where, as the King remarked, 'his abilities will be of material
use, and his conciliating temper will in future aid in keeping
matters smooth with the Chancellor'. The King's speech
announced a triumphant issue of the negotiations with
Spain, for Pitt's firmness had prevailed, and the way was
now open for a Dominion of Canada, which would stretch
from the Atlantic to the Pacific. Opposition was reduced
to grumbling at Pitt's refusal to publish the correspondence.

There would be no war with Spain, but Burke was beginning to turn all his powers of persuasion to bring about a war
with France. He was convinced that no internal remedy,
'whether the drastic purges or the mild aperitive', would
restore order, as he conceived order, in France. Nothing
could be effected without invasion from abroad, and invasion would not be delayed if Governments would accept his
view that 'no monarchy, limited or unlimited, nor any of
the old republics, can possibly be safe as long as this strange,
nameless, wild enthusiastic thing is established in the centre
of Europe'. He was not alone in his call for intervention.
In every Court of Europe French *émigrés* were carrying on
a futile unconvincing intrigue for a return in force to restore
the old order; the Queen of France was suggesting to her
brother that an Austrian demonstration on the frontier
might produce a reaction in France and restore King Louis
to his lost dignity; and the Empress Catherine was attracted
by a scheme whereby the forces of Austria and Prussia
should combine to suppress revolution in France, while she
herself would deal with the dangerous tendencies which she
affected to discover in Poland.

In England little attention was paid to Burke's appeal,
for Pitt had embarked upon another venture which might
well lead to war, but not with France. At the end of March
he announced that 'as our endeavours to effect a pacifica-
tion' between Russia and the Porte had failed we were
forced to arm 'in order to give greater weight to our representation'. The actual point of dispute was whether Russia
should give up part of her recent gains from the Turks and

particularly the fortress of Oczacow. Pitt believed that the
triumph over France in Holland and Spain in Nootka Sound
could be repeated on the Black Sea, and when Fox 'with
more than usual solemnity' asked for details, he rather
abruptly refused to add anything to the formal message.
The debate was resumed next day, and neither House
showed any enthusiasm for the destiny of a town of which
most members had never heard. The Government majority
was safe enough for the moment, but Pitt realized that he
had made a serious mistake and that if he went forward the
Government might collapse. He decided to retreat with a
promptitude which saved him from disaster, but left him
publicly humiliated at home and abroad. The immediate
incident ended a few days later with a debate in which Fox
'charged the minister with insolence, arrogance, incapacity
and wilful imposition on the House of Commons', but it
had shown Pitt that, notwithstanding his majority, his new
peers, and the King's favour, his position was not assured.
His majority might melt at any time as it had melted on
Ireland and electoral reform, and if his Government broke
up, who could tell what new coalition might arise against
him? It is probable that the Oczacow affair inspired him
with a new interest in any cause which might break up the
Opposition.

The prospect of breach in the Opposition was imminent.
Not content with the clearest expression of his own views,
Burke was trying to force his leader into an unreserved
declaration for or against the French Revolution. He even
prepared a long memorandum of instructions to be followed
by the Duke of Portland in a conversation with Fox, drafted
in such a way as to exclude any possibility of reticence or
evasion on either side. The Duke was advised to 'take care
that he does not receive that as a satisfactory explanation,
which is compatible with the presumption which induces him
to ask the explanation', and he is warned that Fox's 'object would naturally be to set the Duke's mind as much as
possible at ease with regard to his intentions, to lull him

with a false security, and, in. the meantime, to go on as usual'. The Duke must not content himself with 'asking if he means to apply the principles of the French Revolution to England, and to acquiesce in the negative answer'. He must ask why, if he does not intend to introduce the French Revolution in England, 'he extols and magnifies it in the language and sentiments of those who do'. And on that point, Burke fancied, 'no explanation can give satisfaction'.

The memorandum was most properly suppressed by Sir Gilbert Elliot, and it never reached the Duke. It shows clearly enough that no personal influence or tact on the part of the Whig leader, no appeal to friendship or loyalty, would have induced Burke to swerve in the smallest degree from his course as self-appointed inquisitor into revolutionary heresy. He had complained that Fox was seldom to be seen, but Fox in daily consultation in London would have effected no more than Fox in rural solitude at St. Ann's Hill against the crusader's exaltation which now possessed the soul of Burke.

The inevitable end came in May. In the Oczacow debate in April Fox had described the new constitution of France, a little irrelevantly, as 'the most stupendous and glorious edifice of liberty which had been erected on the foundation of human integrity in any time or country'. Burke proposed, hardly less irrelevantly, to take occasion in the debate on the Quebec Government Bill to reply to this outburst of enthusiasm, and Fox tried unsuccessfully to persuade him to postpone so public an advertisement of their disagreement to a more suitable occasion. On the 6th of May Burke began a long discourse on the Rights of Man, the atrocious principles of the Jacobins, and their infamous treatment of the King of France. He was constantly interrupted by protests from the Whigs, and the proceedings became a wrangle on the point of order. Tempers rose a little, and Fox supported a motion that 'dissertations on the French constitution, and to read a narrative of the transactions in France, are not regular or orderly on the question that the clauses of the Quebec Bill be read a second time, paragraph by paragraph'. There was a jeer in the tail of his speech which rasped hard on Burke's nerves, already raw from interruptions: 'From his right honourable friend he had learned that the revolt of a whole people could never be countenanced and encouraged; but must have been provoked. Such had at that time been the doctrine of his right honourable friend, who had said with equal energy and emphasis that he could not draw a bill of indictment against a whole people. Mr. Fox declared he was sorry to find that his right honourable friend had since learnt to draw such a bill of indictment, and to crowd it with all the technical epithets which disgraced our Statute Book. . . .' Burke notoriously lacked restraint in debate, and, when he rose to reply, his reserve of self-control was almost exhausted. He complained that Fox had 'ripped up the whole course and tenour of his private and public life, with a considerable degree of asperity'. Then came another irritating interruption from Grey, and Burke's final outburst: 'frequently differed from Mr. Fox in the past . . . never for a single moment interrupted their friendship . . . indiscreet at his time of life to give his friends occasion to desert him . . . now risk all and as public duty and private prudence taught him, exclaim, "Fly from the French Constitution!"' Fox interposed in an amicable whisper that there was no loss of friendship, and Burke to every one's astonishment answered him aloud with a declaration to the House that he 'knew the price of his conduct . . . done his duty at the price of his friend . . . their friendship was over'; and the speech went on with a 'rapturous apostrophe to the infinite and unspeakable power of the Deity'.

It was probably the greatest shock of Fox's life. Friendship was in his nature. His capacity for friendship and his appreciation of the claims of friendship were unbounded. He had already risked his political career and perhaps the interests of his country by refusing to join in an arrange-

ment which failed to provide for the friends to whom he was
pledged, and he continued to do so throughout his life of
opposition. He might quarrel with them again and again,
as he quarrelled with Sheridan about the Regency and with
Grey about the Bastille dinners, but it was unthinkable to
him that any political difference, which did not involve, as
his difference with Pitt had involved, the waging of a
political blood feud, could seriously affect any of his old
friendships. He had expected, and he was probably conscious of deserving, an energetic reply in Burke's most
polemical manner, but the thought that Burke, without
any hint of warning, could publicly denounce their personal
friendship, had never occurred to him. For some time he
tried to speak, but 'his mind', as the reporter tells us, 'was
so much agitated and his heart so much affected by what
had fallen from Mr. Burke, that it was some minutes before
he could proceed. Tears trickled down his cheeks, and he
strove in vain to give utterance to feelings that dignified
and exalted his nature.' What he said when speech returned to him was pathetic. He spoke a little of the French
Revolution, but he returned again and again to his real
subject, the five and twenty years of friendship from boy-
hood, their life of 'most familiar intimacy', his own profound regret for his 'rash and imprudent words', and his
pain at the 'cruel and hard' manner of Burke's treatment.
He implored Burke to think it over, and to let them differ
on the French Revolution as they had differed before on
other subjects. He would 'keep out of his right honourable
friend's way', until 'time and reflection' or the mediation
of friends had restored peace. But Burke was unyielding.
He complained of misrepresentation and 'sincerely hoped
that no member of that House would ever barter the Constitution of this country, that eternal jewel of his soul, for
a wild and visionary system which could only lead to confusion and disorder'. Pitt contributed to the troubles of
the Opposition by opining that Burke had not been, 'even
in the first instance, at all out of order'. In that scene of

eighteenth-century sensibility, so repugnant to modern
tradition of repressed emotion and measured enthusiasm,
the sympathy of the House and of the world was with Fox.
He had appeared in all his usual sincerity, but Burke gave
an impression of something fanatical and almost vindictive. Pitt and Dundas no doubt observed these dissensions
with much complacency. They knew how nearly the Government had fallen on the Oczacow business, and they had
heard rumours that the King showed signs of relenting to
his old enemies and that energetic Whigs believed that
'were Mr. Fox a fresh man, there would be little difficulty
in getting into office'. They knew too that if, as the *Morning Chronicle* suggested, Burke must now retire from his
party, he would probably not retire alone. Nothing could
be more opportune for the Government.

The session proceeded with a debate on the Test Act in
Scotland, in which the reformers encountered the customary
defeat, and Fox's Libel Bill, to correct the doctrine that in
criminal libel it was the duty of the jury to determine only
the question of publication and not the question of libel.
His speech showed more than a debating knowledge of the
subject, and he was supported by the Attorney-General and
Pitt. It triumphantly passed both houses, and it remains
one of the two pieces of legislation for which Fox was
directly responsible. The session ended with wrangling
debates on the Russian Armament, for Pitt was trying to
escape from his commitment with such dignity as could be
saved, and the Opposition was demanding why, if no war
was intended, the expenditure on armaments continued.
The situation was complicated by the visit of Mr. Adair,
a member of the Opposition, to Russia; for the Empress
took pleasure in showing her dislike of Pitt by ostentatious
civilities to a Foxite. Perhaps Adair would have served his
country as well if he had remained at home, but he went
on his own responsibility without any sort of mandate from
his party. The most that he could extract from Fox was
'Well: if you are determined to go, send us all the news'.

Politics were not eventful in those days of steadily increasing prosperity, but there hung, as Burke said, 'a dark cloud over us all'. Refugees from France were landing incessantly with stories of ruined homes and lost possessions, and when on the night of the 21st of June the great travelling coach of King Louis was turned back at Varennes, it was difficult to contend that the French were engaged only in the fashioning of a constitution on the English model. But the 14th of July was approaching, and preparations for its celebration in England were advanced. The Revolution Society of London had taken Ranelagh, and their friends in France had been 'so condescending as to send over a flag of the national colours of France blended with those of *England*, which was to have decorated this great festival, but as it was unfortunately composed of contraband materials it was seized, and is now at the custom house'.

Odd rumours appeared in the press that the Bastille dinners would be the occasion of rioting. In Birmingham, where the warfare between Establishment and Nonconformity was active, the rumours were well founded. A riot, which must have been planned with considerable industry, broke out after the dinner. Some of the most useful citizens of Birmingham spent the night on the roads or in escorting their families to comparative safety in other towns. Every Nonconformist house was burnt, and the magistrates took no serious steps to restore order until, after two days of rioting, the mob got out of hand and no longer confined the looting to the property of Nonconformists.

It was a peculiarly degraded outburst, but it was welcomed by some of the Government supporters as a useful lesson to radicals, dissenters, levellers, and Jacobins; for the idea was now gaining ground that electoral reform, of the kind which the Prime Minister had tried to carry a few sessions ago, was necessarily allied to the cause of the French Revolution and that both causes were necessarily republican. While reformers in England were mobbed on the suspicion of being French republicans, processions of citizens in

Paris, who were demanding a republic, were shot down by
La Fayette's National Guards, for the Assembly was still
impressed by the advantages of a strictly limited monarchy.

> Nous conserverons le roi
> Par pur décence;
> Le peuple fera la loi
> Par toute la France.

It was manifest that Burke would not rest content with the
breaking up of his old friendship. He meant to break up his
party, and in July he published his *Appeal from the New to
the Old Whigs* in which he once more denounced that 'wild
attempt to methodize anarchy; to perpetuate and fix disorder', and once more appealed to right-thinking Whigs to
leave the party, suspected through its leader of dallying
with the accursed thing. But life was not all unrelieved
censure for Fox, for in August he heard the pleasing news
that the Empress Catherine had ordered her ambassador
to send her 'the very best bust of Charles Fox' which, in
token of his talent and eloquence in the cause of peace, she
proposed to place 'dans sa galerie entre Cicéron et Démos-
thène'; and a few days later he was honoured with the
freedom of the City of York 'in token of his brilliant and
unrivalled abilities in support of the British Constitution,
upon the principles of the Glorious Revolution, of the just
rights of every degree of citizen, and the peace, liberty and
happiness of mankind'. Burke was, as might be expected,
much disquieted at this compliment of a Whiggish Mayor.
'It must', he wrote, 'have a reference to something done or
said relative to the principles of the revolution.' It was
even worse; it was a direct rebuff to the New Whig. 'It
was not just at York . . . that I apprehended, in the praises
of another, I should have found, an oblique censure, and the
first vote against me amongst the judges to whom I had
addressed my appeal.'

But Burke was concerned in adventures more stormy
than the intrigues of party politics. Convinced that salvation could be found only in a combined attack on France

by all constitutional nations, he was pursuing ministers for
some gesture of sympathy with 'this cause of sovereigns',
and even drafting messages to guide the Queen of France
herself through the crisis when the King must accept or
refuse the new constitution: 'If the King accepts their pretended constitution you are both of you undone for ever.
The greatest powers in Europe are hastening to your rescue.
They all desire it. You can never think this a time for surrendering yourself to traitors, along with the rights of all
the sovereigns allied to you, and whose cause is involved
in yours.' At Coblenz his son Richard was discussing doctrines of monarchical solidarity with the French princes
and any foreign diplomats who would listen to him.

But the declaration of the Emperor Leopold and King
Frederick William, when they at last agreed on a formula,
was hardly encouraging, for it began with a hope that all
the kings of Europe would combine to restore monarchy.
Then, and only then (*'alors et dans ce cas'*), the Austrian
Emperor and the Prussian King would act promptly. Since
it was perfectly understood that England would not join
in the alliance, the Emperor felt no undue anxiety at the
prospect of war, and Burke's picture of the greatest powers
in Europe 'hastening to your rescue' was imaginary.

But King Louis took other advice and accepted the constitution on the 18th of September amid general rejoicing,
while Parisians chanted to the accompaniment of pealing
bells:

> Not' bon Roi
> A tout fait!
> Et not' bonne Reine
> Qu'elle eut de la peine!
> Enfin les v'là
> Hors d'embarras.

With the new constitution the Assembly was dissolved, and
the French Revolution was said to be over. The Princesse
de Lamballe returned to France, confident that her neck
was now safe from pike or lanterne.

But the new Assembly showed little sign of tamely adopting the work of its predecessor. Its members were, on the whole, new to the problems of government, but few of them felt diffidence on that account. The election had produced a tendency towards the Left, and it had produced also an unduly large number of deputies who were anxious to qualify by revolutionary activity for their eighteen francs of pay.

> On peut tout faire, on peut tout dire:
> Et même détruire un Empire
> Pour dix-huit francs.

The Feuillants of the Left in the old Assembly were now the constitutionalists of the Right, while in the Left appeared a new group of the strangest enthusiasts, doctrinaire Girondins with a developed taste for Roman history and unbounded confidence in their ability to re-fashion not only their own country but the rest of Europe. Even if they had been content to let the new constitution work as best it could, their task would not have been easy, for, as winter came, famine spread in Paris, and the value of assignats fell alarmingly. Threats from abroad were producing their effect, and French opinion began to show a warlike tendency. Deputies also were beginning to think kindly of war, if only as a possible escape from their troubles at home. 'Perhaps', wrote Couthon at the end of the year, 'the Revolution needs a war to ensure its consolidation.'

CHAPTER XI

1792–1793

THERE was no war-fever in England. The King opened
the session of 1792 with the 'pleasing hope' of reduced taxation, and that hope was realized: the Budget proposed the
removal of taxes on female servants, carts, houses with less
than seven windows, and candles. Revenue was increasing,
and Pitt could indulge in a restrained rhapsody of the theme
of our peace and plenty: 'Although we must not count with
certainty on the continuance of our present prosperity
during such an interval, yet unquestionably there never was
a time in the history of this country when from the situation
of Europe we might more reasonably expect fifteen years of
peace than we may at the present moment.'

But in other directions the prospect was less attractive,
and debate was dominated by the thought of the French
Revolution. On five days in April resolutions on the
Slave trade were discussed, and Fox, as always, did his best
in the cause of abolition. But the moment was inopportune
for reform. Stories were reaching England of Black Revolution in San Domingo, where half a million slaves were taking
advantage of the divisions among their French masters, and
the House was easily persuaded that interference should be
'moderate' and progress 'gradual'. In these debates Fox
spoke eight times, and Pitt made the final plea for immediate
abolition in that memorable speech in which the first rays of
dawn, as they lit up the windows of the House after a long
night of debate, were invoked to portray a new Africa, whose
natives would be 'engaged in the calm occupations of industry, in the pursuit of a just and legitimate commerce. We
may behold the beams of science and philosophy breaking in
upon their land, which, at some happy period in still later
times, may blaze with full lustre; and joining their influence
to that of pure religion may illuminate and invigorate the
most distant extremities of that immense continent. . . .

Nos . . . primus equis Oriens afflavit anhelis;
Illic sera rubens accendit lumina Vesper.'

But the cause of humanity was now suspect, and the House was not to be moved by the combined appeals of its greatest orators.

There was no sign of reconciliation between Fox and Burke, who was informing his friends that 'things remain nearly as they were; no approximation on the part of Fox to me, or of me to him, or to or from any of his people, except general civility when seldom we meet'. But Fox was meeting other members of his party at weekly dinners, where he could show his most attractive qualities, 'always pleasant in these sort of small and cosy companies . . . being very much engaged and eager in whatever he was about'. It seemed that in spite of the *Appeal from the New to the Old Whigs*, he might still hold the party together. 'I am glad', wrote Elliot after one of the dinners, 'to find, I think, an appearance of greater moderation about the French affairs, and our own constitution, etc., than there seemed to be last year. The conduct of France is not commended in *everything* as it was, by *anybody* that I have met with, and Fox spoke as ill of Paine's book yesterday as other people, which he did not do last Parliament of Paine's first book. There are certainly a certain number of people in the kingdom who are desirous of confusion; but there always are, and always must be, some such men in every country.' 'Horne Tooke', Elliot thought, 'and such persons' might preach sedition, but they would certainly make no revolution. Francis would have 'no objection to a convulsion', and Sheridan might wish to 'stir the lesser ranks of the people even by the hope of plundering their betters'. But none of them, in Elliot's view, seemed likely to produce any effect, and the Opposition need not be unduly concerned at the activities of its extremists.

Actually the character of the reform movement was changing. The Dissenters, appalled by the fate of their friends in Birmingham and by the general fury aroused against them throughout the country, were less conspicu-

ously active. But a new movement was forming to support
their cause. At the beginning of the year an association of
English workmen was formed in London by Thomas Hardy,
a working shoemaker, as the London Corresponding Society.
It was a political working man's club, and it was the pattern
for other bodies which began to appear in industrial towns.
Its only object was parliamentary reform, and such interest
as it displayed in the progress of the French Revolution and
the Rights of Man was, as its records show, incidental to
that object. But it was something new in English politics
for working men, disregarding the political parties, to band
themselves together in the cause of democracy. Burke and
Tom Paine, from their opposite extremes, were in combined
effect producing a vague impression that in some undefined
manner a demand for representative government was a
demand for a republic. In any case a new movement speaking the language of liberty and democracy could expect
no hearing in those days of suspicion. Had not the French
Revolution with all its horrors sprung from such beginnings?
'Do not', wrote Gibbon, 'suffer yourself to be lulled into a
false security; remember the proud fabric of the French
Monarchy. Not four years ago it stood founded, as it might
seem, on the rock of time, force and opinion, supported by
the triple aristocracy of the Church, the Nobility and the
Parliaments. They are crumbled into dust; they are vanished
from the earth. If this tremendous warning has no effect on
the men of property in England; if it does not open every
eye and raise every arm, you will deserve your fate.'

Men of property in England were confronted by another
association at least as alarming to them as the London
Corresponding Society. In April Grey founded a society
named the Friends of the People. Its objects were 'to restore
Freedom of Election, and a more equal representation of the
People in Parliament' and 'to secure to the People a more
frequent exercise of their Rights of Electing their Representatives'. They insisted that their object was not innovation
but only the restoration of ancient liberties; but to the ruling

class of the country they were distinguishable from Hardy's
Society only by their higher subscription, two and a half
guineas a year against Hardy's penny a week, and by the
fact that being themselves men of property and, some of
them, members of Parliament, they were more dangerous.
They had, in forming their Society, carefully excluded Fox in
order that he might not be compromised. But they none the
less forced the issue in their party, for they so terrified the
Duke of Portland and that group to whom reform was abhorrent, that Fox was compelled to throw in his lot finally
with one side or the other.

The panic and the division of the Whigs were accentuated
at the end of the month when Grey gave notice of a motion
on Parliamentary Reform. Pitt was full of forebodings.
He did not think that 'a Reform at this time can safely
be attempted', he saw 'nothing but discouragement . . .
great danger of anarchy and confusion'. As to the Association it 'affords suspicion that the motion for a Reform is
nothing more than the preliminary to the overthrow of the
whole system of government'. It was not Fox's habit to
see a friend attacked without defending him, and he made
it clear that, whatever he might think of the wisdom of the
new Association, he would by no means disclaim Grey. His
enemies made the most of his declaration. 'For my part,'
commented the King, 'I cannot see any substantial difference in their being joined in debate by Mr. Fox and his not
being a member of that Society; but if men are to be found
willing to overturn the Constitution of this Country, it is
most Providential that they so easily cast off the mask.'

A fortnight later the breach in the party was definite.
Pitt issued a Royal Proclamation against 'divers wicked
seditious writings'. It may have been aimed only at the
second part of the *Rights of Man*, in which case it was an
ill-advised advertisement of a book which had already done
its work; or it may have been aimed also at the Friends of
the People, in which case it is difficult to acquit the Prime
Minister of deliberately exaggerating his alarms in order to

increase the embarrassments of the Opposition. He knew that he had no grounds for accusing Grey of a design to 'overthrow the whole system of government', and the prevailing rumours of seditious activity were by no means convincing.[1]

He consulted the Duke of Portland before issuing the Proclamation, and the Duke consulted his friends. Fox could see no sign of sedition at home, and the party met for further discussion without him. The Duke of Bedford arrived and was told that 'Mr. Fox is not likely to come', to which, in the tradition of his family, he replied, 'Then I am sure I have nothing to do here', and left them. But there remained with the Duke of Portland a large group of Whigs and Northites, and ministers congratulated themselves that their proclamation was backed by the 'most respectable members of the Opposition'.

It was not the right moment to suggest that Fox should moderate his sympathy for the French Revolution, for revolutionary France was now in adversity. The Brissotin ministry had blundered into war with Austria, proclaimed by King Louis 'in the same tone of voice as that in which he might have proposed the most unimportant decree in the world'; the Prussians were advancing on Paris; the French armies were in panic-stricken retreat, and the days of the Revolution seemed to be numbered. At such a moment Fox could do nothing which might suggest desertion. Had

[1] Lord Grenville to the Marquis of Buckingham, 14th November 1792: 'As to what you mention of overt acts, those things are all much exaggerated, when they are not wholly groundless. . . . It is not unnatural, nor is it an unfavourable symptom, that people who are thoroughly frightened, as the body of landed gentlemen in this country are, should exaggerate these stories as they pass from one mouth to the other; but you, who know the course of this sort of reports, ought not too hastily to give credit to them.' The Archbishop of Canterbury to Lord Auckland, 22nd May 1792: 'You have the proclamation, of course; the prevailing opinion at present about it is, that it seems to admit more disposition in the country to tumult than exists in fact.' Reports of the French Ambassador, in which Talleyrand may have had a hand, warn the French Government against reliance on revolutionary feeling in England.

he not written fifteen years ago when other rebels were in
defeat, 'Whatever happens, for God's sake let us all resolve
to stick by them as handsomely (or more so) in their adversity as we have done in their glory'? In the debate on the
proclamation he supported Grey in defending the Friends
of the People. But the Portland section, North, Windham,
Thomas Grenville in the Commons, and Lord Spencer, Lord
Stormont, Lord Rawden, and Lord Porchester in the Lords,
spoke against him, and the Government found a new supporter in the Prince of Wales, who had rallied to the cause
of monarchy. Feeling ran high, and the speeches were followed by a duel in which Charles Fox appeared as second
to Lord Lauderdale.

The division on the proclamation produced a political
crisis with negotiations, interviews, dinners, and conversations, of which full details survive in contemporary diaries
and letters. The position was complicated. Pitt had divided
the Opposition, and he had tested his own position with the
King by successfully insisting on the dismissal of the intolerable Thurlow. But he was anxious to strengthen his Government and avoid any possibility of the Opposition being
again united. He knew that the Portland group were opposed to any sort of reform, and his own party was pushing
him in the same direction. He decided that such reforming
fervour as remained in him must be quenched. He had
already abandoned Parliamentary Reform, and he might
on the same reasoning acquiesce in a postponement of Abolition. On these terms a coalition with the Duke might be
arranged.

The Duke of Portland had no objection to offer. But the
honour of his party must be maintained, and the coalition
must be on equal terms. Above all he was anxious that it
should be a coalition of parties, and not a coalition with a dis-
sentient group split off from the Opposition. The crux of the
question was Fox. If Fox would join them in the negotiations for office, if he could sink his loyalty to the Friends of
the People, the Portland section would be the party, and

Grey and his friends, greatly diminished by the removal of
Fox's protection, would be the outcasts.

At first Fox seemed to like the idea. It was, he said, 'so
damned right, to be sure, that I cannot help thinking it
must be'. But he soon began to see difficulties. There were
old friends, Sheridan, Fitzpatrick, Lord Robert Spencer, to
be provided for, and it was unlikely that a coalition would
leave room for them. And he had growing doubts whether
Pitt's invitation 'ever meant anything but to make a division among us'. These were obstacles to coalition, but there
was another objection which was decisive. On one point
he had made up his mind. He would go very far to avoid
a division of the party, but, if he must choose between Portland and Grey, he would choose Grey. He was no democrat
and his interest in parliamentary reform was faint. But he
believed that the cause of liberty and justice was with Grey,
and by that cause he would stand whatever it might cost
his party and himself.

The negotiations dragged on for nearly two months. Pitt
at first professed himself willing to admit Fox, although 'it
perhaps would not be quite easy to give Fox the Foreign Department *immediately*, but . . . in a few months he certainly
might have it'. He even declared that 'no objection need
be expected from the closet', in which statement he was
perhaps over-confident, for the King's comment on the
approach to the Whigs had been, 'Anything complimentary
to them, but no power'. At a later stage he had to admit
that his friends were 'very averse to an arrangement including Fox', their objections being 'principally grounded on
Fox's declarations and conduct on the proclamation', and
'upon the whole he did not feel the emergency of the times
to be so urgent as to justify him in adopting such a measure,
contrary to the *advice* and *sentiments* of his friends'. The
Duke wanted a 'clear and explicit understanding on Parliamentary Reform, the Abolition of the Slave Trade, the Repeal of the Test Act', to all of which he was opposed, and
'the system to be observed *relative to French politics*'. He

also thought that Pitt should give up the Treasury to a 'neutral man', but negotiations did not reach the stage at which that issue became decisive. There were interviews, with Fox 'silent and embarrassed', and discussions in which he showed 'peevishness and obstinacy', and Burke announced that 'Mr. Fox's coach stops the way'. He was right. Fox could not join on the only terms which would have been acceptable, and the Duke was not yet ready for a coalition without him.

The tempo of events in France quickened during that summer, while a panic-stricken Government tried to improvise an army of defence from the forces in which they themselves had subverted discipline. It was natural that resentment and suspicion should be focused on the King, and republicans were openly demanding his deposition. Other forces were unwittingly helping the republicans, for on the 26th of July the Duke of Brunswick issued his manifesto promising, in the language of royalist refugees, slaughter and destruction to any who might threaten the King. Monarchy had indeed united against Revolution, but it was hardly the sacred crusade of Burke's dreams. 'The re-establishment of order', wrote the Austrian minister, 'is no longer to be considered the most important object of our military operations. The continuance of disorder and of civil war must even be regarded as favourable to our cause, and the return of peace, consequent on the arrangement of a French Constitution of some kind, will be a benefit which France will have to purchase by the sacrifice of the province we shall have conquered.' Pitt and Grenville, who well knew the real nature of this monarchical adventure, had no difficulty in deciding on complete neutrality.

Charles Fox's letters to his nephew reflected his feelings on the events which followed. On the 10th of August the French Monarchy ended with the invasion of the Tuileries and the massacre of the Swiss. The spectacle of Parisian democracy overwhelming the soldiers who had been left to die was not easily endured by a professional soldier; and

Captain Buonaparte, who was looking on, muttered 'Che coglione!' as Marseillais and sans-culottes swarmed over the terrace. 'I do not think', wrote Charles Fox, 'near so ill of the business of the 10th of August as I did upon first hearing it. If the King and his ministers were really determined not to act in concert with the Assembly, and still more if they secretly favoured the Invasion of the Barbarians; it was necessary at any rate to begin by getting rid of him and them. . . . However, it is impossible not to look with disgust at the bloody means which have been taken, even supposing the end to be good, and I cannot help feeling that we are not yet near the end of these trials and executions. . . . And yet, with all their faults and all their nonsense, I do interest myself for their success to the greatest degree. It is a great crisis for the real cause of liberty, whatever we may think of the particular people who are to fight the present battle. I wish they were like our old friends the Americans, and I should scarcely be afraid for them.' It was less easy to take a hopeful view when the invasion of France began, and panic expressed itself in the massacre of the prisons with every circumstance of obscene savagery. 'I had just made up my mind to the events of the 10th of August,' he wrote, 'when the horrid accounts of the 2nd of this month arrived, and I really consider the horrors of that day and night as the most heart-breaking event that ever happened to those who, like me, are fundamentally and unalterably attached to the true cause. There is not, in my opinion, a shadow of excuse for this horrid massacre, nor even the possibility of extenuating it in the smallest degree.' But buoyant enthusiasm returned a few weeks later, when the invaders were stopped at Valmy by the new army of France led by officers whose names were as yet unknown outside the rank and file who had elected them. An unusually wet summer, which spread dysentery through the Prussian army, helped the defence, but the victory may be attributed chiefly to that power of recovery which in war and in politics has so often distinguished the

R

French from other nations. Fox's delight was unbounded:
'As you wished, as you say, ardently against the invaders,
you must be almost as much (for *quite* is impossible) re-
joiced at their flight as I am. No! no public event, not excepting Saratoga and York Town, ever happened that gave
me so much delight. The defeats of great armies of invaders always gave me the greatest satisfaction in reading
history from Xerxes' time downwards; and what has happened in America and in France will, I hope, make what
Cicero says of *armed force*, be the opinion of all mankind,
invidiosum, detestabile, imbecillum, caducum.'

Autumn brought increased political activity in England.
The heavy rains, which had helped in the discomforture
of Brunswick and spoiled Charles Fox's partridge shooting,
had greatly damaged the harvest. Prices were rising, and
discontent was naturally growing; and, as discontent increased and the Duke of Brunswick retreated, the Reformers' Clubs tended increasingly to declare their sympathy
with France and the Revolution. There was, in fact, no
appreciable movement towards revolution in the country. The dominant sentiment, energetically promoted by
Mr. Reeves and the new Associations to assert patriotism, was
one of aggressive loyalty, and in most parts of the country
reformers, who professed radical opinions, did so at considerable personal risk. But it was disquieting to gentlemen of
property, with horrible stories of September massacres in
their ears, to hear of clubs in which enthusiastic members
not only sent congratulations to the Jacobins and the Convention, but among themselves substituted 'Citizen' for
'Mister', put on caps of Liberty, and even planted trees of
liberty. Ladies were active in spreading the alarm. 'To
give you an idea how serious the evil is,' wrote Lady Malmesbury, 'I will say that even Lord Malmesbury foresees the
storm, and you may guess how men's minds are when I add
that Louisa read to-day, written upon the Privy Garden-
wall, "No coach tax; d——n Pitt! d——n the Duke of
Richmond! *no King!*" ... As for Fox and Grey, I wish they

would utter treason at once and be beheaded and hanged.'
Grenville defined the position less emotionally: 'The real
fact is that these people were completely quelled, and their
spirit destroyed, till the Duke of Brunswick's retreat. Since
then they have begun to show themselves again, and nothing
that I know of has been neglected that could tend to put the
law in force against them.'

But ministers had anxieties more urgent than the proceedings of the radical clubs. The armies of France were
not content with repelling Brunswick's invasion. On the
6th of November Dumouriez defeated the Austrians at
Jemappes and on the 15th he entered Brussels. 'I bless
God', wrote Grenville to his brother, 'that we had the wit
to keep ourselves out of the glorious enterprise of the combined armies, and that we were not tempted by the hope
of sharing the spoils in the division of France, nor by the
prospect of crushing all democratical principles all over the
world at one blow. But having sturdily resisted all solicita-
tion to join in these plans, we have been punished for our
obstinacy by having been kept in profound ignorance of the
details by which they were to be executed, and even of the
course of events, as far as that could be done, which occurred
during the progress of the enterprise. Now that it has failed
we may expect these deep politicians to return to the charge,
and to beg us to help them out of the pit into which they
wanted to help us. . . . The Austrians and Prussians thought
they were marching to certain victory. The emigrants, who
had given them this idea, confirmed them in it till the facts
undeceived them. The Duke of Brunswick, who joins to
great personal valour great indecision of mind, and great
soreness for his reputation, hesitated to take the only means
that could have insured success—a sudden and hazarded
attack. The more he delayed the more difficult his position
grew. He then attempted to buy a man who, under other
circumstances, would have been very purchasable; failed
in this; lost time; excited distrust and jealousy among his
allies, dispirited his own troops; and ended his enterprise

by a disgraceful retreat, which coffee-house politicians are, as usual, willing to attribute to all sorts of courses except the natural and obvious one. The subsequent successes of the French are natural.'

It was less easy for Lord Grenville to maintain his complacent detachment as the French army advanced, and the tone of France changed from a desperate appeal for the defence of the fatherland to a call for a crusade of democracy with ominous insistence on Victory and Glory.

> Tant que sur la Terre
> Vit un oppresseur
> Qui peut de la guerre
> Plaindre la rigueur ?
> Il faut à la gloire
> Savoir immoler
> Ce que la victoire
> Viendra réparer.

The taking of Brussels was followed by a declaration that exclusive navigation of the Scheldt and Meuse was 'contrary to the laws of nature', and on the 19th of November, the Convention proclaimed its purpose to 'grant fraternity and assistance to all people who wish to recover their liberty'. Reports from Holland suggested that the French were intriguing to produce a revolution there; French agents were known to be active in England, and it was unfortunate that at this moment a deputation of English radicals was received at a sitting of the Convention. The declaration of fraternity and assistance might be nothing more than one of those revolutionary gestures, which have become familiar to statesmen of our own time; but the opening of the Scheldt, whatever the laws of Nature might provide, involved the treaty obligations of Great Britain.

It was a matter for skilled diplomacy, but King Louis was being tried in Paris, and while that trial proceeded it would not have been easy to find a basis of agreement. In any case French diplomacy in London was far from skilled. The French representatives included the most adroit statesman

in Europe, but Talleyrand's status in the mission was uncertain, and Chauvelin, the official chief of it, had all the
faults of incompetence and conceit. Fox and his friends
worked hard for peace, imploring the French to come down
to earth and face realities. But revolutionary governments
are seldom well informed, and the Convention listened more
readily to delegates from radical clubs than to the less
flattering suggestions of Whig leaders. Pitt and Grenville
were as anxious as Fox to avoid war, but the Scheldt was
not a minor issue, and Chauvelin was trying to secure
recognition of the republic and insist on British neutrality
in Holland. Perhaps a way out of the difficulty might have
been found by a statesman of more revolutionary sym-
pathies, but the responsibility for the failure lay beyond
question with the French.

The danger of war may have distracted Pitt's attention
from the study of affairs at home, for he was undoubtedly
misinformed as to the extent and significance of the revolutionary movement, and needlessly alarmed at its progress.
His alarm bore fruit on the 1st of December in a proclamation calling up part of the militia on the ground of 'acts
of riot and insurrection'. Fox was convinced that the proclamation was an infamous device to complete the ruin of
the Whig party by the discovery of an imaginary plot, and
his note to the Duke of Portland, on hearing the news, was
explosive: 'I send you enclosed a note I have just received
from Adam. If they mention danger of insurrection, or
rather (as they must do to legalise their proceedings) of
rebellion, surely the first measure all honest men ought to
take is to impeach them for so wicked and detestable a
falsehood. I fairly own that if they have done this I shall
grow savage, and not think a French *Lanterne* too bad for
them. Surely it is impossible if anything were impossible
for such monsters, who for the purpose of weakening or
destroying the honourable connections of the Whigs, would
not scruple to run the risque of a Civil War. I cannot trust
myself to write any more for I confess I am too affected.'

He had much cause to grow savage, for he saw clearly enough that the new proclamation would be even more disastrous to his party than the proclamation against sedition in May, and he was entirely convinced that neither proclamation was justified by the state of the country. In this view he was probably right. The aims and methods of the radical reformers have recently been examined in some detail by historians,[1] and the evidence entirely supports Fox's view that the associations and clubs represented a genuine demand for reform and were not either in purpose or method a revolutionary movement. In such matters Fox might well be a better judge than Pitt, for his political apprenticeship had been served to an accompaniment of riots and window-breaking, and no one was better qualified to appraise the significance of popular unrest; but Pitt, who came into public life at a later and more restrained period, had no such experience. The motives of Pitt in this, as in other matters, remain obscure; but there is no reason to doubt that the constant rumours of revolutionary activity—deputations to the Convention, vast sales of the *Rights of Man*, Bastille dinners, and a mysterious order for 3,000 daggers in Sheffield—had profoundly impressed him, and his alarms were genuine. After a long Cabinet meeting in December he suddenly asked the Secretary of the Foreign Office what he thought of the position at home, and himself supplied the gloomy answer, 'Probably by this time to-morrow we may not have a hand to act, or a tongue to utter'.

Parliament, summoned on the same grounds, met on the 13th of December, and Fox's apprehensions of the effect of the proclamation on his party were fully realized. His speech on the calling up of the Militia is among his most eloquent. It is well reported, and three passages from it are typical of him at his best:

[1] See G. S. Veitch, *Genesis of Parliamentary Reform*; H. W. Meikle, *Scotland and the French Revolution*; P. A. Brown, *The French Revolution in English History*; G. M. Trevelyan, *Lord Grey of the Reform Bill*.

A RIGHT HONOURABLE *alias* A SANS CULOTTE

From a cartoon in the author's possession

'The next assertion is, that there exists at this moment an insurrection in this kingdom. An insurrection! Where is it? Where has it reared its head? Good God! an insurrection in Great Britain! No wonder that the militia were called out, and parliament assembled in the extraordinary way in which they had been. But where is it? Two gentlemen have delivered sentiments in commendation and illustration of the speech; and yet, though this insurrection has existed for fourteen days, they have given us no light whatever, no clue, no information where to find it. . . . I will take upon me to say, sir, that it is not the notoriety of the insurrections which prevents these gentlemen from communicating to us the particulars, but their non-existence.

'I am not so ignorant of the present state of men's minds, and of the ferment artfully created, as not to know that I am now advancing an opinion likely to be unpopular. It is not the first time that I have incurred the same hazard. . . . I will act against the cry of the moment, in the confidence that the good sense and reflection of the people will bear me out. I know that there are societies which have published opinions, circulated pamphlets, containing doctrines tending, if you please, to subvert our establishments. I say that they have done nothing unlawful in this; for these pamphlets have not been suppressed by law. Show me the law that orders these books to be burned, and I will acknowledge the illegality of their proceedings: but if there be no such law, you violate the law in acting without authority. You have taken upon you to do that for which you have no warrant; you have voted them to be guilty. What is the course prescribed by law? If any doctrines are published tending to subvert the constitution in church and state, you may take cognizance of the fact in a court of law. What have you done? Taken upon you by your own authority to suppress them—to erect every man, not merely into an inquisitor, but into a judge, a spy, an informer—to set father against father, brother against brother, and neighbour against neighbour, and in this way you expect to maintain the peace and tranquillity of this country! / You have gone upon the principles of slavery in all your proceedings; you neglect in your conduct the foundation of all legitimate government, the rights of the people; and, setting up this bugbear, you spread a panic for the very purpose of sanctifying this infringement, while again, the very infringement engenders the evil which you dread. One extreme naturally leads to another. Those who dread republicanism fly for shelter to the Crown. Those who desire reform, and are calumniated, are driven by despair to republicanism. And this is the evil that I dread. / . .

'But, it may be asked, what would I propose to do in times of agitation like the present ? I will answer openly. If there is a tendency in the dissenters to discontent, because they conceived themselves to be unjustly suspected and cruelly calumniated, what would I do ? I would instantly repeal the test and corporation acts, and take from them by such a step all cause of complaint. If there were any persons tinctured with a republican spirit, because they thought that representative government was more perfect in a republic, I would endeavour to amend the representation of the Commons, and to show that the House of Commons, though not chosen by all, should have no other interest than to prove itself the representative of all. If there were men dissatisfied in Scotland or Ireland, or elsewhere, on account of disabilities and exemptions, of unjust prejudices, and of cruel restrictions, I would repeal the penal statutes, which are a disgrace to our law books. If there were other complaints of grievances, I would redress them where they were really proved; but above all, I would constantly, cheerfully, patiently listen.'

But the minds of the Portland section were no longer open to argument,[1] and only fifty members voted with Fox.

---

[1] Contemporary letters show that supporters of the Government were as sceptical as Fox as to the existence of 'insurrection'. Sir Gilbert Elliot to Lady Elliot, December 13th: 'As no insurrection has

The next move lay with the Duke of Portland, who was being hotly pressed by the more energetic members of his group to make a public announcement transferring his support from Fox to Pitt. But the Duke was very reluctant to take the final step. It was bitter to him to destroy the 'honourable connexions of the Whigs', and it was even harder to break from the personal sway of Fox. Again and again Elliot and Malmesbury lectured him on his duty and urged him 'as friends sincerely and affectionately loving him, and attentive to his honour and reputation, to come to a fair and short explanation with Fox, and separate from him *amicably* but decidedly'. He would hear them without answering, 'admitting, however, all you say and sobbing grievously'. He would sit 'benumbed and paralysed' while his ordeal proceeded with 'intervals of ten and fifteen minutes silence', and when at last they got him to the point of a declaration in the House of Lords, his 'predilection and tenderness to Fox' would undo their work at the last moment. He clung desperately to the hope that Fox might still join them, although Fox had declared 'that there was no address at this moment Pitt could frame, he would not propose an amendment to, and divide the House upon'. But the Duke's followers were less patient, for events in

taken place in England, which seems, I think, rather more quiet than usual, they lay it all in the *insurrections* which have taken place in Scotland, and, I believe, Ireland. The Scotch insurrections consist of planting the Tree of Liberty at Perth, and the Dundee mob, and some others of less note. This is certainly ridiculous to those who live in Scotland and know the truth. . . . Yet, with all these objections, I think it the peculiar duty of the present hour to support the Government in measures right in themselves, though irregular in their form.' The Archbishop of Canterbury to Lord Auckland, 3rd February 1793: 'You will have observed, since my last, indications in abundance, firm and decisive, of the increased loyalty and zeal of this country in support of the King and constitution. It pervades the country to such a degree, that whatever there is of a different sort in the kingdom is silent and concealed, and I am persuaded it is of very small extent comparatively speaking. . . . This spirit is not confined to London, nor to great towns only. It is the spirit of the country at large.'

France were moving quickly, and war seemed certain. At last Loughborough accepted the Great Seal, and in the course of January 1793, although the Duke still made no public declaration, his group became supporters of the Government.

The weeks of suspense on the brink of war ended at the same time. Chauvelin had attempted to explain away the decree of fraternity and assistance, but he could find no answer to Grenville's insistence on the treaty obligations and the integrity of the Netherlands. On the 1st of January King Louis was found guilty, and six days later the great green coach carried him for the last time through silent streets to the square where Santerre's drums and Sansom's knife awaited him. London was profoundly moved when the news arrived, and protests were heard against the opening of theatres. It was too late for diplomacy, and Chauvelin was ordered to leave within eight days. On the 1st of February the Convention declared war against Britain and Holland.

CHAPTER XII

1793–1797

I<small>F</small> Charles Fox had been nothing but a party man, or if his chief motive had been, as Burke was fond of suggesting, nothing but ambition, the outbreak of war would have given him a good chance of extricating the party and himself from their difficulties. Alleging the need for national unity in time of national crisis, he could have called upon his followers, with no abandonment of principles, to proclaim a truce, and it is probable that, leaving Burke apart, he might have patched up some sort of agreement. But he was the last man to abandon any detail of his political principles because the country was at war. He profoundly hated war, and above all he hated a war of coercion, an aggressive war designed to force upon an independent people the will of an invader. In advance of his age, he was a convinced nationalist, and he could admit no sort of right in any country to interfere in the internal affairs of another. This view, which became the unquestioned doctrine of the nineteenth century, was by no means accepted in the days of Fox, when the ruling principle of European relations was dynastic, and countries were partitioned and exchanged as ruling monarchs might decide. Even if Burke's Crusade of Kings had been in fact a crusade to restore religion and monarchy in France, and not a raid to annex provinces and extort compensation, Fox would have denounced it as an intolerable interference in the rights of a free nation.

The immediate cause of war filled him with suspicion. No doubt we were bound to protect Holland, but had Holland called on us for protection? And why had our anxiety to protect a threatened country displayed itself when Holland was attacked by France, but not when Poland was attacked by Russia and Prussia? And why had we not answered the declaration of Pilnitz by an announcement that no interference in the internal affairs of France would

be permitted ? It was known that ministers were personally
hostile to the Revolution. Was not this war simply a pretext
to join in the murder of Liberty ? In these suspicions he
was probably wrong. Pitt was beyond doubt anxious for
peace, but the independence of the Netherlands has at all
times been a vital question to this country, and it was not
the first nor the last occasion on which Great Britain would
go unwillingly to war to maintain it. What might have
happened if Pitt had so far departed from neutrality as to
intervene after Pilnitz is conjectural, but it was in fact
hardly conceivable that Pitt could have persuaded his party
and the country to support such an intervention. The feeling of the ruling class was in the opposite direction. But
Fox was certainly right in his view that, whatever might be
the occasion for the war, this country would in fact be fighting in alliance with the forces of oppression, the kings who
had divided Poland and were planning to despoil France ;
and a victory, whatever might be the purpose of this
country, would be a victory for despotism.

Operations began, a little unexpectedly, on the 25th of
February when three battalions of Guards marched from
London to Greenwich for active service under the Duke of
York. Dumouriez was invading Holland, and an expeditionary force was to go to the rescue. It was a stirring
moment when the King 'on a fierce white charger' with the
Prince of Wales, 'very handsome and theatrical' in his new
Light Horse uniform, followed by the Royal Dukes, came
to see the Guards march off. The column was received on
its route with such sympathetic enthusiasm that only the
leading files remained steady, and a procession of carts
laden with the casualties of intoxication brought up the
rear. They landed in Holland with neither transport nor
reserve of ammunition.

The British Army was not readier for war than this unpromising beginning might suggest, but the state of the
French Army was worse. They were in no condition for
attack or for defence, and their commander was secretly

negotiating the terms of his desertion to the Allies. They were defeated by Coburg at Neerwinden, and by the beginning of April they had been driven out of Belgium. The immediate purpose of Great Britain, the freeing of the Netherlands, had been achieved.

A determined advance by the Allies would probably have restored the monarchy in Paris, but the Governments associated in what has been strangely named the First Coalition were far from displaying that unity of purpose which should inspire an attack. The Emperor Francis was interested in a plan to annex Bavaria, and give Belgium, enlarged at the expense of France, to the Elector of Bavaria in exchange. The Empress Catherine and the King of Prussia were meditating another division of Poland. But on one point our Allies were in accord. If their armies were to march against France, England must find the money.

The plans of the British Government were of the vaguest. Should we concentrate for invasion on the French front? Or make sudden attacks on the coast of France, where a counter-revolution might be encouraged? Or turn our attention to the French islands in the West Indies? Ultimately —it was partly through force of circumstances—all three plans were adopted to the ruin of each one of them. The island of Tobago was taken. The Duke of York was reinforced by troops whose military value seemed questionable, and it was decided that he should attack Dunkirk. 'The early capture of Dunkirk by a Prince of the Blood', wrote Dundas, 'would give much éclat to the commencement of the war.' In Paris the new Committee of Public Safety was struggling desperately to organize the defence of France by methods which included the guillotining of generals whose performance did not come up to expectation. The Girondins were falling, and Robespierre was waiting to proclaim his doctrine that the 'springs of popular government' in time of revolution 'are both *in virtue and in terror*'. 'People here', wrote Fox to his nephew in June, 'begin to be heartily tired of the war, in some degree owing to the disgust pretty generally felt at the scandalous conduct of the Empress and Prussia in respect to Poland; but chiefly to the extreme distress which is felt at home. I do not know whether there is not some comfort in seeing that, while the French are doing all in their power to make the name of liberty odious to the world, the despots are conducting themselves so as to show that tyranny is worse. I believe the love of political liberty is *not* an error; but, if it be one, I am sure I shall never be converted from it— and I hope you never will.'

But he had his consolations in those gloomy days. A committee of his friends, 'respectable', as their secretary described them, 'as fortune, rank, and character could make it', decided to raise a subscription to relieve him from debt and provide a sufficient income for the future. It was a good moment for such an enterprise for some of them, who were regretfully leaving the party, were glad to make a personal offering to their forsaken leader. In other cases it was rumoured that zealous promoters of the scheme were perhaps unduly insistent in their applications. Of these things Fox of course knew nothing. He heard first of the scheme when the decision of the respectable committee was formally communicated to him by Adair, and he accepted the gift considering it 'as an additional obligation upon me, if any were wanting, to continue steady in the principles which I have uniformly professed'. The names of the subscribers and their contributions are unknown, but the amount of the fund, which was sufficient for its purpose, must have been enormous. 'You will hear from others', he wrote to Lord Holland, 'of what has been done, and is doing for me. I may, perhaps, flatter myself; but I think it is the most honourable thing that has ever happened to any man. The sum which has been raised is such as will pay all my debts that are in any degree burthensome, and give me an income upon which I can live comfortably without contracting any more.' His play had for some time been infrequent, and he now finally abandoned it for the blameless hazards of gardening.

The outbreak of war had brought the Portland group into closer touch with Pitt. In March the Prime Minister was 'all civility, and desired that we would never make the smallest scruple of applying for any information we wished, or suggesting anything we thought useful, promising to attend to it with great care'. The Duke was still wavering, and Sir Gilbert complained that he had 'behaved as usual about the Whig Club business' when he had apparently made no protest, although 'in their speeches and toasts we are treated as deserters from friends and principles'. But the rank and file of the group were less diffident than their leader, and a few weeks later they could contemplate the attractive prospect of office.

In June Fox moved the first of his peace resolutions. He supported the war 'for the object of defence and security, and for those objects only', tried to commit the House to a declaration that 'any plan of aggrandizement, founded on the present distressed situation of France, much less any purpose of establishing among the French people any particular form of government, never would have their concurrence or support', and called upon the Government, now that the French were behind their frontiers, to negotiate for peace. The Opposition vote was 47. Probably Pitt was right in his answer that, with France preparing for war, the moment for negotiations was not yet; but Pitt could not in any case accept the declaration against aggrandizement. Ministers were already discussing pleasant schemes of 'indemnisation' to the horror of royalist émigrés, and speculating 'on the slices which may be required from France'. 'Our line seems perfectly plain', wrote the King to Grenville. 'The war being once begun, the expense already entertained, France must be greatly circumscribed before we can talk of any means of treating with that dangerous and faithless nation.'

There was nothing more to be done that summer in the cause of peace. Mainz and Valenciennes fell to the Allies; black revolution flamed up in Haiti; Toulon opened its port to Lord Hood 'in trust only for Louis XVII'. In Paris the Committee of Public Safety had discovered a young officer of engineers with a gift for military administration. His name was Carnot, and he began his career by sending the Duke of York in full retreat from the siege of Dunkirk. It had been an expensive siege, although the resources of the expeditionary force included a plan of attack drafted by the Lord Chancellor himself, and it ended with the loss of all the siege guns. Charles Fox, dividing his time between St. Ann's Hill, visits in Hampshire, and partridges at Thetford, was filled with gloom. 'Everything in the world', he wrote in August, 'seems to be taking a wrong turn; and, strange as it sounds, I think the success of the wretches who now govern Paris is like to be the least evil of any that can happen.'

He had good cause for distress without looking abroad, for the Government, undecided on military problems, was entirely decided upon one question. There was to be no concession to the reformers, and any protests or representations which could be construed as seditious would be treated with the fullest severity. When Grey moved a resolution for Parliamentary Reform in May, he secured only 41 votes, and Pitt wrought upon the already quivering nerves of his followers with a dark reference to a 'small, but not contemptible party, who aspired at something more than a moderate reform, whose object indeed was nothing less than to introduce here those French principles which from their consequences, I could not regard but with horror'. It was useless for Fox to point out that the small but not contemptible party asked only for those reforms which a few years before Pitt himself had pressed upon the House. Members had now come to regard a reformer as hardly distinguishable from the levellers, jacobins, regicides, and sansculottes who were banded to overthrow civilization, and serious discussion on the subject was no longer possible.

The repression of sedition began with prosecutions of obscure enthusiasts, who were heavily sentenced for un-

guarded remarks in sermons or ale-house conversations.
Everywhere the magistrates were on the alert and Government informers were busy. In Scotland the hunt was ruth-
less, and the trials of Muir and Palmer before Lord Braxfield,
the 'Scottish Jeffreys', showed to what lengths frightened
authority could go. Gems from Lord Braxfield's dicta from
the Bench are celebrated among the curiosities of legal
literature. The most famous of them is his declaration that
'a government in every country should be just like a corporation; and in this country it is made up of the landed
interest, which alone has a right to be represented; as for
the rabble, who have nothing but personal property, what
hold has the nation of them?' Muir was sentenced to
transportation for fourteen years, and Palmer, a few weeks
later, for five years. The trials were manifestly unfair and
the sentences obviously unjust, but the Prime Minister,
who as a lawyer well knew that justice had been denied,
refused to interfere. 'Prosecutions intolerable', commented
Fox, 'both here and in Scotland are going on every day,
and nobody seems to mind them. The very name of Liberty
is scarce popular.'

The autumn brought no comfort. In October Jourdan
defeated the Prussians at Wattignies, and England, accustomed now to news of horror from France, heard with new
horror of the trial and execution of the Queen of France,
'attended', as Fox wrote, 'with every circumstance that
could contribute to make the act more disgusting and detestable than any other murder recorded in history'. He
saw no hope of peace. 'Everything happens', he went on,
'to disgust everybody with the war, but whether some persons whom I most wish to be convinced are so, I much
doubt; that the public in general wishes for peace I have
no doubt. . . .'

Parliament had made it abundantly clear that electoral
reform would not be considered. But the reformers of the
new democratic school were not deterred. Unaccustomed to
public life, they believed that by constantly demonstrating

s

the justice of their cause they would ultimately convince a House of Commons which would not listen to Fox or Grey. For this purpose they determined to hold in November a Convention in Edinburgh. The name Convention was not wisely chosen in a world shuddering at a Queen's trial before a Convention in Paris; nor was any place within the jurisdiction of Lord Braxfield a prudent choice for such a gathering. Early in December Robert Dundas found their proceedings 'so strong that we agreed to take notice of them', and the Lord Provost dispersed the Convention and arrested seven of the delegates. 'Behold the funeral torches of Liberty,' said Gerrald, an English delegate, as they saw the lights of the Government officers approach their meeting place, and his subsequent encounter with Lord Braxfield gave him no reason to modify his view.

In France the Terror was developing. Madame Roland with pensive aphorisms followed the Queen to the scaffold, and her Girondin friends, who had so hopefully set forth to build their Republic of Virtue, were hunted to death throughout France. Toulon was lost to the Allies, and the expedition to La Vendée was too late.

For Charles Fox the year ended in the gloom of despair, and a letter to his nephew expresses his hopeless feelings: 'In short there is such a barefaced contempt of principle and justice in every step we take, that it is quite disgusting to think that it can be endured. *France is worse* is the only answer, and perhaps that is true in fact, for the horrors there grow every day worse. The transactions at Lyons seem to surpass all their former wickedness. Do you remember Cowper?

'"Oh for a lodge in some vast wilderness!" &c.

'It is a much more natural wish now, than when it was uttered. If I had written yesterday, I should have said poor O'Hara! To-day I am glad that he is a prisoner, as it has exempted him from being concerned in the evacuation of Toulon. We do not know to what number, but it is certain that thousands of poor wretches who had been deluded by our promises are now left by us to the guillotine. It must be a strong case of necessity which can justify such a proceeding, and at any rate it is fortunate for a man not to be concerned in it. That therefore which was thought a misfortune, I now esteem a great happiness for O'Hara.... At home we imitate the French as well as we can, and in the trials and sentences of Muir and Palmer in particular, I do not think we fall very far short of our original, excepting inasmuch as transportation to Botany Bay is less severe (and to a gentleman that is not much) than death, I do not think any of the French *soi-disant* judicial proceedings surpass in injustice and contempt of law those in Scotland; and yet I hear from good authority what, till I heard it from authority, I resolutely disbelieved, that not only those proceedings are to be defended in Parliament, but that the sentences are to be executed, and that *sedition*, the most vague and loose in its description of all misdemeanours, is to be considered as punishable, and actually to be punished in Scotland, as a felony. It is evident that those who execute the supposed law in Scotland must *wish* it were law here too, and such are the times that what they wish they may easily obtain if they have the courage to ask it. You will easily believe I shall not acquiese in this tyranny without an effort, but I am far from sanguine as to success. We live in times of violence and of extremes, and all those who are for creating or even for retaining checks upon power are considered as enemies to order. However, one must do one's duty, and one must endeavour to do it without passion, but everything in Europe appears to my ideas so monstrous that it is difficult to think of things calmly even alone, much more to discuss them so, when heated by dispute.'

The new year brought no relief. An amendment to the address asking for peace negotiations was defeated by the plain statement that no peace could be made with the existing government of France. In London the Government called a conference to discuss policy, for ministers, who are often readier to detect military genius in foreign commanders than among their own, were greatly impressed by the proposals of a newly promoted Austrian, General Mack, whose name was not yet disastrously joined to that of Ulm. The discussion turned upon man power, and, in the case of Prussia, man power depended on British subsidies. 'The question', wrote Malmesbury impatiently, 'reduces itself to a very narrow compass. Can we do without the King of Prussia or can we not? If we can, he is not worth the giving of a guinea for; if we cannot, I am afraid we cannot give too many.' After much bargaining, it was agreed that the armies of the Coalition were to be raised to 340,000 men, but only the more credulous statesmen could believe that such a force would really take the field.

Ministers were much more successful in their repression of the reformers at home. Three of the delegates arrested at the Edinburgh Convention were sentenced to transportation for fourteen years, and Lord Braxfield propounded the remarkable doctrine that sedition can be committed unintentionally. It was 'to all intents and purposes' sedition to arouse dissatisfaction, which 'will very naturally end in overt rebellion'. But when the conduct of Braxfield was questioned in a debate on the cases of Muir and Palmer, the Prime Minister had no doubt 'of the propriety of the manner in which the Lords of Justiciary had exercised their discretion upon the occasion'. Fox could only review Braxfield's dicta with the comment, 'God help the people who have such judges!' The repression in Edinburgh was, indeed, a little embarrassing in its success. 'Entre nous', wrote Robert Dundas after the trials, 'I would prefer a commission . . . in place of that violent and intemperate great man'. But the warning of Scotland was plain, and Thomas Hardy showed uncommon courage in proposing to his Society that a new Convention should be called in England to press once more for electoral reform. He well knew that he was risking his liberty and perhaps his life, but he could see no other way of serving the cause of reform. Ministers now gave way to something like a panic. Hardy and the leaders of the London Corresponding Society were arrested in May, and were, if we may accept their stories, melodramatically questioned by the Privy Council. A secret Committee was appointed to examine the books and papers of the Society, and the Habeas Corpus Act was suspended in a single sitting. 'I think', wrote Fox, 'of all the measures of Government this last nonsense about conspiracy is the most mischievous and the most foolish. . . . If they succeed in committing and hanging any of these fellows whom they have taken up, it will be considered as a corroboration of the conspiracy, and a pretence for more extraordinary powers; if they fail, as I rather think they will, then, the consequence that always belongs to men who have been falsely accused and acquitted will attach to Horne Tooke, Thelwall, and others like them, and possibly that danger that was only imaginary may in time become real by these wise manœuvres, which unaccountably to me, my old friends think calculated to dispel it.'

Progress abroad was not encouraging. Fox was right in his forecast that the Prussian subsidy was money thrown away. A few weeks after it had been paid the Prussian army began to move against a new insurrection in Poland. The Treaty was broken, and in May the Austrians began to with-draw. 'Thugut', wrote our representative in Vienna, 'said of the King of Prussia to-day, with some truth and some humour, that all he wanted was to save the whole of his army to conquer Poland without the loss of a man, and, in reward, to receive from us a pension of a million and a half per annum.'

At the end of May, Fox made another hopeless effort in the cause of peace. The real purpose of his fourteen resolutions was to compel Pitt to declare whether or not the object of the war was to interfere with the internal government of France. It was exactly the point on which any precise answer would have infuriated some section of Pitt's allies and supporters, and the Prime Minister was forced to take refuge in an impenetrable labyrinth of 'ifs' and 'provideds'.

His answer might have been less obscure if he had spoken a few days later, when the news had arrived that the Glorious First of June had saved the country from any immediate danger of invasion. Following a long series of blunders and defeats, the victory, which had the additional attraction of a win against numerical odds, was celebrated with boundless enthusiasm.

> Of French ships there were twenty-six
> When first upon them we did fix.
> We valued not their Gallic tricks,
>   We had but twenty-five sail;
> But being British sailors bold,
> Who value honour more than gold,
> Our courage has been tried of old,
>   We ever will prevail.

In London the celebrations included a massed attack on the house of Hardy, the shoemaker, in Piccadilly. The house was undefended, for Hardy was in prison awaiting trial as a leader of the London Corresponding Society. Only his wife was at home; she was expecting a child, and the shock killed her.

But popular enthusiasm was only temporary, and Fox was probably right in his estimate written from St. Ann's Hill at the end of the month: 'I believe the country is heartily tired of the war, but men dare not show themselves. . . . It is a great comfort to me to reflect how steadily I have opposed this war, for the miseries it seems likely to produce are without end. . . . However in these bad times, here am I with Liz., enjoying the fine weather, the beauty and (not its least beauty) the idleness of this place, as much as if those horrors were not going on. When one has done all one can, as I think I have, to prevent mischief, one has a right I think to forget its existence if one is happily situated, so as not to be within its reach; and indeed I could not name any time of my life when I was happier than I am now, but I do not believe I should be so, if I had acted otherwise than I have done.' He was indeed 'happily situated' at St. Ann's Hill,

where he could for a moment forget, in the song of the
nightingales and the peace of his books, the cumulative
horrors of the Terror, the misery of the war, the collapse
of his party, his own ruined career and his lost popularity.
For the Man of the People was now the object of a hue and
cry by the Patriotic Associations and cartoonists. He had
now constantly to see himself depicted as a traitor, a sans-
culotte (literally construed), a would-be regicide. For the
opinions of his critics he maintained his customary indifference, but he had always lived on friendly terms with his
neighbours, and the general animosity of the attack was
distressing to him.

Events in Europe moved with bewildering speed. Carnot's organization of victory was now taking shape, and the
armies of France no longer stood on the defensive. The
Duke of York himself was hunted by French dragoons after
Turcoing, and, although reinforcements including a young
Colonel Wesley arrived at Ostend, the Duke was in July
driven out of Belgium, the brigade of Henry Fox, now a
Major-General, marching in the retreat. In Paris the Feast
of the Supreme Being followed that of Reason with no
apparent effect upon public conscience or behaviour. The
Girondins were gone, and Danton had followed them to the
guillotine with his muttered 'Danton, no weakness', as he
faced his last audience. For month after month the long
procession of victims, priests, peasants, soldiers, women,
drove slowly to the guillotine, until after a day of frenzy
and thunder in July, the tumbrils carried the wounded
bodies of the Tiger himself and his fellow terrorists, a last
fournée of twenty-two; and the Terror was over. It had
lived on the fear of invasion and it died when the country
was safe. Would a new régime be better disposed to peace?

At home the administration was at last enriched by the
inclusion of the Duke of Portland, Lord Fitzwilliam, and
Lord Spencer. The final defection of Fitzwilliam was a
blow to Fox. 'I have nothing to say', he wrote to his nephew,
'for my old friends, nor indeed as politicians have they any

right to any tenderness from me, but I cannot forget how long I have lived in friendship with them, nor can I avoid feeling the most severe mortification, when I recollect the certainty I used to entertain that they would never disgrace themselves as I think they have done. I cannot forget that ever since I was a child Fitzwilliam has been, in all situations, my warmest and most affectionate friend, and the person in the world of whom decidedly I have the best opinion, and so in most respects I have still, but as a politician, I cannot reconcile his conduct with what I (who have known him for more than five-and-twenty years) have always thought to be his character.' But in a few weeks he had recovered his cheerful buoyancy, and was even writing from Holkham of the possibility of re-establishing the party. 'The master of this House, the Duke of Bedford, Guilford and Derby, and some others with myself, make undoubtedly a small basis, but then how glorious it would be from such small beginnings to grow into a real strong party, such as we once were. The times are, in some respects, favourable to such an attempt; at the commencement of the American war, though we had a greater number of splendid names, we were not more numerous in Parliament, and we grew to what we afterwards were by events. This war must grow to be disliked by all classes of people, as much, or more than the America war, and we may profit, as a party, by such an opinion becoming prevalent.'

But that small and aristocratic group which followed Fox had more urgent matters to consider in the autumn of 1794 than their possible return to power. The trials of Hardy, Horne Tooke, and the members of the London Corresponding Society, arrested in May, began in October, and the Whig leaders were uncomfortably conscious that if justice broke down in England, as it had broken down in Scotland, they might expect no mercy.

'The first trial,' wrote Grey to Miss Ponsonby, 'which will be Hardy's, comes on on Thursday. I believe I shall attend it in order to learn how to conduct myself when it

comes to my turn. You see by these new constructions of
treason they have found a much better way of disposing of
obnoxious persons than by sending them to Botany Bay,
and one which will save both you and me a great deal of
trouble. I am not, however, very ambitious of being classed
even with Algernon Sydney.'

But the judges of England were not Braxfields, and the
prisoners were defended by Erskine, who had shown in the
trial of Walker at Manchester that in an English Court spies
could not lie with impunity. The Attorney-General opened
with a speech of nine hours, which drew from Thurlow the
comment, 'Nine hours! Then there is no treason, by God.'
The Court was crowded, Grey sitting on the Bench by the
Judge 'who I am not quite sure does not think I ought to
be in Mr. Hardy's place at the bar'. For nine days Scott
and Erskine, each a future Lord Chancellor, exchanged recriminations, while Government spies told their tales, and all
over the country crowds waited for the coaches with news
from London. The Crown lawyers did their best, but the
spies broke down before Erskine, and no evidence of acts
which any judge but Braxfield could have called treasonable, was forthcoming against Hardy. The Lord Chief
Justice was unbiased in his summing up, and, after an
absence of three hours, the jury brought in a verdict of
Not Guilty, which Hardy acknowledged with a simple 'My
fellow countrymen, I return you my thanks'. The test had
been severe, but English justice had born it. Although
London was as fervently anti-Jacobin as Mr. Reeves and
his Association could wish, the verdict was received with
an outburst of enthusiasm, almost equal to the rejoicings
for the Glorious First of June. With Hardy's acquittal
anxiety for the others was removed, and Horne Tooke
played his part in a spirit of high comedy. To the formal
question how he would be tried he gave the formal answer,
'by God and by my country'. But he gave it with intona-
tion—'I *would* be tried by God and by my country . . .'—
with a pause and a sardonic glance to the jury. He

continued in the same tone, calling Pitt as a witness to answer awkward questions about reform, and asking that a tune might be hummed to enable the jury to determine whether it was seditious. The result was never in doubt, and after two more trials the case against the remaining prisoners was dropped.

Pitt's motives in prosecuting the reformers remain conjectural. The evidence now available suggests that although a few of them may have aimed at something more than electoral reform, and may have contemplated the use of something more than argument, the reform movement as a whole was in no sense seditious. The suggestion that Pitt deliberately misrepresented it in order to destroy the Opposition need not be considered. Pitt evidently believed that revolution was threatened, and he apparently believed it, not only in the crisis of the war, when distracted ministers may be pardoned for ill-considered experiments in government, but in tranquil 1792 when he saw no prospect of war. Under the stress of war and increasing illness his original misapprehension became a dangerous obsession. But, however it may be explained, the facts leave little doubt that, in his appreciation of the purpose and mind of the reformers, Fox was almost entirely right, and Pitt was correspondingly misguided.

The end of the year brought an unexpected ally to the cause of peace. When Parliament met, Wilberforce, to the visible discomfort of the war party, moved an amendment to the Address asking for peace negotiations. His case was, on the whole, Fox's—the folly of interfering in the affairs of another nation, the desire of our allies for peace, the hopelessness of an indefinite war. Pitt retorted with the impossibility of peace without security, and the amendment secured 73 votes. For a moment it seemed that the Opposition had gained Pitt's closest friend and most trusted counsellor. Fox hastened to call on him, and assure him that he would 'soon see that he must join us altogether'. But the hope was soon quenched. Wilberforce's conscience had

compelled him to vote against the war, which was indeed
the main concern of Government policy, but it did not compel him to vote against Pitt on other matters. In any case
there could be no question of his going over, for he had
conscientious doubts of the 'moral practice' of the Opposition, and that with Wilberforce was final. But it was a
heavy blow to Pitt in the loneliness of his responsibilities,
and it is recorded by biographers as one of the infrequent
events which deprived him of his customary sleep.

The year 1795 followed its dismal course, broken only by
the pleasing news of the Prince's marriage. But it was soon
apparent that even here the prospect was clouded, for
Prinny, at the first sight of his bride, 'retired to a distant
part of the apartment', saying 'Harris, I am not well;
pray get me a glass of brandy', and the scandal of Queen
Caroline began. In Europe the Coalition was broken. Prussia made peace; Spain might follow at any moment; and
Holland, now dominated by France, declared war on England. The strain of war was now terribly apparent at home,
for food was short and prices rising. Everywhere Pitt's
failure seemed to be complete, and Lord Auckland felt sure
that if Fox's party were not 'dreaded and disliked' as
avowed Jacobins, the Government would be out. But Fox
could see no ray of hope. Peace seemed as remote as ever.
In spite of the State Trials the House clung as firmly as
ever to repression and the suspension of Habeas Corpus.
The Opposition was not gaining ground, although there was
some hope that Fitzwilliam might return to them, for Fitzwilliam had been sent to Ireland as Viceroy by Pitt, and he
had now been recalled after misunderstandings and recriminations on the immediate issue of Catholic Emancipation and on general policy, which made it most unlikely that
he would settle comfortably in his new party. Fox was
beginning to play with the idea of a withdrawal from
politics. He was inclined 'every day to think less of
public affairs'. He would like to persuade himself that secession was the right course, but he could not help feeling that it

was 'the measure a shabby fellow would take in our circumstances'. And there was the question of public duty.
'One may be of opinion that persevering is no use; but
ought a man who has engaged himself to the Public to trust
so entirely to a speculation of this sort as to go out of the
common road, and to desert (for so it would be called) the
public service? . . . I fear the general opinion would be that,
having lost all hope of place, we left the country to take
care of itself.' If only he could persuade himself on the
point of duty, he would have no hesitation. 'I am perfectly
happy in the country. I have quite resources enough to
employ my mind; and the great resource of all, literature, I
am fonder of every day; and then the Lády of the Hill is
one continual source of happiness to me.'

That continual source of happiness was now assured to
him. On the 28th of September he was secretly married
to Mrs. Armistead. The certificate, which describes her as
Elizabeth B. Cane, sheds no light on her antecedents or
history.

Bad news accumulated as the year went on. The Qui-
beron expedition to raise counter revolution in Brittany
failed horribly, and ended with a massacre of royalist
prisoners at Auray. Spain made her peace with France.
Louis XVII, or his substitute, died miserably in the Temple.
Fox was now convinced that the country was 'nearly
unanimous for peace', that peace was 'the wish of the
French, of Italy, Spain, Germany and all the world', that
it could be made by 'a negotiation of a few hours, and by
saying "done and done", like a bet at Newmarket', but
'Great Britain is alone the cause of preventing its accom-
plishment, and this not for any point of honour or even
interest, but merely lest there should be an example in the
modern world of a great and powerful Republic'. With this
rather cursory appreciation of the international position,
he departed for Holkham and partridges, leaving Mrs. Fox
at St. Ann's Hill, for his marriage was not announced and
Coke of Norfolk still drew the line at Mrs. Armistead.

During the autumn hunger increased. In Paris the Sections were rising alarmingly, and General Barras found a man, 'the little Buona-Parte', who could command the artillery, if artillery could be found to protect the Government. There were guns at Les Sablons, and the new commander ordered a cavalryman, Joachim Murat, to gallop with his chasseurs and, by hard riding, bring back the guns before the Sections could seize them. That ride, which in the end put both officers on thrones, was a decisive event, for the guns of Vendemaire crushed mob government and brought General Bonaparte into history. In England the discontent was manifested less dramatically. Bread riots became noisier; and the King was mobbed on his way to open Parliament, when his coach window was broken by a pebble discharged, it was believed, from an air-gun. He was, as always, unmoved by personal danger, and announced his escape to the Lord Chancellor with a quiet 'My Lord, I have been shot at'. But ministers did not share their master's Hanoverian *sang-froid*. Pitt, who a few days later gloomily remarked, 'My head would be off in six months were I to resign,' saw in the disturbance the realization of all his fears. For such a situation he had only one remedy, and he had no difficulty in persuading Parliament to pass a Seditious Meetings Bill and a Treasonable Practices Bill. Fox fought them at every stage. 'You may prevent men from complaining,' he said on the second reading of the Bills, 'but you cannot prevent them from feeling. Either your Bills must remain waste-paper, or they must be carried into execution with circumstances of the greatest oppression./ Depend upon it, if men speak less, they will feel more, and arms will be left them as the only resource to procure redress to themselves, or exercise vengeance on their oppressors.' But only twenty-two members agreed with him, and he gloomily prepared to warn the country of its impending loss of liberty by public meetings, while meetings might still be held. 'There appears to me', he wrote, 'to be no choice at present but between an absolute surrender of the liberties of the people and a vigorous exertion, attended, I admit, with considerable hazard, at a time like the present. My view of things is, I own, very gloomy; and I am convinced that in a very few years this government will become completely absolute, or that confusion will arise of a nature almost as much to be deprecated as despotism itself.'

A faint gleam of hope penetrated the gloom of that October. To the voluble indignation of Burke, Lord Auckland published a pamphlet on the *Apparent Circumstances of the War in the fourth week of October*. It was the first step to prepare the public mind, accustomed to Pitt's repeated refusals, for the opening of negotiations. To Burke a Regicide Peace could mean only 'utter and irretrievable ruin to the Ministry, to the Crown, to the Succession, to the importance, to the independence, to the very existence of this country'. But Burke was no longer the Burke of the *Reflections*, and Pitt contemptuously reviewed his letter as being 'like other rhapsodies from the same pen, in which there is much to admire and nothing to agree with'. Peace was no longer a hopeless dream of the Opposition.

The year ended with a meeting of 'the different factious societies' in Marylebone Fields, where a vote of thanks to Fox was carried for his recent declarations in Parliament. 'I cannot but be glad of this,' wrote Lord Malmesbury spitefully, 'as whatever explanation he may think proper to give them, it is very clear how they are understood by these societies.'

In March Pitt began his negotiations with an approach to the French minister at Bâle. The answer of the Directory was discouraging. They did not believe in the honesty of the British purpose, and they would not surrender their new Belgian provinces. Fox seems to have shared the suspicions of the Directory, for in a letter on the prospects of Abolition he wrote, 'What a rogue Pitt is! it is quite unpleasant to think that a man with such parts should be so totally devoid, as he seems to me, of all right feelings.' In a speech of over four hours on the 10th of May he ranged over the whole history of the war, the failure of each venture in turn, and charged the ministers with insincerity in their desire for peace.

But the French were not thinking of peace, and each week was bringing relief to that bankruptcy in which Pitt had seen the best hope for negotiation. General Bonaparte, the hero of Vendemaire, had been given command of the hungry, unclothed, unpaid rabble known as the Army of Italy; and he had made the only appeal which could reach them: 'Soldiers, you are ill fed and ill clothed. . . . The Government owes you much but can give you nothing. . . . I shall lead you to the most fertile provinces of the world. . . . There you shall find honour, glory and riches.' And at once the victories began, Montenotte, Dego, Millesimo, and Mandovi in April; then another thrilling appeal ('In the space of a fortnight you have won six victories. . . . But, soldiers, you have done nothing, for you still have work to do . . .'), and the Bridge of Lodi and Milan, with a stream of money pouring into bankrupt France. Peace could not easily be made with Directors who adorned themselves with eagles' plumes to celebrate Festivals of Victory.

The news became worse during the summer, for Spain became an ally of France, and Prussia signed a treaty of amity. But ministers drew such comfort as they could from the thought that a general election once more returned them with undiminished strength. In Westminster Fox was unopposed by the Government, but Horne Tooke again appeared as a democratic candidate and kept the poll open for fifteen days. In the prevailing state of public opinion it was fortunate for Fox's little group that so many of them sat for close boroughs.

In the autumn Pitt made another attempt at peace. Lord Malmesbury, the Lion, as his contemporaries called him from his rather formidable appearance, was sent to Paris. For a moment negotiations seemed possible, for the Archduke Charles in Germany had provided a set-off to the conquest of Lombardy. But Bonaparte's harvest of victory was resumed—Lonato, Castiglione, Roveredo, Bassano, Arcola—and the mood of exaltation was restored. The Directors were busy with plans for the immediate invasion of Ireland, and perhaps of England, which might lead to a peace on terms very different from those which Lord Malmesbury wished to discuss. Meanwhile they refused to consider any idea of surrendering the Netherlands, and, after weeks of useless discussion, abruptly requested Lord Malmesbury to leave France, when their expedition had already started for Ireland. It was Hoche's ill-fated raid on Bantry Bay.

No doubt Pitt was anxious for peace, but the negotiations in Paris were conducted in a way which gave Fox some reason for his suspicion that Lord Malmesbury was sent 'merely to show his diplomatic dexterity . . . to evince his superior skill and adroitness in the management of argument and the arts of finesse . . . to make the cause of this country appear the better cause'. The country was pledged not to make peace without the consent of Austria, except on the terms that France should restore all that Austria had lost. It was perfectly certain that France would not restore Belgium. What then could be the purpose of negotiating without Austria?

The new year began unpromisingly with Rivoli, a French invasion in South Wales, and the suspension of payment by the Bank of England. This sequence of gloom was broken only by the news that at Cape St. Vincent Jervis and Nelson had removed the immediate threat of invasion from the country's perils. It was a welcome victory, and the Government made the most of it, for the war was becoming daily less popular, and the hope of any tolerable peace receded as Alvinzi's broken army swarmed over the Brenner and Bonaparte's cavalry rode into Mantua. 'To desire war without reflection,' wrote Grenville bitterly, 'to be unnecessarily elated at success, to be still more unreasonably depressed by difficulties, and to call for peace with an impatience which makes suitable terms unattainable, are the established maxims and the regular progress of the popular mind in this country.'

The part of the Opposition grew increasingly distasteful, for the country was now in danger, and critics were exposed to all the storm of abuse and charges of treachery which a Government can use in times of crisis. It was not a pleasant task in those days to denounce the obvious blunders in Pitt's negotiations for peace or to comment on the want of foresight which had made possible the crisis of the Bank. To Fox it seemed that political liberty, justice, parliamentary government were doomed to extinction, to Euthanasia as he called it, and he was meditating a closer alliance with the democratic reformers as the only faint hope of salvation. 'At present', he wrote to his nephew, 'I think we ought to go further towards agreeing with the democratic or popular party than at any former period; for the following reasons: we, as a party, can do nothing, and the contest must be between the Court and the Democrats. These last, without our assistance, will be either too weak to resist the Court—and then comes Mr. Hume's Euthanasia, which you and I think the worst of all events—or, if they are strong enough, being wholly unmixed with any aristocratic leaven, and full of resentment against us for not joining them, will go probably to greater excesses, and bring on the only state of things which can make a man doubt whether the despotism of monarchy is the worst of all evils.'

But other councils were at work among the Whigs in that winter of dismay. Grey was now married and, like Fox, he grudged every moment taken from his home for the hopeless business of politics. Other Whigs, the Duke of Bedford, Lord Lauderdale, Erskine, Whitbread, had persuaded themselves that, since opposition in Parliament was now impotent, the most effective gesture of protest was to withdraw and take no further part in the proceedings. It was not a unanimous view. Sheridan was against it, but Sheridan's advice no longer carried its former weight. He was in close alliance with the Prince, and some of his colleagues were inclined to question his loyalty to the party.

The faithful Fitzpatrick and Lord Guilford also opposed the idea, and Lord Lansdowne, restored to the Whigs in their distress, gave his opinion that 'secession means rebellion or it is nonsense', while Tierney, a new member of unbounded energy, refused in any case to withdraw. For Fox the temptation was great. Secession was exactly what he most passionately desired. Four years before, when the party had paid his debts, he had proposed to withdraw, but Fitzpatrick and his nearest friends had persuaded him to remain in public life; and two years later he had again played with the idea of secession and dismissed it as 'the measure a shabby fellow would take in our circumstances'. But now, when the crisis of affairs was worse, and every cause for which he had stood was threatened, he allowed himself to be persuaded, as Lord Holland sadly recorded, 'from indolence rather than from judgement'. He warned his tempters that if he once withdrew they might find it difficult to bring him back, if they should tire of their exile, but he did not give them the one decisive answer that in his heart he knew secession to be wrong. It was decided that in the Commons Grey should move for Parliamentary Reform, while the Duke of Bedford moved in the Lords on the State of the Nation, and that in each debate the Whigs should announce their withdrawal.

Unfortunately for its public effect this manœuvre was carried out at a most unfavourable moment. In April, when a French invasion was preparing, with the fleets of Holland and Spain in support, began the naval mutinies of Spithead and the Nore, and for many weeks the public mind was occupied by more urgent matters than Mr. Hume's Euthanasia. The reformers fell naturally under suspicion of arousing discontent, but the most hopeful inquiry could find no trace of complicity in any one connected with English politics. Perhaps French agents may have had a hand in the intrigue which produced unanimous revolt in so many ships, but the cause of the mutinies was beyond doubt. The treatment of the sailors was intolerable, and they could find no other way of expressing their grievances.

> The reason unto you I now will relate:
> We resolved to refuse the purser's short weight;
> Our humble petition to Lord Howe we sent,
> That he to the Admiralty write to present,
> Our provisions and wages that they might augment.
> . . . .
> But soon to our grief, as you shall understand,
> They refused to comply with our humble demand;
> Although to the Army they granted more pay,
> While we sons of Neptune neglected did lay,
> But the 15th of April soon roused them straightway.

With the red flag flying at Sheerness and rúmours of a mutiny in the Artillery at Woolwich and even in the Guards at St. James's, it is not surprising that the demonstration of the Whig Opposition attracted only a small share of public attention.

On the 26th of May Grey moved for Parliamentary Reform, as arranged at the Whig conference. His motion took the form of a request for leave to bring in a Bill, of which he gave the heads; and he announced that if the House rejected his motion he would not speak again. When Fox spoke he declared that he would henceforth devote more time to 'the leisure that I love'. Ninety-one members voted for the resolution, and the great secession of the Whigs began.

CHAPTER XIII

1797–1803

THE Secession is one of the mysteries of Charles Fox's life. To his enemies, who see nothing in that life but a moral and political Rake's Progress, it is simple enough. He was the Spoilt Child of History, and he sulked when he could not have his way. He was consumed by ambition, and he gave up Parliament when it would no longer serve his ambition. He was a gambler, and he threw up the game when it was no longer worth the candle. But to those who are not convinced of his universal worthlessness the solution is less easy. They must admit that as a leader he had made some disastrous blunders, and they must admit that as a leader he felt such complete confidence in the excellence of his political principles that he was sometimes ready to support them by rather questionable means. The attack on the King's right of Dissolution and the affair of the Regency illustrate both faults. He had certainly committed many blunders, but this was something worse than a blunder. He knew well enough that secession was wrong. He might complain of the suppression of free speech, but free speech could not be suppressed in the House of Commons, and he was leaving the House of Commons. He might talk of Mr. Hume's Euthanasia and the approaching death of Liberty, but he knew that at any moment the death of the King or Pitt or Lord Chatham might alter everything. Secession was 'the measure a shabby fellow would take in our circumstances'. Why then, did he take it?

It is difficult to find any single answer. He was, no doubt, attracted by the delights of rural domesticity at St. Ann's Hill. But his honeymoon had already lasted for some thirteen years, and most of them had been spent at St. Ann's Hill. He was, no doubt, overpersuaded by Grey and other supporters of the scheme. But a leader is not infrequently surrounded by persuasive enthusiasts, and it is not for him to follow them. No doubt all these things had their effect, but even cumulatively they should not have prevailed on the man who had written when another cause was tottering, 'Whatever happens, for God's sake, let us all resolve to stick by them as handsomely (or more so) in their adversity as we have done in their glory. . . .'

Perhaps a glance at Fox's pictures may suggest an explanation. We see him as Sir Joshua painted him in 1783,[1] with the India Bill in his hand when he had 'divided the Kingdom with Caesar'. He was then 34, and his appearance might without flattery be called youthful. He was painted again in 1793 by Hickel,[2] and his appearance then could hardly by flattery be called middle-aged. The Nollekens Bust,[3] still displayed with honour in Whig houses, was of the same year, and it tells the same story. He had passed with extraordinary speed from youth to old age, with hardly a pause for the years of middle age. He was now old, a hale and hearty old man with immense appreciation of life, but none the less an old man; and the forlorn unending fight for peace in a country mad with war is hardly to be borne by old age. If we may believe the portraits, the sudden descent of old age may have turned the scale, already heavily weighted by his passion for St. Ann's Hill, his despair in the state of politics, and the persuasion of his friends.

The years which followed were the happiest of his life. He had experienced most of the triumphs and emotions which life can offer, and now he desired nothing but the ordered simplicity of living which had become his ideal. John Trotter, who became his Secretary, has told us how he lived at that time: 'In summer he rose between six and seven; in winter before eight. . . . After breakfast, which took place between eight and nine in summer, and at a little after nine in winter, he usually read some Italian author with Mrs. Fox, and then spent the time preceding dinner at his literary studies, in which the great poets bore a principal part. A frugal but plentiful dinner took place

[1] See frontispiece.   [2] See p. 278.   [3] See p. 326.

at three, or half-past two, in summer, and at four, in winter; and a few glasses of wine were followed by coffee. The evening was dedicated to walking and conversation till tea-time, when reading aloud, in history, commenced, and continued till near ten. A light supper of fruit, pastry, or something very trifling, finished the day; and at half-past ten the family were gone to rest; and the next and succeeding dawn ushered in the same order and elegance. . . .'

For such a life St. Ann's Hill was ideal. It was a small country house with a garden of sloping lawns and shrubberies, and some thirty acres of land. There he could idle to perfection, lying motionless on the lawn for hours until the birds ignored his presence; anxiously consulting the weather-wise on the chances of rain and the prospects of his hay; tramping rapidly over the Surrey lanes; shopping economically for the household; and playing battledore and shuttlecock with Mrs. Fox. He possessed that talent for idling which Sir Philip Francis associated with greatness. When Francis read Fox's correspondence with the scholar, Wakefield, he described it as 'a curiosity, not for the value of the criticisms, but as it indicates the propensity of a great mind to be easily interested or amused. I never knew a second-hand man, who, without labour or occupation imposed upon him, could in the proper sense of the word, be *amused* or find amusement for himself. Such people, having no resources of their own, are generally a burden to themselves and, of course, to others.' By this test Fox was great indeed. When a friend on a hot day in the Manager's Box suggested that it was just the day to lie on the lawn with a book, his agreement was qualified: 'But why a book, why a book?'

Mr. Trotter's time-table shows several hours of the day devoted to reading, and Fox's reading was not of a kind which would to-day suggest indolence. He had all his life been an insatiable reader of poetry, and above all of Greek and Latin poetry. Now he could make up for lost time, and his letters of those years show how he did it, for it was his

CHARLES JAMES FOX, 1793

From an engraving by J. G. HUCK *after the portrait by* ANTON HICKEL

pleasant habit to discuss his reading in his letters, in the
hope that his correspondents might share his interest in the
book of the moment. His letters to Lord Holland are concerned mainly with books, and they range over Homer
('You see I have never done with Homer; and indeed, if
there was nothing else, except Virgil and Ariosto, one
should never want reading'), Polybius, Dryden ('wants a
certain degree of easy playfulness that belongs to Ariosto'),
Aristotle's *Poeticus* ('a great deal very obscure, and in some
parts (if one dared say it) rather confused'), Spencer and his
use of the word 'that', Pope ('I think he is as miserable a
moralist and as superficial and faulty a reasoner as ever
existed, and that all the merit of his satires consists in his
poetry and his wit, of both of which he had a good share'),
Don Quixote ('loses more by translation in the grave than
in the humorous parts'), Medea ('I am clear it is the best
of all the Greek tragedies upon the whole, though the
choruses are not so poetical as in some others'), and Chaucer,
to name only a few.

The correspondence with Gilbert Wakefield begins in
1796 when Wakefield's edition of Lucretius was dedicated
to Fox, and it ended in 1801 when the unfortunate scholar
was released from Dorchester Gaol, where he had spent two
years for an injudicious pamphlet. They discussed the
authenticity of the twenty-fourth book of the *Iliad*, the
place of Ovid among poets, the significance of words for
colour in Latin poetry, a scheme for a new Lexicon, and a
host of other questions. Fox's letters show a charming
deference to his imprisoned elder combined with his usual
force of argument. Occasionally they turn from the classics
to the less enthralling matters of the day. In 1799 Fox's
hand was wounded by the bursting of a gun while he was
shooting partridges, and Wakefield took occasion to lecture
him on pleasures which 'misbecome a man of letters'. Fox
tried to defend partridge shooting ('if it is lawful to kill
tame animals with whom one has a sort of acquaintance,
such as *fowls*, *oxen*, &c., it is still less repugnant to one's

feelings to kill wild animals; but then to make a pastime of it—I am aware there is something to be said on this point'); but he received a terrific rejoinder from Wakefield ('Is it philosophical and humane to leave numbers of them to perish by pain and hunger, or to occasion the remainder of their lives to be perilous and miserable? For such I presume are the inevitable consequences of *shooting* . . .'), and he had to admit himself beaten but unconverted ('I believe I had best not continue the controversy about field sports . . .').

The letter which best reveals its writer is to Grey: 'In defence of my opinion about the nightingale, I find Chaucer —who of all poets seems to have been fondest of the singing of birds—calls it a *merry note*, and though Theocritus mentions nightingales six or seven times, he never mentions their note as plaintive or melancholy. It is true that he does not call it anywhere merry as Chaucer does, but, by mentioning it with the song of the blackbird, and as answering it, he seems to imply that it was a cheerful note. Sophocles is against us; but even he only says *Lamenting Itys*, and the comparison of her to Electra is rather as to perseverance day and night than as to sorrow. At all events a tragic poet is not half as good an authority in this question as Theocritus and Chaucer.

'I cannot light upon the passage in the Odyssey where Penelope's restlessness is compared to the nightingale; but I am sure it is only as to restlessness or watchfulness that he makes the comparison. If you will read the last twelve books of the Odyssey, you will certainly find it, and I am sure you will be paid for your hunt whether you find it or not: the passage in Chaucer is in the "Flower and the Leaf", p. 99. The one I particularly allude to in Theocritus is in his epigrams—I think in the fourth.

'Dryden has transferred the word *merry* to the goldfinch, in his "Flower and the Leaf", in deference, maybe, to the vulgar error; but pray read his description of the nightingale here—it is quite delightful.'

The impressive catalogue of Fox's classical reading has been used by his admirers to suggest that scholarship, in the strict and narrow sense, should be added to his other accomplishments. No such claim was made by Fox himself, whose diffidence in such matters is noticeable in all his letters to Wakefield. The only point on which he tended to claim authority was his conviction that as an Etonian he was peculiarly fitted to appreciate Greek and Latin verse. 'I do not wonder', he wrote on a point of Greek prosody, 'Marsh does not know so much about it, for he was not, I believe, at Eton, and though it sounds impertinent to say so, I think that none but those who have been there ever have a correct notion of Greek or even Latin metre.' Apart from this modest claim he would have agreed entirely with the disparaging view of Sir Philip Francis that 'his Greek studies were not very deep, and had gone but a little way beyond Homer and Euripides, the minor poets, and the political orations of Demosthenes'. It is certainly true that his classical studies were an amusement and not a vocation, and he never allowed himself the opportunity for that kind of reading which would be needed before his quality as a scholar could be tested. But it is also true that he possessed remarkable gifts of rapid assimilation, effortless memory, and sense of language, and if with such gifts he had devoted his life to classical studies, he might well have achieved fame as a scholar.

Even zealous Foxites can hardly pretend that English literature lost a master when Fox took to politics. He had written a poem to Mrs. Crewe in his youth, and he now addressed jingles to Mrs. Fox to celebrate his fiftieth birthday or to sooth her alarm as they drove to London after the bursting gun had wounded his hand:

> Where's the sorrow that thy smile
> Knows not sweetly to beguile?
> Sense of pain, and danger flies
> From the looks of those dear eyes. . . .

Perhaps this verse displays, as Mr. Trotter suggests, 'an

exquisiteness of feeling, rarely met with (unhappily for the world) in those statesmen who rule mankind'; but it displays no greater literary merit than its diffident author would have claimed for it. His more serious venture in writing was a History of James II. In this he was inspired by something more than the strange fascination which the writing of history seems so often to exercise upon disappointed statesmen. He believed that in a History of the Revolution he would explain and justify the actions of himself and his party in their conflict with George III, and he toiled doggedly with his authorities, although, as he remarked in his letter on the nightingale, 'I am afraid I like these researches as much better than those that relate to Shaftesbury, Sunderland, &c., as I do those better than attending the House of Commons'. But that style which had made him the greatest of debaters, throwing himself 'into the middle of his sentence and leaves it to God Almighty to get him out again', is rarely successful in the writing of prose, and the *Historical Fragment*, which was published after his death, is a rather heavy and depressing tome.

In this contemplative existence he was not entirely detached from the events of public life. He constantly gave opinions on current events to his political friends, and he was occasionally persuaded to come to London for a public utterance. But much persuasion was needed to move him from St. Ann's Hill. Now that secession was an accomplished fact, approved at last even by Lansdowne, his mind was turning to complete withdrawal from public affairs. 'I indeed,' he wrote to Lord Lauderdale in November 1797, 'even supposing Royal prejudices out of the way and all other objections of the kind, feel such an extreme aversion to the situation of First Minister that I am sure I should act very ill a part I so much dislike. I have not diligence or activity enough for the situation—*je ne suis pas à la hauteur des circonstances*; and I am quite seriously convinced that if yourself, Guilford, Bedford, and Grey could get the Government, and would accept it, you would

do much better without me than with me, having of course
the advantage, whatever it may be, of my name and my
support in the House of Commons.'

History moved quickly in the first months of the secession. In July Burke died, disappointed of all his hopes, while
Lord Malmesbury at Lille was doing his best to negotiate
a regicide peace. A friendly message of inquiry from Fox
obtained only the chilling reply that 'it has cost Mr. Burke
the most heartfelt pain to obey the stern voice of his duty
in rending asunder a long friendship, but that he deemed
this sacrifice necessary; that his principles continue the
same; and that in whatever life may yet remain to him, he
conceives he must look to others and not to himself'.

The war raged on. A threatened invasion from Texel
was frustrated by adverse winds, and in October the Dutch
Navy learnt at Camperdown that something more than a
fair wind was needed for the conquest of England. In
November Pitt trebled the Assessed Taxes on inhabited
houses, windows, male servants, horses, and carriages. The
outcry was terrific and the Prime Minister was hooted in
the City on his way to the thanksgiving service for the
naval successes. Fox, who had flatly refused to attend the
opening of Parliament, was persuaded by Sheridan to return for the second reading and predict gloomily that the
Bill tended to 'the immediate destruction of our trade, to
the annihilation of our fortunes and possibly to the loss of
liberty to our persons'. The Assessed Taxes were unpopular,
but they did not destroy confidence in Pitt. An appeal for
'Patriotic Contribution', which was tacked on to the Bill,
produced subscriptions of £2,300,000. Fox, pressed for
advice on the duty of a good Whig, saw no objection to
voluntary subscriptions assuming that 'subscription does
not tend to put more money in the Minister's disposal, but
only to relieve non-subscribers of part of the burden laid
upon them, and is not therefore so objectionable in cases
where persons suppose themselves to be too little taxed in
proportion to others'. But it could not greatly matter in

the general collapse. 'I am so sure that we are going to certain ruin as we are now going on, that perhaps any event which may disturb us is good. . . .'

The new year brought an unwelcome interruption to the repose of St. Ann's Hill. On the 24th of January 1798 the birthday of Charles Fox was celebrated by a public dinner at the Crown and Anchor Tavern. The Duke of Norfolk, whose behaviour was frequently unexpected, proposed from the chair the toast of the evening in a speech which compared Charles Fox to Washington: 'Not twenty years ago the illustrious George Washington had not more than two thousand men to rally round him when his country was attacked. America is now free. This day full two thousand men are assembled in this place: I leave you to make the application.' This, with Ireland in revolt, was a dangerous sentiment, and the Duke apparently tried to dilute its potency in a series of loyal toasts. But at the end of the evening, inspired perhaps by the toasts and by three new songs composed for the occasion by Captain Morris, he responded to his own health with an invitation to the Company to 'drink our Sovereign's health—the Majesty of the People'. This in the context of current history was considered, as Pitt observed, 'a speech . . . which, I think even the Crown lawyers will hardly prove to be much short of treason', and the Duke was instantly dismissed from the command of his militia regiment and from the Lord Lieutenancy of the West Riding. 'The toast relating to the sovereignty of the people', wrote Fox to the Duke, 'will be universally and I believe truly considered as the cause of your removal, and thus you will be looked up to as the marked champion of that Sovereignty, under which alone King William and the Brunswick Kings have held their throne. The Ministers call for unanimity, for suspension of party disputes, for the purpose of repelling a foreign enemy, and then they dismiss your Grace from not only a Lieutenancy, but a Regiment, for an opinion certainly of a theoretical nature at any rate, but an opinion which to

have controverted in the times of the first two Georges
would have been deemed a symptom of disaffection.'

But a letter of sympathy was not enough for Fox, and
at a meeting of the Whig Club early in May he pointedly
repeated the Duke's toast to the Sovereignty of the People.
The effect was sensational, for Ireland was in a blaze, and
Ministers talked of the Tower. 'I understand', wrote Pitt,
'there is a strong feeling among many of our friends that
some decided notice must be taken of Fox's speech. An
idea has been suggested which I think deserves consideration. It is to begin with one of the measures we talked of,
that of ordering him to attend. If he disavows, prosecuting
the printer. If he avows, ordering him to be reprimanded,
and then (which is the new part of the suggestion) if he
offers a fresh insult at the next Whig Club, instead of gratifying him by an expulsion, to send him to the Tower for
the remainder of the session; which, though I hope it would
prove a very short punishment, would be enough to assert
the authority of the House.'

It was Pitt at his pettiest, for he knew the history of the
toast, and he knew that Fox could not with any truth be
called seditious. But with war abroad and rebellion in Ireland, a Minister in the grip of illness is not to be censured
for such loss of self-control. The Government prudently
decided on the less spectacular course of removing Fox's
name from the Privy Council. Fitzpatrick offered, by way
of protest, to resign from the Privy Council, but Fox, whose
mind was full of the precedents of 1762, in which he seemed
to forget his father's role of executioner, would not hear of
it. The Government was not alone at that time in threatening him with captivity. A Government spy had discovered,
or pretended to discover, in France a project for a Directory
in England. It allots high office to various champions of
liberty and equality, but Fox is awarded transportation as
'faux patriot; ayant souvent insulté La Nation Française
dans ses discours et particulièrement en 1786'.

It is not surprising that in those days of terror and dismay appeals for the return of Fox were frequent, for in 1798 rebellion broke out in Ireland with all the horrors of repression and reprisal which are associated with Irish warfare, and in August Humbert's ill-fated expedition landed in Killala Bay. Had they landed a few months earlier when Sir Ralph Abercromby was proclaiming that his forces were 'formidable to every one but the enemy', history might have been changed. But Bonaparte had returned to Paris, and, distrustful of schemes for the invasion of England, had asked for an expedition to Egypt; and the Directory, with no liking for Bonaparte at close quarters, had enthusiastically accepted the project, sending the army of Egypt on that romantic venture which ended with Nelson and Aboukir. In London the papers of the London Corresponding Society were once more seized, and Habeas Corpus was once more suspended. On Wimbledon Common Mr. Pitt and Mr. Tierney exchanged harmless shots. But Fox was, as he had predicted, hard to move. 'I should', he wrote in March, 'dislike to a degree I cannot express to attend again myself; indeed, if there is a point upon which I cannot bring myself to give way it is this. . . .' And in October he would 'not be at all sorry to find myself the sole seceder, but a seceder I will be till I see a very different state of things from the present, and indeed if they were to alter more materially than can be expected, it would be with more reluctance than I can describe, or than is perhaps reasonable, that I should return to politics'. But he was persuaded in June to support Sheridan and Lord George Cavendish in a motion on the state of Ireland.

For many months he believed that the Directory's Armée d'Angleterre would invade England, and one of the horrors of invasion would be the obligation of actively supporting the Government. 'It is bad enough', he wrote to Lord Lauderdale, 'to be passively obedient to the present system, but when one has just made up one's mind to that, to feel oneself in a situation when one must make active exertion in support and for the establishment of such a tyranny is the very Devil. And yet I cannot help feeling that if the French come, this is what we must do.'

His purpose remained inflexible during the next year— it was 1799—although he saw much to criticize in two of the measures, Income Tax and Union with Ireland, which were before the House. Income Tax would, he feared, be 'dreadfully oppressive upon persons from £200 to £600 a year, but I have long suspected that persons of this class have long become quite ciphers in respect to political power, and indeed they are most of them too dependent, either on account of what they actually have, or of what they expect for themselves and children, to dare to stir against the government and the higher ranks.' His preliminary objection to Union was on the curious ground that union was revolution, and beyond the 'competence' of Parliament, because Parliament could not 'destroy the constitution which it is instituted to support, even though it should place a better in its stead. . . . I cannot think for instance that Parliament is competent to declare Great Britain an absolute monarchy; or a republic, though it should be of opinion that any change would be for the better.' But his objections were not strong enough to bring him to London for the debates in which Sheridan fought hard for the Irish Parliament, and his absence from the House, when the Union was being carried in Ireland by bribery, threats, and a vague indication of Catholic Emancipation to come, is one of the least easily forgivable results of the Secession. It was easier from rich experience to give good advice to Fitzpatrick, who persisted in his old affection for the dice: 'Ought a wise man who has lived half a century of years, to allow himself to depend upon such events? But it is in vain to preach.'

That year, on the whole, went well for Pitt's new coalition. Melas and Suwaroff reconquered Italy; and although the Russians were defeated in Switzerland and the 'grand old Duke of York' failed in Holland, France was clamouring uneasily for the return of Bonaparte and the days of spectacular victory. His return from Egypt and the days of

Brumaire had all the dramatic qualities to appeal to the French, and, by the end of the year, the First Consul was offering peace in a personal letter to King George III.

The refusal of that offer on the grounds of 'security' and the acrimoniously unpleasant form of its refusal are matters which concern the careers of Pitt and Grenville. When the Government's answer was debated on the 3rd of February, Fox was persuaded 'against inclination, common sense, and philosophy', to return to the House, and his nephew 'saw tears steal down his cheeks' when the debate was postponed and he had to lose another day from St. Ann's Hill. The speech was among his greatest, and his mockery of the Government's anxiety to be sure that the Consulate should be stable before opening negotiations is perhaps the best reported of his speeches and the best example of his ironic manner:

'We are called upon to go on merely as a speculation—we must keep Bonaparte for some time longer at war, as a state of probation. Gracious God, Sir! is war a state of probation? Is peace a rash system? Is it dangerous for nations to live in amity with each other? Is your vigilance, your policy, your common powers of observation, to be extinguished by putting an end to the horrors of war? Cannot this state of probation be as well undergone without adding to the catalogue of human sufferings? "But we must pause!" What! must the bowels of Great Britain be torn out—her best blood be spilt—her treasure wasted—that you may make an experiment? Put yourself—oh! that you would put yourselves—in the field of battle, and learn to judge of the sort of horrors that you excite. In former wars a man might, at least, have some feeling, some interest, that served to balance in his mind the impressions which a scene of carnage and death must inflict. If a man had been present at the Battle of Blenheim, for instance, and had enquired the motive of the battle, there was not a soldier engaged who could not have satisfied his curiosity, and even, perhaps, allayed his feelings—they were fighting

to repress the uncontrolled ambition of the grand monarch.
But, if a man were present now at a field of slaughter, and
were to enquire for what they were fighting: "Fighting!"
would be the answer; "they are not fighting, they are pausing." "Why is that man expiring? Why is that other
writhing with agony? What means this implacable fury?"
The answer must be: "You are quite wrong, Sir, you deceive
yourself. They are not fighting—do not disturb them—they
are merely *pausing!* This man is not expiring with agony,
that man is not dead—he is only pausing! Lord help you,
Sir! they are not angry with one another; they have now
no cause of quarrel—but their country thinks that there
should be a pause. All that you see, Sir, is nothing like
fighting—there is no harm, nor cruelty, nor bloodshed in it
whatever—it is nothing more than *a political pause!*—it
is merely an experiment—to see whether Bonaparte will
not behave himself better than heretofore." ...'

Only 63 members voted with him, and he returned contentedly to St. Ann's Hill. In July Grey gives us a glimpse
of him at Woburn with his Whig friends: 'I did not find as
large a party as I expected. It at present consists of Fox,
Lord Robert, Fitzpatrick, Lord John Townshend, Francis,
Dudley North, Richardson, and myself. Sheridan and
Adair are expected to-day, and Hare to-morrow. Fox is in
the highest spirits. It is quite delightful to see such a man
in the midst of a society which he appears to like, so unas-
suming, good humoured and cheerful. Everything seems to
be a source of enjoyment to him, and I hardly know which
to envy most—his amiable disposition or his unrivalled
talents. . . . He is enthusiastic about poetry, and admires
Spencer as much as we do. . . .'

His friends tried again in 1800 to bring him back, but his
methods of resistance had improved and he was beyond
persuasion. He would write freely to Grey on the prospects
of Reform and the possibility of moving Reform without
frightening Fitzwilliam; but he would not come to Parliament, and at St. Ann's Hill he remained while the Union Bill

U

became law, while Mr. Hadfield shot at the King from the pit of Drury Lane, and at Marengo the First Consul taught the allies that they might as well have accepted his offer of peace.

But at the moment when Pitt's majority seemed to be the one stable feature in a changing world, it was suddenly announced that Pitt was gone. It was a complete surprise, for outside the Cabinet little was known of Pitt's move to carry Catholic Emancipation as part of the consideration for the Union; and the story of Lord Loughborough's treacherous intrigue against his colleagues, and the rigidity of the King's conscience in the matter of the Coronation oath had not become public. There was some gossip of a royal outburst at the Levée, then a pause while King and Minister exchanged notes, and it became known that Pitt had resigned and with him Grenville and Dundas; and with even greater astonishment it was learnt that Addington was to take Pitt's place. The thought of the Doctor, as he was called in memory of his medical father, as Prime Minister was fantastic. From Hare the news called forth 'such a fit of laughter that he laughed the whole way from the Horse Guards to the Stable Yard, and was obliged to sit down on a bench in the park to rest'. Fox shared the general amazement: 'If I do believe it, it must be *quia uncomprehensibile.*' But he was soon able to survey the position: 'In the Lansdowne language, I say *Simplicity and Consistency.* Pitt was a bad Minister; he is out—I am glad.'

The appointment of Addington—it was the King's choice —was certainly an amazing event, but not, in Fox's view, the beginning of a great change. He had no doubt that the King would support the Doctor, and, in the making of a Government, the King and not Pitt held the final power. 'The King's power is, as we know, great; and when exerted in conjunction with his ally, the Church, and therefore in the way and upon the points which he likes best, and upon which he will enter with the greatest spirit, will not easily be foiled; and you may be sure the Ministry is quite one to his heart's content.'

But even as he wrote events were outstripping him. The King's emotion, frequently expressed in incoherent soliloquy, had been profoundly disturbed. By the middle of February the habitual ejaculations became noticeably louder; a few days later he was wandering; and before the end of the month he was beyond question mad. The roles of all parties had been well rehearsed in 1788, and there was no revival of the Regency Crisis. Pitt, *de facto* minister until he could resign the seals, called upon the Prince, and informed him that if a Regency should become necessary the restrictions of 1788 would be imposed; Fox, whose enthusiasm for the prospective Regent had considerably waned, remained discreetly aloof; Parliament was induced to be silent on the crisis; and the Prince submitted.

In the first week of March the King recovered sufficiently to use his illness ('What has not *he* to answer for who is the cause of my having been ill at all') to extort from Pitt an undertaking not to propose Catholic Emancipation again during his reign. Convalescence seemed to raise His Majesty's political sagacity to its highest level, and this was a triumph of dexterity. Seldom has an access of lunacy been used with greater presence of mind.

After such submission he might safely recall Pitt to office, but he had the highest opinion of Mr. Addington, already described in a royal note as the King's 'own Chancellor of the Exchequer'; and Mr. Addington had no doubt of his own superior ability. To the open fury of Canning, Leveson Gower, and active young Tories the Doctor remained in office.

Fox saw no reason to alter his manner of living. He attended Parliament unwillingly on the 25th of March for Grey's motion on the State of the Nation, 'on the ground', as he told his nephew, 'that having absented myself because the influence of the late Ministers had made the proceedings of the House of Commons a farce, I return to put the House to the test, whether they will by an implicit confidence make themselves the same abject tools of the present Government

as they were of the last'. The result was conclusive. Grey's
motion secured 105 votes, and Fox returned cheerfully to
St. Ann's Hill to obtain such consolation as the news of
Copenhagen might afford. His only other appearance was
on behalf of his old enemy at Westminster, Horne Tooke,
who had at last got a seat and, ineligible as a priest, was in
danger of losing it. 'Mr. Fox', said Tooke, 'has taken a
severe revenge. I have passed my life in attacking him, and
he has now, for the second time, defended me nobly against
the arm of power.' Once more opposition seemed hopeless,
and Fox was able to console Grey, who disliked the thought
of leaving the Commons on succeeding to his father's peerage.
'It is undoubtedly a provoking event; but according to my
notion the constitution of the country is declining so rapidly
that the House of Commons has in great measure ceased,
and will shortly entirely cease to be a place of much importance.'

His reluctance disappeared when it was announced early
in October that Preliminaries of Peace were signed. It was,
as Sir Philip Francis put it, 'a peace of which everyone is
glad, but nobody is proud'. But Grenville, Canning, and
Windham found no cause for gladness in the loss of the
Cape, Malta, Martinique, and all the recent conquests except
Trinidad and Leghorn, and they openly rebelled against their
leader's support of the terms. Fox had no doubt on the
subject, and at a meeting at the Shakespeare Tavern to
celebrate the anniversary of the Great Westminster Election, he belauded the French Republic with a fervour which
drew a mild protest from Grey. In the correspondence
which followed he had to admit that he had 'gone something
further in hate to the English Government than you and the
rest of my friends are, and certainly further than can with
prudence be avowed'.

But his friends were disquieted by this typical example
of impulsive frankness, and Lady Bessborough describes the
leader's penitent embarrassment when he came to London
in November for the debate on the peace terms: 'At Hare's

dinner he was begging Grey and Sheridan to speak first, and promising to say nearly whatever they did, that he might not get into a scrape; for he says he never opens his lips now, let his intention be what it will, but he gets scolded and rated on all sides, offends everybody, and has so many different meanings and words forced upon him that he hardly knows at last what was his own or what he meant either as to words or sense. Grey and Sheridan scolded him till he almost cried about his speech in the Whig Club. . . .' It was perhaps owing to this tuition that he escaped disaster in the debate, where he is said to have spoken 'extremely well and with perfect discretion', supporting Pitt, defending Lord Granville Leveson Gower from a charge of inconsistency, and meeting a spiteful attack from Lord Temple by 'unexpected and amiable civility'.

It was a victory, but an uncomfortable victory, for the new Minister, and he began to look for recruits from the Opposition. He had some grounds for hope, for Sheridan had for some time displayed warlike tendencies which might divide him from his friends, Tierney was believed to think kindly of the new Administration, if only because it had supplanted Pitt, and Erskine had indicated a desire to hold some high office 'which my birth and acquired place render fit for me'. But the Doctor chose Grey and the Duke of Bedford for his offers, with the results which he might have foreseen. He had grounds for anxiety, for he was becoming increasingly an object of caricature, a figure of fun, and in English public life it is not easy to survive sustained ridicule. His Cabinet was a weak one, for every leader of political thought was outside it, and neither the favour of the King nor the flattering applause of his brother-in-law in the House could save him from the sarcasms of Canning:

> If his speeches lag most vilely,
> Cheer him, cheer him, Brother Hiley!
> If his speeches vilely lag,
> Cheer him, cheer him, Brother Bragge!

Even a single unguarded phrase in a speech— 'to doubt is to decide'—would bring down on him an ode from the same formidable enemy:

> If Pitt should hear his Country's voice,
> Say, would'st *thou* point thy Sovereign's choice
>   To worth and talents tried?
> Shake not thy empty head at me,
> Thy modest doubts too plain I see—
>   'To doubt is to decide'.

During that winter, while Addington tried to demonstrate his merits to the sceptics of London, Lord Cornwallis at Amiens faced the task, which was no less difficult, of turning the preliminaries into a treaty. At last it was done, and on the 27th of March 1802 the Treaty of Amiens was signed. The Session and the life of Parliament ended with a triumph for Pitt, for the House of Commons voted him thanks by name, and for the dinner of celebration, which followed, Canning produced his 'Pilot that weathered the Storm':

> And O! if again the rude whirlwind should rise,
>   The dawning of peace should fresh darkness deform,
> The regrets of the good and the fears of the wise
>   Shall turn to the pilot that weathered the storm.

The Election did not materially alter the state of parties. Once more at Westminster Fox had the annoyance of a poll, which he now headed. At Thetford the Duke of Norfolk earned the thanks of letter-reading posterity by bringing in Mr. Thomas Creevey.

After the Election it was open to sympathetic Whigs to take advantage of the peace and visit Paris. They went in large numbers, with the same enthusiasm which has impelled their successors to visit revolutionary Russia, and their excited gossip fills contemporary letters and diaries. There were so many strange celebrities to be seen and heard— M. de Talleyrand, whom they had known as an impecunious refugee in London and met now in the dullest and most ornate splendour; M. Fouché, who had once been seen, it was whispered, to 'ride full gallop to preside at some celebrated massacre with a pair of *human ears* stuck one on each side of his hat'; Madame Cabarrus, with her procession of husbands and lovers; Madame Récamier, posed in her celebrated bed with muslin and gold curtains, looking-glasses and incense, to receive her guests; the soldiers whose names were now famous over Europe—Moreau, Massèna, Berthier, Duroc; and perhaps a few words with the First Consul himself and occasional glimpses of him on his way to review an army.

To France also went Fox at the end of July accompanied by Mrs. Fox and his secretary. To avoid misunderstandings abroad, the marriage was now made public, to the astonishment of his friends. 'All his friends', wrote Lady Bessborough, 'are very angry with him. I cannot see anything but what I always knew of him—that he is kindness and weakness itself to everything that he loves. . . . The odd thing is that people who were shock'd at the immorality of his having a mistress are still more so at that mistress having been his wife for so long.'

The journey began with a tour in the Low Countries—Ghent, Antwerp, Utrecht, Amsterdam, Haarlem, Leyden, The Hague, and Brussels—with long days of driving and much conversation about the books taken for the journey, the *Aeneid* and *Ariosto* for Fox and *Joseph Andrews* and *Tom Jones* for Mrs. Fox and Trotter.

They found Paris full of friends, the Hollands, Fitzpatrick, Lord Robert, Adair and General Fox, all intent on a round of gaiety. But Fox had come for the sterner purpose of research for his history, and to the Foreign Office he went day after day to peruse the letters of Louis XIV and Barillon. In the intervals of his studies he found to his extreme annoyance that he was regarded as a popular hero. At the theatre he sat in confused silence while the audience applauded his presence, and he was dismayed to observe among his French hosts a tendency to welcome his arrival for dinner with an outburst of eloquence on his international destiny as a statesman. His manner on such occasions was apt to convey a wrong impression. He was, according to Hare, 'reckon'd very proud from not being delighted with the fine speeches made him, and only answering them by his little short bows, which look more like nods of approbation than anything else'. But in spite of these occasional embarrassments, the days passed very pleasantly amid dinners with Talleyrand, Madame Cabarrus, where he was unexpectedly embraced by a 'black-looking oldish man' afterwards identified as the Chevalier de Boufflers, Berthier, where he discussed Napoleonic strategy with Massèna, and long conversations with Siéyès, Kosiusco, and La Fayette.

There were also meetings with Bonaparte, and the record of them suggests an impression of uneasiness on both sides, as if each were a little pained to observe in the other a departure from the preconceived type. Neither answered quite in the part which the other had given him. At their first meeting Bonaparte lamented the necessity for a great military establishment, and Fox, instead of producing the expected compliment on a military establishment being the true safeguard of Liberty, answered morosely that a great military establishment was *toujours odieux* and that every Government which existed by force was *oppressif et mauvais*. This was not an encouraging beginning, but the First Consul persevered with compliments and they conversed amicably, until Bonaparte, still anxious to please, began to abuse Windham and Pitt. Lady Bessborough recorded for the benefit of Lord Granville the end of that conversation as she heard it from Lord Robert: 'Buonaparte questioned Mr. Fox concerning Windham, saying he understood his talents were mediocre, and that he was an unfeeling, unprincipled man. Mr. F. interrupted him, and said: "On vous a trompé. Il n'y a pas sur la terre un être plus noble, plus humain, plus rempli d'honneur et de talents que Monsr. Windham, intégre jusqu'au scrupule, jamais sa conduite ne dément ses sentiments, j'ai le malheur de ne pas m'accorder avec lui sur tous les points, mais je l'estime et je le revère." B. did not like it, but after a little frown and pause, said:

"C'est très bien pour vous qui n'avez que quelques démêlés publiques. Mais pour moi je le déteste, lui et ce Pitt qui ont tous deux attenté à ma vie." Mr. Fox stared. Bte. went on saying he would have forgiven open enemies in the Cabinet or the field, but not cowardly attempts to destroy him, such as *subornéing* his own Guards, and setting on foot the Infernal Machine. Mr. F. again with great warmth assur'd him he was deceiv'd, that Mr. Pitt and Windham, like every other Englishman, would shrink with horror from the idea of secret assassination. "Vous ne connaissez pas ce Pitt," said Buonaparte. "Oui je le connais," replied Mr. F., "assez du moins pour savoir qu'il est incapable d'une pareil action et je risquerois ma tête sur cette croyance." Buonaparte after a moment walk'd away in silence, and so they parted.'[1] Fox's own bulletin of that interview was 'Oh, he was very civil', and we may imagine him a little doubtful of the First Consul as a champion of liberty, and more than a little doubtful whether he was quite the sort of person whom he would wish to add to his friends.

He came home much impressed by his experiences, and, unlike other visitors to Paris, persuaded that Bonaparte wanted peace and was 'to the last degree' afraid of war with Britain. It was a little difficult to reconcile such a view with the proceedings of the First Consul during the peace—Piedmont and Elba annexed and Switzerland 'mediated'. And it was not easy to detect fear of war in the vehement protests from France against the refusal of our Government to suppress M. Peltier and his propagandist Ambigu, to expel emigrants from Jersey and to turn the Bourbon princes out of England. A little later the protests became even sharper against our continued occupation of

[1] Parisian manners had evidently not emerged from the revolutionary phase, for on another occasion Fox was obliged to intervene when Pitt was maligned in public. Madame Junot has described the scene: 'M. Fox change de physionomie avec une rapidité que l'on ne peut décrire. Ce n'était plus le tribun, le chef de l'opposition, c'était le frère de M. Pitt, le secourant de sa parole au milieu d'un cercle d'ennemis.'

Malta, contrary to the terms of the treaty, for the Government, confronted with the Consul's aggressive activity, had not been energetic in arranging the cession of Malta to the Order of St. John. The Peace of Amiens was manifestly in danger, and the prospect of war had its effect on the ferment of parties. Addington, with support from Tierney, Sheridan, and a few of the Whigs, was believed to want peace. Grenville, Canning, and the displaced Pittites who wanted to restore Pitt, were believed to be warlike. Pitt remained inscrutable. Would he support Addington as before, or attack him as a public danger when war was threatened, or remain aloof in convalescent secession? And in all these uncertainties what should an uncertain Opposition do?

Parliament met on the 16th of November, and Fox, without persuasion from his friends, attended 'for a very short time, I swear . . . not with any hope of dissuading the warlike, but for the chance of being of some use in encouraging those who are said to be pacific, especially the Ministers'. He expected to be 'abused for pacific language now, as I was ten years ago', and Mr. Creevey feared that his leader had been 'damned imprudent' in Paris, where he was said to have talked publicly of 'Liberty being *asleep* in France but *dead* in England'.

But Creevey's fears were not realized. Pitt remained at Bath and Fox's speech consisted of repeated protestations that peace could and should be preserved. 'His conduct', wrote Creevey delightedly, 'and his speech were, in my mind, in every respect *perfect*; and if he will let them be the models of his future imitation, he will keep in the Doctor and preserve peace. God continue Fox's prudence and Pitt's gout!'

Hopes of peace fell in the new year, when the *Moniteur* published a military report on the Levant which showed that expansion in the East was one, if not the first, of the French ambitions. Negotiations in Paris became more difficult, and on the 9th of March Fox supported the Govern-

ment in increasing the Navy and embodying the militia.
There followed Bonaparte's explosive interview with Lord
Whitworth, when the Consul, 'his countenance perfectly dis-
torted with passion', shouted his complaint at the ambassador to the horror of waiting diplomats. It was evident
that war was near, but Fox still believed that the Consul
wanted peace and that war might be avoided. He had no
wish to defend the invasion of Switzerland, which was 'no
doubt very disgusting, but there is no remedy'; nor could
we think of expelling the Bourbon princes to please republican France. But renewal of war would not save Switzerland or Piedmont, and the retention of Malta against the
terms of the treaty would everywhere put us in the wrong.

As a war minister Addington was clearly impossible, and
once more the question of Pitt's intentions became urgent.
He had crushed a clumsy intrigue by Canning and Lord
Malmesbury to organize a petition by his party for his
return. A little later Addington made a move by sending
Dundas, now Lord Melville, with a proposal that Pitt
should join a Cabinet headed by Lord Chatham, but the
conversation languished after a tentative preliminary, and
Pitt 'had not the curiosity to ask what I was to be'. The
distracted Prime Minister then himself sought an interview,
and found that Pitt was quite willing to return if the King
sent for him, but his return would bring Grenville and
Windham with him, and Addington himself might look
forward to dignified leisure as Speaker of the House of
Lords. The Cabinet, a little belatedly, asserted its dignity
in a repudiation of these terms, and Pitt acknowledged the
end of negotiations in a single sentence.

It was a difficult moment for Fox. He would have preferred to act with the Grenville group 'as men of spirit,
but the line they have taken with respect to war, and their
profound desire for reinstating Pitt, made any junction with
them impracticable for the present'. As to Addington, his
'folly and hollowness . . . is, you know, my aversion'; but
it might be unpleasantly necessary to support the Doctor

in the cause of peace. In that case Sheridan's line would be doubtful, and Moira and Tierney would certainly join a new opposition.

In France there was no lack of decision. An ultimatum was sent on the question of Malta, and on the 12th of May Lord Whitworth left Paris. Four days later Lord Hawkesbury ('convulsed with fear and could hardly articulate from the violence of his agitation') moved consideration of the message announcing the failure of negotiations. The Prime Minister on that day turned tragedy into farce by appearing in the full dress of the Windsor uniform, and the House hardly needed Sheridan's reference to 'a sheep in wolf's clothing' to salute him with a burst of laughter. 'We are now actually at war,' wrote Grey, 'and we can only say God send us a safe deliverance! which under such Ministers can hardly be hoped.'

CHAPTER XIV

1803-1806

Britain was again at war, but it was now a very different war. No longer were ministers in the happy position of selecting allies for subsidy from the kings in Europe and discussing alternative proposals for indemnities and annexations. Without a single ally Britain had now to await the attack of Bonaparte's army with its already legendary reputation. For the next two years the country was to live in almost daily expectation of invasion, with the Armée d'Angleterre encamped along the French coast, their ferry boats ready for the crossing, and their squadrons waiting in the ports to slip past the blockade and command the Channel for the few hours which the Army needed. Bonaparte's real plan remains unknown; and Fox was among those who believed that the French would 'find it very difficult to get out of their ports, and still more so to reach England and land in safety; and upon these difficulties my boldness rests'. But such hesitating confidence depended entirely on the supremacy of the Navy, and not every one felt happy about a navy controlled by the Doctor. It was indeed difficult in the crisis to avoid a dismal comparison between leaders on the opposite shores of the Channel, between Addington, ridiculous in Windsor uniform, and Bonaparte, already a figure of awe in the redingote grise; between the imperturbable Talleyrand and the unhappy Lord Hawkesbury; between the soldiers whose names now rang across Europe—Berthier, Massèna, Lannes, Murat, Augereau, Marmont, Duroc—and the less inspiring products of seniority and patronage—Dundas, Dalrymple, Cathcart—who would withstand them. It was not a reassuring comparison.

The debate on the renewal of the war began on the 23rd of May and Fox, with less than his usual laments, came to London to define his views. Simple living at St. Ann's Hill had improved his health, and Creevey found himself

'perfectly astonished at the vigour of body, the energy of mind,
the innocent playfulness and happiness of Fox. The contrast between him and his old associates is the most marvel-
lous thing I ever saw—they having all the air of shattered
debauchees, of passing gaming, drinking, sleepless nights,
whereas the old leader of the gang might really pass for the
pattern and the effect of domestic good order.' Leigh Hunt
as a child saw him 'fat and jovial' in these days of his
return to Parliament looking 'something quaker-like as to
dress, with plain-coloured clothes, a broad round hat, white
waistcoat, and, if I am not mistaken, white stockings', as
he stood in Parliament Street 'making two young gentlemen laugh heartily at something which he seemed to be relating'. Pitt had also emerged from his retreat for the debate,
and Creevey was relieving his feelings by recording that
'this damned fellow Pitt' was 'done'. He certainly looked
ill, if we may trust Creevey, who reported cheerfully that
'his face is no longer red, but yellow; his looks are dejected;
his countenance I think much changed and fallen and every
now and then he gives a hollow cough. . . . I saw no expression but melancholy on the fellow's face—princes of the
blood passing him without speaking to him, and, as I could
fancy an universal sentiment in those around him that *he
was done. . . .*' It was assumed that he would support the
war; but would he also support Addington? Canning
believed that he would '*fire over the heads* of the Government—i.e. not to blame or praise them, but to support the
war measures', and he would then return to Walmer.

The debate quickly disposed of Creevey's hope that Pitt
was 'done'. Taking his place on the third bench on the
Government side amid general acclamation of 'Pitt! Pitt!'
he proceeded to fire over the heads of the cowering ministers
one of his greatest speeches calling the nation to war. Its
effect on all parties was prodigious. 'Detesting the dog,
as I do,' wrote Sheridan to Lady Bessborough, 'I cannot
withhold this just tribute to the scoundrel's talents.' He
was answered on the next day by Fox in a speech worthy

of the occasion. 'The truth is', wrote Fox later, 'that it was my best.' Fox made it clear that there could be no question of approving the conduct of France during the peace. The invasion of Switzerland was a 'violent act of injustice', and the treatment of Holland was 'an act no less despicable for its meanness, than hateful for its atrocity'. As to the First Consul's complaints, we should never abandon the liberty of the press to please a foreign country, nor would we expel the Bourbon refugees. 'No one, perhaps—and I hope not to be suspected at this time of bearing hard upon an unfortunate and fallen family, when I say it—no one, perhaps, politically speaking, has less respect than I have for the house of Bourbon; yet I am ready to declare, that for that family, nay, for the worst prince of that family, if among them there should be a bad one, I should be ready to draw my sword and go to war, rather than comply with a demand to withdraw from him the hospitality to which he had trusted.' There could be no excuse for the conduct of France, but Ministers had left Holland and Switzerland to their fate, and were now putting their country in the wrong by allowing the question of Malta, in which England was in default, to be the occasion of war. The minority was 67, and they included Wilberforce.

A few days later Fox, with Pitt's support, made a last effort for peace with the Tsar as mediator. But he had little hope. 'Ministers', he wrote to Lord Holland, 'gave in so handsomely to my proposition of the Russian mediation, that many people conceive hopes from it; and so should I if it were not for two reasons; first, that "non vuolsi cosi colà"; next, that the business requires some address, and, above all, some moderation—of neither of which I see any traces in the conduct of these people.' It was not in any case a good moment for mediation, for on the day of Fox's speech the First Consul arrested all British subjects in France.

The summer passed with the enrolment of volunteers against invasion, Emmet rebellion in Dublin, and increasing ridicule of the wretched Addington. He and his family seemed to exist as a target for satire, and even the prudent erection of blockhouses on the Thames was turned against them:

> If *blocks* can from danger deliver,
> Two places are safe from the French:
> The one is the mouth of the river,
> The other the Treasury Bench.

It was evident that outside the Court the Doctor had few friends. 'Si ce Ministère dure,' remarked the Tsar's ambassador, 'la Grande-Bretagne ne durera pas.' But the future was obscure. 'The House of Commons', wrote Fox in June, 'continues still divided into three, or rather four distinct parties; for Pitt separated himself both from Addington and the Grenvilles. From the divisions the result would be —that there are Pittites 58, Grenvillites 36, Foxites 69, and all the rest Ministerial. Things cannot long continue in this precise state; but for this session I think they will; and how they will jumble afterwards God knows.'

The session ended in August with Pitt, a conscientious Lord Warden, at Walmer drilling his volunteers and providing gunboats for coastal defence, while Fox at St. Ann's Hill faced the problems and anxieties of English farming. His agricultural difficulties were many, for part of his 'potato oats' had 'totally failed, owing as they say to a damned worm of some sort'; his Swedish turnips were coming up well, but they were encumbered by weeds, 'and particularly of what we call Catlock, which unskilful hoers cannot distinguish from the turnips themselves'; his rye grass had 'got quite the better' of his clover, and 'some croakers talk of a *silver blight*, which I never heard of before'.

Alarms of French landings were frequent. In August it was rumoured that the French transports were out, and 'all women, etc.', were ordered from the coast. Lady Malmesbury was suggesting that women should be armed for the defence of their homes ('Amongst the lower ranks their physical strength is certainly sufficient'). Lord Minto found everywhere the strongest expectation of invasion, and could not 'remember in my life a season of such real and well founded anxiety'. This constant alarm of invasion was among the chief influences in the politics of 1803, and it accounts for the surprising transformation in the structure of parties which was then beginning. There was no panic, but the urgencies of national defence overshadowed politics. The alarms increased as the year went on, and in December the false report of a French landing on the Border enabled Lord Napier's butler to announce imperturbably that 'supper is on the table—*and*—the beacons are lighted on the hills', while Lady Minto and her daughters 'sat at the window and watched the fires with sick hearts'. A succession of such alarms over a year taught the country to think in terms of invasion.

Preparations for defence were energetic but hardly reassuring, for the Government had no arms for the volunteers who were waiting to be drilled. Lord Buckingham's infantry was, as he frequently pointed out, unequipped, and Fox in August observed to Grey that 'here we have Volunteers in plenty learning on the green to *stand easy*, and so forth; but not a single weapon, gun, or pike among them all, and this they call training!' It was known that Pitt was disquieted, and a letter of Lord Granville Leveson Gower reports his chief's gloomy appreciation of the country's danger and the efforts of ministers to save it:

'He says that if they had merely been passive, if they would have allowed the country to save itself, it might have been made impregnable, but that the Ministers have by their inconceivable blunders been actively thwarting every measure which could contribute to the Salvation of the Kingdom: . . . that Spain they have allowed to bring home all her Treasures from South America to supply France with money to carry into Execution her Plans of Invasions: that they never thought of blocking up the mouth of the Seine, which is the most convenient place for the building and fitting out vessels, till it had been completely filled with every sort of Naval Store Bonaparte could wish for. He says also that the dilatoriness and blunders of the Admiralty can only be conceived by those who live upon the Coast. . . .'

No one except the King had any confidence in Addington for the defence of England, but it was not easy for a leader of Opposition to decide what line he should follow; and in the days before Parliament opened Fox anxiously discussed four alternatives with Grey. They might support Ministers; but that was impossible, because to speak a word in their praise 'would be a base falsehood on our part'. Or they might 'attack past and present conjointly'; but that would be 'sacrificing our ease for nothing', and it might even strengthen the hands of the King. Or perhaps they might succeed in forming a party 'against the Court, composed of the old and new opposition'. Or they might do nothing. The last course was the most attractive. But was it not their duty to try the third? Although 'nothing will induce Pitt to make the *saut perilleux* and jump into opposition', yet some of his supporters might 'by degrees, make up their minds to be in opposition without him'. Fox had in fact an uneasy feeling that the pleasant days of secession were now ending.

But in spite of his forebodings nothing would induce Pitt to declare his opposition to the Doctor, and when the session opened in November the Government was still arousing Mr. Creevey's contempt: 'When there is anything like a general attack on them, they look as if they felt it all; they blush and look at one another in despair; they make no fight; or, if they offer to defend themselves, no one listens but to laugh at them. When the House is empty and their enemies are scattered, they rally and fall in a body upon Windham, call him all kinds of names, and adopt all kinds of the most unfounded misrepresentations of his sentiments. Upon these occasions they are quite altered men; they talk loud and long, and cheer one another enough to pull the house down.'

But if Pitt would do nothing his friends were not content

to remain passive. The ever-exuberant Canning had his
hopes of uniting Pitt and Fox in Opposition, and he was
making an approach to Fox at third hand through Lord
Granville Leveson Gower and Lady Bessborough. But it
was difficult even for Lady Bessborough to extract anything definite from Fox. He meant to avoid politics as long
as the case for secession remained unaltered, 'but if there
is any good to be done, *alors comme alors*'. The confederates
felt sure that joint action could be arranged with immense
advantage to the country if they could only overcome 'Mr.
Fox's indolence'. But he was, as Lady Bessborough found,
'*un enfant difficile à pateliner*', and it was quite impossible
to induce him to make the first move. There was no hope
of its being made by Pitt.

Meanwhile Lord Grenville and his friends were at work
independently. Alarms of invasion were increasing, for it
was now known that, in spite of the blockade, 2,000 boats
for the crossing had been collected, and at Boulogne 100,000
men were waiting to cross. Lord Grenville had little in
common with the Foxites; the causes of Liberty and Reform
had no attraction for him. But he was, as Fox discovered,
'a very direct man', and, when he had decided that a new
grouping of parties was necessary to save the country, he
took steps to bring it about. By the end of the year he had
made up his mind, and he wrote to Pitt inviting him to join
forces with Fox, turn out the 'manifestly incapable' Government, and replace it by 'an administration comprehending
as large a proportion as possible of the weight, talents and
character to be found in public men of all descriptions, and
without any exception'. For such an alliance 'co-operation'
seemed a more attractive word than 'coalition'. The answer
was a refusal, and Grenville, intent on his purpose, opened
negotiations with Fox. The intermediary was his younger
brother, Thomas, who had never ceased to frequent the
Whigs, and the proposal was direct and unequivocal. It
was an important moment, for the discussions involved not
only Grenville and his family connexion, but some of the

Whigs—Fitzwilliam, Carlisle, Spencer, Windham—who had with the Duke of Portland unwillingly transferred allegiance and would now return enthusiastically to the fold. Fox at once asked the advice of Fitzpatrick and Grey, with a clear indication of his own view:

'There was an openness and appearance of cordiality in the manner of making the proposal that much pleases me. Upon the subject of Pitt there was no reserve; it was stated that he, for himself, peremptorily refused entering into anything that could be called opposition, and that . . . all political connexion between them was off. . . . I own I lean very much to a junction—but then, what they say is true, that it is idle to look for the full effect of it unless both you and I attend; the inconvenience of this to both of us is certainly very great, but is it not perhaps right to sacrifice our convenience?'

But Grey hesitated: 'They are certainly able men: their conduct is direct and open; we agree with them in opinion both as to the character and measures of the present Administration; and the overture which they have made, appears from what you say, well calculated to inspire confidence.

'But on the other hand, their opposition has appeared to proceed rather from personal disappointment than from public principle; they are extremely unpopular, and it is not till they have failed, first, in their endeavours to set up Pitt as the only man who can govern the Country, and next to gain the Country and inflame it in support of a War, which they hoped to conduct, that they have recourse to us.'

On the whole Grey thought it wise to answer 'expressing a general inclination to support' but not committing them to 'a regular and systematic attendance', and Fox, against his better judgement, agreed that the alliance should be informal.

The mind of Pitt in these transactions remained a mystery to all men and a source of despair to his friends. 'They say', wrote Fox, 'that P. has a notion that these Ministers must

go, and that, in that case, he may return to power, without
the odium at Court of having been in Opposition; I cannot
think he can be weak enough to have such a hope, "but
Love will hope where reason would despair" and Sancho
Panza could never quite give up the idea of his island after
he had discovered the vanity and illusion of his master's
plan.' Pitt's own explanation, as revealed to Lord Malmesbury in conversation a few days later, does nothing to solve
the mystery, but it throws some light on the way in which
the Pilot proposed to weather the storm of 1804. He believed
that the crisis was acute and that the ministers were incom-
petent, but, after reflecting 'maturely and leisurely', he had
decided 'that in all simple and plain questions it was his
resolution to support the Government; but when Government omitted anything he thought the state of the country
required to be done, or did it weakly and inefficiently, he
then should deliver his sentiments clearly and distinctly, but
not even then in a spirit of opposition, since he would never
do it till he had ascertained Government would persist in
what he condemned, and not adopt what he thought essentially necessary'. It was a surprising plan of action from a
statesman who had eight years' experience in the conduct
of war.

No doubt the King's health had its influence on the negotiations, for insanity had returned after a chill in the middle
of February, and there seemed to be every prospect of a
regency with Fox as minister. Pitt was loyally anxious to
avoid any action which might affect the King's recovery, and
going into opposition might on these grounds be an action
to be avoided. But it seemed to the agonized Canning, when
he discussed matters with Lady Hester Stanhope, a short-
sighted view: 'I think he has thrown away the greatest
situation that ever Man had offered to him—by not acced-
ing to the proposal made to him by Ld. G. etc. Had he done
that a fortnight ago, there would not have been at this
moment the *possibility* of a New Government being formed,
not only without him, but without him at the head.'

Once he had faced the decision, Fox returned to politics with his old energy, although, as his occasional laments to his nephew show, he could not recover his taste for it: 'I dislike it to a degree you can hardly conceive, but I feel it is right, and resolve to do it handsomely, and therefore make it a rule not even to grumble, only to you who are so far off I may.' His writing was suspended with Monmouth's execution, on which he hoped that he had 'not made as bungling a piece of work with him as did the hangman'. Much of his reading had to go the way of the history, but he made unwillingly an exception in favour of his friend Lord Lauderdale's work on Public Wealth, and was even inveigled into correspondence on the subject, with a characteristic outburst on economists and their terminology:

'One of my grand objections to this most nonsensical of all sciences is that none of its definitions are to me intelligible. Your notions (I do not mean yours only, but *vous autres*) of value seem to me stark nonsense. You use that as a positive term which never can be other than a relative term. We grammarians are much wiser; we say a thing is valuable, i.e. capable of being valued or compared to some other thing. But we have no substantive to express value; we say such a thing is worth a shilling, or a pot of porter, etc. . . . I cannot leave this subject without noticing your constant use of the word *supplant* where we would say *supply the place of* or *be a substitute for*. I remarked it the more because it occurred to me how unfortunate it would be, if, on recommending a Regency, you should have said that your intention was to *supplant* the personal exercise of the royal functions.'

The new alliance was quickly effective, and early in April Addington sent a despairing message to Pitt, with the discouraging result which he might have expected. Pitt would, if invited, put his views before the King, but not before Mr. Addington; and in due course, through the medium of Lord Eldon, an indication was conveyed to His Majesty that Mr. Pitt now found it his duty to oppose the

Government. This belated support was not without inconvenience to the 'co-operation', for Grenville complained
that Pitt 'does not seem to know his own mind for two
days together', and Fox was 'worried and disconcerted by
always having to pursue a concurrence which he never
obtains'. But on Addington with his falling majority it was
decisive, and on the 29th of April Addington resigned.

The King asked for Pitt's suggestions in writing, and
Pitt replied with a memorandum, sent through Lord Eldon,
suggesting a ministry to include Fox and Grenville. The
reply, so far as concerned Fox, was an expression of the
King's astonishment that Mr. Pitt 'should one moment
harbour the thought of bringing such a man before his
Royal notice'. It was accompanied by a note to the Lord
Chancellor suggesting that Pitt would no longer seek an
audience but probably would 'rather prepare another essay
containing as many empty words and little information as
the one he had before transmitted'. This was discouraging,
but Pitt respectfully pressed for his audience, and on the
7th of May he was received. It was an unfortunate moment
for such an interview, for the King was in one of his worst
moods of intermittent sanity. Only a few months before
that interview Ministers had with difficulty dissuaded him
from opening his Speech from the Throne with the surprising words, 'My Lords, and Peacocks of the House of Commons', and, only a few days after it, he is said to have
greeted his subjects with cheerful cries of 'Hot buns!' from
the window of his coach in Bond Street. As was customary
with him in that condition, his mind was unusually suspicious and, for political purposes, unusually acute. Pitt,
with all honesty, put his case for Fox and the Grenvilles,
and secured with much difficulty an assent to the return of
the Grenvilles. But never Fox. He might perhaps be made
an ambassador, but in the Cabinet never. 'Never', remarked
Pitt afterwards, 'in any conversation I have had with him
in my life has he so baffled me.' The refusal was no surprise
to Fox. He had already declared that he had no ambition

for office, and he had written to Thomas Grenville that 'he was sure the King would exclude him; but that this ought not on any account to prevent the Grenvilles from coming in, and that, as far as his influence went, it should not prevent his own friends'. To Leveson Gower he explained that he was 'too old to care now about office, but I have many friends who for years have followed me. I shall advise them now to join Government, and I trust Pitt can give them places.'

Fox had said precisely what he meant, and Pitt thankfully availed himself of the opportunity. But not one of the New Opposition, Foxite or Grenvillite, would desert Fox. Grey, intended by Pitt to be Secretary at War, declared that 'no earthly consideration would make me accept office without Fox', and Grenville, that very direct man, declined to become 'parties to a system of Government which is to be formed at such a moment as the present on a principle of exclusion'. Pitt decided to proceed with such ministers as he could get, 'though I think my health such that it may cost me my life'. The result was a Cabinet, half of it Addingtonian , 'eked out', as Grenville remarked, 'with Roses and Dundases'.

Across the Channel the Government had also changed, but the new régime would lack neither efficiency nor precision. On the 18th of May the First Consul was proclaimed Emperor.

The remainder of the session was a severe trial to Pitt. His ministry was manifestly feeble, and he was himself far too ill to bear the burden of government alone. The Opposition groups were not displeased with the turn of events. 'In summa', wrote Fox, 'nothing could have fallen out more to my mind than what has happened: the party revived and strengthened, Pitt lowered, and, what is of more consequence in my view, the cause of *Royalism* (in the bad sense of the word) lowered too.' And Creevey, who had loudly deplored the return of Pitt, decided in June that 'considering we have certainly been out-jockeyed by the villain Pitt, we are doing famously. Pitt, I think, is in a damnable dilemma; his character has received a cursed blow from the appearance of puzzle in his late conduct. . . .'

There seemed for a moment to be some faint hope of peace. When Livingston, the United States minister, arrived in London full of his pacificatory conversations in Paris with Joseph Bonaparte and Talleyrand, Fox and Grey at once conducted him to Pitt, who received him with civility; but his proposals for mediation were nebulous, and Pitt was probably right in his view that 'if France had any serious intention of putting an end to the war, the new Emperor would have found some less exceptionable channel of communication. . . .' The new Emperor, untrammelled by questions of party politics, was in fact engaged on a project of rallying the fleets of Toulon and Rochefort to the Channel. 'Let us be masters of the Channel for six hours and we are masters of the world!' It was in the summer of Napoleon's invasion medal, *frappé à Londres en 1804*, and it was most unlikely that the new Emperor had any thought of peace.

Autumn passed in a crescendo of volunteer drilling and the hurried construction of the curious buildings known as martello towers for the defence of the south coast. The year ended gloomily for the Government. Spain declared war, and Pitt felt bound to make a tentative offer of a seat in the Cabinet to the despised Addington. Opposition spirits were rising. They no longer believed in invasion, and they had regained with the Grenvilles some of the strength which Burke had taken from them. The return of Windham, Fitzwilliam, and Carlisle was an immense gain, although the party could not hope to regain its old strength either in votes or in power. For the Duke of Portland would stay where he was, and Sheridan was no longer the Sheridan of the Begum days. He had struggled nobly for Ireland and for Parliamentary reform, but he was closely allied to the Prince, and Holland House was full of rumours suggesting that he was no longer a loyal Foxite. Probably they had no better foundation than other rumours proceeding

from Holland House, but Fox suspected him of leaning
unduly towards war. Grey was, of course, a tower of
strength, but could they count on him to attend? The
secession was ended, but he was still difficult to move.
'Opposition', wrote Fox to him in December, '*seems* now
restored, at least to what it was before the Duke of Portland's desertion, and the other adverse circumstances of
those times. Mind, I say *seems*, for if *you* stay away, it will
be very far from being so; and whatever is gained, will be
thought by all, and most certainly by me, a bad exchange
for you. . . . Do, for God's sake, make up your mind to one
unpleasant effort, and come for the first two months at
least of the session. . . . I love idleness so much and so dearly,
that I have hardly the heart to say a word against it; but
something is due to one's station in life, something to friendship, something to the country. . . .'

Such an appeal could not be ignored, and Grey came down
disconsolately from Northumberland to find the hapless
Addington, his terms accepted, in the Cabinet as Viscount
Sidmouth. It was an accession of numbers rather than
of strength, and it did not quell the rising hopes of the
Opposition. But Pitt, even with the feeblest colleagues,
was impregnable in debate, and withstood Grey's harryings
on the production of correspondence with Spain and Sheridan's attack on the Additional Forces Bill. In one division
he voted with Fox, when, against his advice, Wilberforce
again moved for Abolition, and found that he could now
rely upon the vote but not upon more active support from
his friend.

The first blow to the Government came from within.
Dundas, Lord Melville, was now Pitt's only colleague of
first-rate ability, and in March a Commission of Naval Inquiry in its Tenth Report charged him with misapplying
public money. The Opposition saw their chance; the Cabinet
was divided; and on the 9th of April ended that fatal debate
when Wilberforce's conscience impelled him to speak and
vote with the Opposition, and the Speaker 'deathly white',

after an agonizing hesitation of ten minutes, gave his casting vote on the same side. It was victory of a kind least attractive to Fox, and his feelings, when the vote was declared, and Pitt pressed down his 'little cocked hat' to hide his tears, while elated Whigs yelled triumph, cannot have been pleasant. He had the strongest distaste for the investigation of scandals, as Creevey found a week later when he tried to involve the Opposition in an inquiry into some rumour affecting the financial probity of Pitt himself. 'Could the most pertinacious derider of Fox's political folly', wrote the angry little Whig, 'have dared to conceive that Fox on such an occasion should acquit Pitt of all corruption, and should add likewise this sentiment to his opinion, that to have so detected him in corruption would have made him (Fox) the most miserable of men?'

It was a deadly blow to the Government, for it meant not only the loss of Melville but a quarrel with the Addington group, for Pitt, instead of reshuffling his cabinet in such a way as to promote the expectant Brother Hiley or Brother Bragge, decided to fill the vacancy at the Admiralty by appointing Sir Charles Middleton. This veteran, disrespectfully referred to by Creevey as a superannuated Methodist, could contribute to public life the ripe experience of some eighty years. The threatened resignations were at last withdrawn on an undertaking, which might perhaps have been taken for granted, that the octogenarian's appointment should be regarded as temporary. It was perhaps fortunate for the Opposition that the Government was then in such adversity, for Fox had encouraged a deputation of Irish delegates to re-open the case for Catholic Emancipation, and he had called upon the Opposition to support their petition in Parliament. It was characteristic of him that he should regard this move as 'the best possible thing for the country and ourselves'. It was a generous declaration of principle for a cause which then seemed hopeless, but in sordid terms of party warfare it was not helpful.

Diplomats had worked hard during that busy session.

There were conversations between Pitt and M. de Novosilt-zoff in London, more difficult negotiations between Lord Granville Leveson Gower and Prince Adam Czartorisky in St. Petersburg, and in April a treaty of prospective alliance was signed. It depended for its effect upon the accession of Austria, which remained improbable, until Napoleon, by annexing the Republic of Genoa and crowning himself King of Italy, offered such shocks to the dignity and security of Vienna that on the 9th of August Count Stadion, in return for the now customary subsidy, pledged his country to the Third Coalition. From the first moment Fox saw no hope in this new venture. 'I suppose', he wrote to Lord Lauderdale, 'we shall have to pay enormously. I know our Allies have said £5,000,000 will by no means do. . . . I think the most probable event is the success of the French and a second treaty of Campo Formio in a few months. . . .'

The session ended with the final resignation of Lord Sidmouth and his supporter, Lord Buckinghamshire, on Pitt's absolute refusal to find places for the minor Addingtonians. The new division increased the political uncertainty. For a moment it seemed that 'yelping underlings', as Lady Bessborough described some of the wirepullers, might induce Fox to ally himself with the displaced Addingtonians. He certainly played with the idea, but only in the form of admitting the Doctor to Opposition. There were, he believed, 180 'supporters of the Chancellor of the Exchequer for the time being', 150 supporters of the Opposition, 60 Pittites, and 60 Addingtonians. The first group might expect to lose members who took a gloomy view of the King's prospects of recovery, and the Opposition from the 'increasing weight of Carlton House' might expect to gain. On this calculation Pitt must be driven to surrender. 'And yet', reflected Fox, 'it does sometimes come across me (and I wish others would not quite forget it) that the Ministry with which this very Pitt set out in the year '84, was in all respects as weak and contemptible as the present.' He was quite ready to

discuss an alliance with Pitt, but it would be now necessary
to protect the Government against the inclusion of some of
those Government supporters who were 'properly speaking
the *âmes damnées* of the Court of Corruption'.

Pitt did not leave them long in doubt. He knew that
neither his majority nor his health could endure, and in
September he once more sought leave from the King to
negotiate for a united Government. The King was at Weymouth, where his health was believed to be vastly improved.
He assured his Minister that he had done well in the past
session, and that 'there existed no necessity whatever' for
agreement with the Opposition. Further discussion produced, according to one version, the statement that he
'would rather risk a civil war than admit Mr. Fox to his
councils'. Whether Pitt could have had his way by threatening to resign, and whether such a threat would have driven
the King mad, are matters of conjecture. It is known only
that he accepted the King's decision, and returned to London to bear the burden alone. 'It was enough to kill a man,'
said Lady Hester Stanhope, 'it was murder.'

The event was not delayed. On the 3rd of November it
was known that Mack, that ingenious Austrian, who had
so greatly impressed Ministers in 1793 as the man to beat
the French, had surrendered to Napoleon at Ulm with an
army of 30,000. It was a day of gloom, but not of despair,
for the Russians still remained. Four days later came the
news of Trafalgar, and the danger of invasion was over.
And on the 9th the failing voice of the Prime Minister was
heard at the Guildhall in the last and most memorable of
his speeches:

'I return you many thanks for the honour you have done
me; but Europe is not to be saved by any single man.
England has saved herself by her exertions, and will, as I
trust, save Europe by her example.'

There was a respite of a few weeks before a December sun
struggling through the morning fog showed Napoleon the
field of Austerlitz.

Il va, tachant de gris l'état major vermeil;
L'armée est une mer; il attend le soleil;
Il le voit se lever du haut d'un promontoire
Et, d'un sourire, il met ce soleil dans l'histoire.

That greatest of Napoleonic victories was the end of Pitt's coalition and the end of Pitt. For a week or two he struggled on wearing his Austerlitz look; then his health collapsed, and on the 23rd of January he died, lamenting, as well he might, the misfortunes of his country.

CHAPTER XV
1806

'THE trumpet's silver sound is still, the warder silent on the hill.' The death of Pitt was, outside his immediate friends, unexpected, and it came with a shock of dismay to a country still attuned to the alarm of invasion. But among politicians a change of Government was by no means unexpected. Ministers had long realized that at any moment a Regency might turn them out, and, since Sidmouth's resignation, the hopes of the Opposition had risen. It was manifest that with the removal of Pitt the Opposition must now come in; there was no possible alternative. But once more the King laboured frantically to escape from Fox.

'The first day', wrote Lady Bessborough, 'the shock was so great that affliction only was to be met with, and stopp'd even the clamour of reports and conjectures which were only whisper'd. Friday people began giving lists of Administration; Ld. Castlereagh, Lord Wellesley, and the Pope,[1] were successively talked of. . . . Friday night Lord Hawkesbury went to the D. of Pd. and was closeted for two hours with him, (two such heads could not fail of producing great wisdom): in the morning the D. of York and one of his Brothers also closeted the poor old Duke, who is half dead in consequence. Lord Hawkesbury was shut up with the King for three hours, and it is everywhere reported is Minister. . . . Since I wrote this Lord Hawkesbury has seen Bess and own'd to her that he was Minister for two hours, but had not the courage to go on: that Lord Mulgrave press'd the King to let them try. But this plan was given up, and he would not even hint what was to supply its place. . . .'

But it all availed nothing, and on the 27th of January

---

[1] Canning.

Lord Grenville was invited to form a Government. Lord Grenville, direct as ever, came at once to the point with 'I can do nothing without consulting Mr. Fox', to which the King, with apparent composure, answered 'I suppose so, and I meant it to be so', leaving it to conjecture whether the same firmness on the part of Pitt in 1804 might not have achieved the same result without unduly deranging His Majesty's mind.

The process of joint cabinet building began. The difficulties were in any case great, and tempers had been slightly ruffled by an unfortunate incident during the interregnum. A Yorkshire member, Mr. Lascelles, consulting no man, put down a motion for a public funeral to Pitt and a memorial 'to the memory of that excellent statesman'. The words were those used for Chatham's funeral, and, once notice had been given, nothing would induce the friends of Pitt to accept any alteration. Fox was most anxious to avoid discord, but he felt bound in the debate on the motion to speak the truth. He could not now declare that Pitt was an excellent statesman, when most of his political life had been spent in saying the opposite:

'If the mark of public respect were such as did not compromise my public duty in the compliance, no person would join in it more cheerfully and eagerly than I would. . . . But it is a different thing to be called upon to confer honours upon Mr. Pitt as an "excellent statesman". It cannot be expected that I should so far forget the principles I have uniformly professed as to subscribe to the condemnation of those principles by agreeing to the motion before the House.'

A week later, when it was proposed that Pitt's debts should be paid from public funds, he was able to prove that he meant what he said: 'Never in my life did I give a vote with more satisfaction than I shall do this night in support of the motion.'

Early in February the Ministry of All the Talents was completed:

Prime Minister and First Lord of the Treasury	Lord Grenville
Lord Chancellor	Lord Erskine
Foreign Secretary and Leader of the House of Commons	Mr. Fox
Home Secretary	Lord Spencer
Secretary of State for War and Colonies	Mr. Windham
First Lord of the Admiralty	Mr. Grey
Chancellor of the Exchequer	Lord Henry Petty
Lord President of the Council	Lord Fitzwilliam
Lord Privy Seal	Lord Sidmouth

Among minor appointments Fitzpatrick became Secretary at War, and Sheridan, with a certain acrimony on both sides, was made Treasurer of the Navy. The Foxite Whigs had their full share, but the inclusion of the Doctor brought its measure of indignation and scorn. 'We must admit the Dr. and all his people,' wrote Lady Bessborough furiously. 'Why? Is he grown wiser or better than when it was reckon'd disgrace to sit on the same side of the House with him? Oh no, but it will conciliate the K., and he commands 40 votes. Oh voilà bien de quoi renier tout ce qu'on a pensé, tout ce qu'on a dit pendant sa vie entière!' Canning supposed that 'the Doctor is like the measles—everybody has him once', but the real explanation was confided by Fox to his nephew. He was afraid to exclude any substantial group to which the King might turn, and he took in Sidmouth because it would 'stop up all the earths'.

In a coalition government it is impossible to distribute posts without disappointing the hopes of many deserving candidates, and the difficulties are increased when one of the coalescent parties has looked forward to office after long years of opposition. Fox had to refuse many old friends whose claims were strong. 'It is a damned thing,' he had to tell Lord Lauderdale, 'but it could not be otherwise. I saw it would not do and one must not be impatient.' He

Y

disliked refusing, and it was painful to him that his accession to power must be accompanied by so many disappointments. 'Your note', he wrote to the Duchess of Devonshire,
'has distressed me to the greatest degree. . . . Can I give
up Jack Townshend, or Courtenay, or Fitzpatrick, or Lord
Robert for any of these young lords ? Indeed, indeed, my
friends are hard upon me.' Apart from the high offices he
took little interest in patronage, to the dismay of many of
his friends and relations who had looked forward to some
harmless little jobs. But his Aunt, Lady Sarah Napier, had
sufficient greatness of soul to make allowances even when
she could get nothing for her soldier sons, whose claims had
every merit to support them. 'I dare say it will be the old
story again,' she concluded, 'for I hear that C. Fox is so
thoroughly occupied with the *essential* Business of England,
viz. with Bonaparte, that he lets Lord Grenville take a
much larger share of loaves than belongs to him. It is very
much like Charles to be above the 2 dary business. I admire
him very much for it, tho' his friends will lose by it, not his
pressing friends, but I don't like to immitate *them*, and
I had rather be disappointed S. N. than the cormorant
Mrs. Bouverie, and I love C. the better for being duped to
the end of the chapter.'

He might be languid in patronage, but there was no lack
of energy in his other duties, and signs of his activity appeared from the first days of the new Government. He had
made up his mind that Catholic Emancipation must wait.
It could not be carried against the King by a divided
Cabinet, and he tried to persuade his Irish friends to defer
their Catholic petition. The Government would do for
them 'all that is consistent with existing bad laws'; they
would remove notoriously oppressive Justices of the Peace;
Fox himself would support the petition if the promoters
insisted on presenting it, but 'if we are beat, which may be
the case, you run the risk of a Ministry being formed on the
avowed principle of defeating your claims. . . .'

Foreign politics seemed even less hopeful than Irish. The

danger of invasion was certainly removed for the moment, but Pitt's Coalition was defeated, and there seemed to be no limit to Napoleon's conquests on land. Fox had made it clear—it was one of his terms of alliance—that there would be no question of surrender to France. But if peace without submission could be obtained, it would be folly to lose any possible chance of it. He soon had an opening for negotiation. Always the most accessible of ministers, he found himself one day conversing at the Foreign Office with a mysterious stranger ('*un quidam*'), who revealed to the horrified Minister that he had called to discuss arrangements for the murder of the Emperor Napoleon. The intruder was ignominiously ejected, and, after he had gone, Fox, reflecting that he had allowed a potential assassin to remain at large, wrote a letter of warning to his old friend, Talleyrand, now Prince of Benevento. Talleyrand answered with effusive compliment, and in spite of the King's criticisms, which were 'as unpleasant as possible', the correspondence developed into a discussion of peace. The Emperor, it appeared, desired peace and repose, and was willing to negotiate in the basis of the Treaty of Amiens. But the matter went badly from the beginning, and in April it seemed that negotiations would break down on the French claim to treat with Britain separately instead of jointly with Russia. Talleyrand gave way on this point and negotiations began on the basis of *uti possidetis*. But it soon became clear that Napoleon could not be trusted. He dismissed the principle of *uti possidetis* as *des formules latines*, and claimed that Sicily should be added to the kingdom of Naples. This was, of course, in Fox's view, out of the question. 'It is not so much the value of the point in dispute', he told Lord Holland, 'as the manner in which the French fly from their word, that disheartens me. It is not Sicily but the shuffling insincere way in which they act, that shows me they are playing a false game; and in that case it would be very imprudent to make any concessions which by possibility would be thought inconsistent with

our honour, or furnish our Allies with a plausible pretence
for suspecting, reproaching, or deserting us.' His tone in
the correspondence was quite in his old *fagôt d'épines*
manner, which had distressed Vergennes twenty years ago,
and the publication of one of his letters was greeted by
Windham as 'Mr. Fox's brilliant *war whoop*'. His firmness on the principles of international honesty did him
honour, for in April he warned the Prime Minister that he
could see nothing but disaster in the continuance of war:
'If Bonaparte does not by an attempt at invasion, or some
other great imprudence, give us an advantage, I cannot
but think this country inevitably and irretrievably ruined.
That is no reason for our quitting our stations, especially
as we took them with something like a certainty of the
evils I dread coming on; and yet to be Ministers at a moment
when the country is falling, and all Europe sinking, is a
dreadful situation, especially if we can make no great and
striking efforts for safety.'

But one great cause remained, in which a great and striking effort seemed possible. Pitt had allowed the Slave Trade
to survive in the Anti-Jacobin panic. Fox determined that
if he could do nothing else, he could and would remove the
obstruction which had for nearly twenty years defeated
Abolition. There were consultations with Wilberforce, delighted at the prospect of success, but evangelically distressed at Fox's remoteness from true religion ('Poor fellow, how melancholy his case! He has not one religious
friend or one who knows anything about it'); and it was
decided to proceed at once with a limited measure, prohibit-
ing importation in British ships to colonies annexed during
the war and colonies of a foreign country. The Bill was
introduced on the 31st of March, and under the compelling
guidance of Fox and Grenville passed both Houses without
difficulty. There remained no time in that session to introduce a Bill for complete abolition, but it was possible to commit Parliament beyond retreat, and on the 10th of June Fox
moved that the House should 'with all practicable expedi-

tion, proceed to take effectual measures for abolishing' the
African Slave Trade. It was one of his great occasions, and
he was worthy of it: 'If, during the almost forty years that
I have now had the honour of a seat in parliament, I had
been so fortunate as to accomplish that, and that only, I
should think I had done enough, and could retire from public
life with comfort, and conscious satisfaction, that I had done
my duty.' The House was with him, and they pledged themselves by 114 votes to 15 that the Slave Trade should be
abolished.

It was a heavy session and the burden of it fell on Fox.
At the Foreign Office he was working with an energy which
brought from the King the unusual testimonial that 'the
office had never been conducted in such a manner before'.
It was work of incessant anxiety in an endeavour, which
seemed almost hopeless, to save the country from destruction. As leader of the House he had the difficult task of
maintaining harmony among the rather discordant elements
which were united to support the Ministry of All the
Talents. There was also the troublesome business of Lord
Melville's impeachment, the scandal of the Princess and
the Delicate Investigation, and the embarrassing zeal of
Mr. Paull to discover matter for impeachment in the Indian
administration of Lord Wellesley, a zeal which was not
shared by ministers who could look back to an earlier investigation of Indian charges and the long wrangle of Warren
Hastings. It was a heavy burden for any man's strength,
and Fox no longer possessed his old toughness of constitution. In 1804 an unaccountable failure of health had driven
him to Cheltenham for a cure, and he was now visibly unfit
for continual strain.

To his public anxieties a personal sorrow was added. In
March the Duchess of Devonshire, 'the kindest heart in England' as he called her, who had made Devonshire House and
Chatsworth homes for him and the Whigs, died after long
days of illness and pain. The shock to Fox was extreme,
for she was among his most loyal friends, and friendship

meant more to him than almost anything in the world.
The Bishop of Down, the William Dickson who had walked
with him from Oxford when the watch was pledged at
Nettlebed, had died in 1804, but apart from Dickson and
Hare, who died in the same year, Fox had lost few of his old
friends. His will, made in 1804, contains a list of those whom
he regarded as his 'oldest connexion'—Lord Holland,
General Fox, General Fitzpatrick, Lord Robert Spencer,
Lord Fitzwilliam, Mr. Isaro, the Bishop of Down, Lord
John Townshend, Miss Fox, and Mrs. Bouverie—and al-
most all of them were alive and had been near him all his
life.

In May his health became worse with symptoms of dropsy,
which to any of his family were necessarily alarming. He
had some difficulty in walking, and he took the air in a bath-
chair pulled by his secretary, Trotter, while Prince Starem-
burg, the Austrian ambassador, walked beside them, bend-
ing low to hear his views on the prospects of Europe. It
became evident that the illness was serious, and the doctors
told him that his recovery would depend on complete withdrawal from work. There was some suggestion of a peerage
and a possible transfer of the Foreign Office to Lord Holland. But he would not give in even for his nephew's advancement: 'Don't think me selfish, young one. The Slave
Trade and Peace are two such glorious things, I can't give
them up, even to you. If I can manage them, I will then
retire.' A peerage in any case would be inacceptable: 'The
peerage, to be sure, seems the natural way, but that cannot
be. I have an oath in Heaven against it; I will not close
my politics in that foolish way, as so many have done
before me.'

He became worse in July, and early in August an operation was tried with no lasting success. Dropsy returned,
and he could no longer direct the Foreign Office, which in
his absence became involved in the strange adventure of
sending an armed mission under Lord Rosslyn and Lord St.
Vincent with instructions which included the rescue of the

Lavater's conclusions from his study of Fox's face:

'*Front.* Inépuisable : plus de richesse d'idées, et d'images, que je n'ai jamais vu peint sur *aucune physionomie au monde. Sourcils.* Superbes, regnants, dominants. *Nez.* Médiocre. *Les Yeux.* Remplis de génie, perçans, fascinants, magicques. *Les Joues.* Sensuels. *Bouche.* Pleine d'une volubilité surprenante et agréable ; et le bas du visage doux, affable, sociable.'

From the bust by NOLLEKENS *in the possession of* MRS. HENRY LASCELLES

Regent and royal family of Portugal from a French invasion. If Fox had been at the Foreign Office he might have
felt some doubt about that part of the plan which provided
that the shipping on the Tagus should be seized and 'saved'
from the French, if the Portuguese Regent, who was said
to be in a state of 'fearful acquiescence' and to feel the
'greatest horror of the sea', should be unwilling either to
defend his country or to escape to Brazil on Lord St.
Vincent's ships.

On the 17th of August he went to the Duke of Devonshire's Palladian villa at Chiswick as a break in his journey
to St. Ann's Hill. There another operation was tried, again
without success. He knew then that his recovery was uncertain, and he discussed with Lord Holland the arrangements to provide for his wife, ending characteristically with
'Now change the conversation, or read me the Eighth Book
of Virgil'. For a few days Lord Holland and Trotter read
to him, while fantastic remedies were tried, as he lay in
the little room looking on to the avenue, and his friends
—Fitzpatrick, Spencer, Townshend, Fitzwilliam—waited
anxiously for news, which was at once dispatched by relays of messengers to the Whig houses, where other friends
were anxiously waiting. He was troubled only by the
thought of his wife's sorrow, and he tried again and again
to comfort her as she sat by him in those hot days at the
beginning of September, which had so often been his happiest days of partridge shooting with his friends. On the
13th of September he died, trying to tell her that 'it don't
signify'.

The final scene followed nearly a month later, when the
streets were packed with a silent crowd to see Mr. Fox
carried through his constituency in the last of his Westminster Processions. In many ways it resembled his old
processions, with its alternation of bands and marshalmen,
banners and deputations, bannerols and trumpets, mourn-
ing peers and members, horsemen in cloaks, state carriages,
kettledrums. But instead of taking the old route to Covent

Garden and the hustings, they turned down Whitehall to a grave which was waiting in the Abbey by Chatham and Pitt.

.   .   .   .

The memorials and their inscriptions were in the flamboyant style of the processions. In Whig houses all over the country funereal urns and Nollekens busts were erected with inscriptions which outdid one another in celebrating the political and moral perfection of the dead leader. 'Beloved, esteemed, renowned, lamented' began Lord Robert, setting out a catalogue of virtues, public and private, which could hardly be credited in any human being. The others were in the same exalted strain, only Fitzpatrick on the urn at Woburn showing a real appreciation of his friend's life:

> A Patriot's even course he steered,
> Midst faction's wildest paths unmoved;
> By all who marked his mind revered,
> By all who knew his heart beloved.

It was natural that they should exaggerate beyond the utmost exaggeration of tombstones, for they felt the loss of such a friend as only he could be, and they felt that after a generation of waiting for power their leader had been taken from them at the moment when he was at last to show that their belief in his genius was well founded. It was natural that they should try to establish in marble the glory which they felt sure he was about to establish for himself, but it was natural also that their panegyric should provoke a reaction, in which critics would exaggerate in their turn. To a later generation Fox was presented chiefly as an attractive failure, and historians found it possible to sum up his life in the amazing ineptitude that 'he had three passions—women, play, and politics. Yet he never formed a creditable connexion with a woman; he squandered all his means at the gaming-table, and except for eleven months he was invariably in opposition.' Even Scott's famous appreciation in *Marmion* is in the tone of one doing the best he can for the sinner who has made a gratifying repentance:

Mourn genius high, and lore profound,
And wit that loved to play, not wound;
And all the reasoning powers divine,
To penetrate, resolve, combine;
And feelings keen, and fancy's glow—
They sleep with him who sleeps below;
And if thou mourn'st they could not save
From error him who owns this grave.
Be every harsher thought suppressed,
And sacred be the last long rest!
Here where the end of earthly things
Lays heroes, patriots, bards and kings;
.   .   .   .
If ever from an English heart
O here let prejudice depart,
O partial feeling cast aside,
Record that Fox a Briton died!
When Europe crouched to France's yoke,
And Austria bent and Prussia broke,
And the firm Russian's purpose brave
Was bartered by a timorous slave,
E'en then dishonour's peace he spurned,
The sullied olive-branch returned,
Stood for his country's glory fast,
And nailed her colours to the mast.

But the career and quality of Fox are not to be measured
by his victories or his defeats as a party leader. His greatness rests on the vindication after his death of those principles and causes for which he lived. And history has supplied an epitaph to satisfy his most devoted friends. On
that day in 1832 when without revolution or bloodshed the
Reform Bill became law; on that day two years later when
eight hundred thousand slaves became free; and when,
more than a century after his death, Parliament in the
greatest of wars met discontent by projects for an extension of the franchise, posterity added its tribute to the
'immortal memory of Mr. Fox'.

NOTE ON AUTHORITIES

A LIST of books containing useful information about the second half of the eighteenth century would be immense, and it is unlikely that reference in detail to the authorities consulted for a biography of Fox would be of any value. But it may be useful to indicate the principal sources of information. Apart from the many histories and historical studies of the period, the main sources of information about Fox and his life are his own letters, the records of Parliamentary debates, biographies of Fox, published letters and diaries of contemporaries and some of the biographies of contemporaries.

Most of Fox's letters were published in the *Memorials and Correspondence of Charles James Fox* by Lord John Russell in 1853. A few letters which do not appear in *Memorials and Correspondence* are to be found in Sir George Trevelyan's *Early History of Charles James Fox*, *The American Revolution*, and *George III and Charles Fox*, Lord Ilchester's *Henry Fox, First Lord Holland*, *The Windham Papers*, and Professor G. M. Trevelyan's *Lord Grey of the Reform Bill*. Unpublished letters in the British Museum do not substantially add to the information already available.

The parliamentary records are incomplete and the reports of speeches are often insufficient. They are supplemented by published collections of speeches and by political journals such as those of Horace Walpole (*Memoirs of the Reign of George III* and *Last Journals*), Wraxall, and Bland Burges.

The biographies of Fox are many. They include, in order of date, *Memoirs of the Latter Years of the Right Honourable Charles James Fox* by John Bernard Trotter (1811), *The Life and Times of Charles James Fox* by Lord John Russell (1859), *The Early History of Charles James Fox* by Sir George Otto Trevelyan, O.M. (1880), *The Life of Charles James Fox* by Henry Offley Wakeman (1890), *The American Revolution* by Sir George Otto Trevelyan, O.M. (1899), *Charles James Fox, a political study* by J. L. Hammond (1903), *George III and Charles Fox* by Sir George Otto Trevelyan, O.M. (1912), *Charles James Fox* by John Drinkwater (1928), and *Fox* by Christopher Hobhouse (1934).

Published letters and diaries are the main source of information about contemporary opinion. Much of the correspondence and many of the diaries of Fox's contemporaries are of great value, and full use has been made of them as a source of information and for quotations. Those most frequently used, in the order of the periods which they cover, are the *Letters of Horace Walpole* edited by Mrs. Paget Toynbee (1903), *Life and Letters of Lady Sarah Lennox* by the Countess of Ilchester and Lord Stavordale (1901), *The Autobiography and Political Correspondence of Augustus Hervey, Third Duke of Grafton* (1898), *The Works and Correspondence of the Right Honble. Edmund Burke* (1852), *Memoirs of the Marquis of Rockingham* edited by George Thomas, Earl of Albemarle (1852), *Historical Manuscripts Commission: Carlisle Papers* (1897), *Courts and Cabinets of King George III* edited by the Earl of Buckingham and Chandos (1853), *Letters of Edward Gibbon* edited by R. E. Prothero (1896), *Diary and Letters of Mme d'Arblay* edited by Austin Dobson (1904), *Historical Manuscripts Commission: Dropmore Papers (Fortescue)* (1892), *Letters of King George III* edited by Sir John Fortescue (1927), *The Windham Papers* (1913), Sir Nathaniel Wraxall's *Historical Memoirs* (1815) and *Posthumous Memoirs* (1836), *The Journal and Correspondence of William, Lord Auckland* edited by the Bishop of Bath and Wells (1861), *Letters of the First Lord Malmesbury* edited by the Earl of Malmesbury (1870), *Life and Letters of Sir Gilbert Elliot* edited by the Countess of Minto (1874), *Diary and Correspondence of the Hon. George Rose* edited by the Rev. L. V. Harcourt (1860), *The Private Correspondence of Lord Granville Leveson Gower* edited by Castalia, Countess Granville (1916), *The Creevey Papers* edited by Sir Herbert Maxwell (1903).

Among the biographies of Fox's contemporaries, those which have been most frequently consulted, in the order of the periods which they cover, are *Henry Fox, First Lord Holland* by the Earl of Ilchester (1920), *Life of William, Earl of Shelburne* by Lord Edmond Fitzmaurice (1875), *Edmund Burke, an Historical Study* by John Morley (1867), *Sheridan* by Walter Sichel (1909), *Coke of Norfolk and his Friends* by A. M. W. Stirling (1912), the biographies of Pitt by Earl Stanhope (1861) and by Lord Rosebery (1891), *Wilberforce* by Reginald Coupland (1923), and *Lord Grey of the Reform Bill* by G. M. Trevelyan (1920).

Among the authorities consulted on particular subjects, in addition to the authorities mentioned above, are those referred to under the following chapter headings. No reference under those headings is made to the many extracts taken from the letters and diaries already mentioned, but extracts from letters taken from biographies of contemporaries are referred to under the chapter headings.

CHAPTERS I AND II. Several extracts from letters of the Holland family have been taken from *Henry Fox, First Lord Holland* by the Earl of Ilchester. For Fox's progress at Eton, *Eton College Lists 1678–1790* by R. A. Austen Leigh was consulted. The Prince of Wales's essay and letters to Lord Bute are quoted from *England in the Age of the American Revolution* by L. B. Namier. That authority and the same author's *Structure of Politics on the Accession of George III* have also been consulted for contemporary politics.

CHAPTER III. For Fox's work at the Admiralty the Admiralty Correspondence at the Public Record Office was consulted. Lady Holland's letter is taken from *Henry Fox, First Lord Holland*, and extracts from Mme du Deffand's letters from *Lettres de la Marquise du Deffand à Horace Walpole* edited by Mrs. Paget Toynbee (1912).

CHAPTER IV. *The History of the British Army* by Sir John Fortescue, vol. iii (1902), *Washington* by Woodrow Wilson (1897), and *Revolutionary New England* by Truslove Adams (1923) were consulted for the American War. Extracts from Mme du Deffand's letters are taken from *Lettres de la Marquise du Deffand à Horace Walpole* edited by Mrs. Paget Toynbee (1912).

CHAPTER V. *The Autobiography of Augustus Hervey, Third Duke of Grafton* (1898) was consulted for the relief of Gibraltar, the Foreign Office Papers in the Public Record Office for the negotiations for peace, *The History of British India* by James Mill (1826) for the India Bill, and *The Parliamentary Papers of John Robinson* by W. T. Laprade (1922), *Historical Manuscripts Commission: Abergavenny Papers* (1887), and *Lord North, Second Earl of Guilford* by Reginald Lucas (1913) for the Coalition and the transactions which ended it.

CHAPTER VI. *The Parliamentary Papers of John Robinson* by W. T. Laprade (1922) and *Historical Manuscripts Commission: Abergavenny Papers* (1887) were consulted for the contemporary estimates of the result of the election, and *The History of the Westminster Election* (1784) for the Westminster election.

CHAPTER VII. The extracts from Herr Moritz's journal are taken from *Travels by Carl Philipp Moritz in England in 1782* (Pinkerton's *Voyages*, vol. ii). *The American Revolution and the British Empire* by R. Coupland (1929) and *William Pitt and the*

National Revival by J. Holland Rose (1911) were consulted for Pitt's proposals for reform.

CHAPTER VIII. *Warren Hastings* by Sir A. L. Lyell (1889) and *Warren Hastings and Philip Francis* by S. Weitzmann (1929) were consulted for the impeachment of Hastings. Extracts from the Begum speech and from the Duchess of Devonshire's diary are taken from Sichel's *Sheridan*.

CHAPTER IX. *The Diaries of Robert Fulke Greville* edited by F. McKno Bladen (1930) were consulted for the King's madness, *George IV* by Shane Leslie (1926) for a description of the Prince of Wales, and *The Life of Thomas Coutts* by E. H. Coleridge (1920) and the old ledger of Messrs. Coutts for Fox's financial arrangements. Extracts from the Duchess of Devonshire's diary are taken from Sichel's *Sheridan*.

CHAPTER XI. *La Revolution* by Louis Madelin (1911) and *Chansons Revolutionnaires et Contre revolutionnaires* (1820) were consulted for the French Revolution, and the *Genesis of Parliamentary Reform* by G. S. Veitch (1913) for the first repercussions of the French Revolution in England.

CHAPTERS XI AND XII. *The Genesis of Parliamentary Reform* by G. S. Veitch (1913), *Scotland and the French Revolution* by H. W. Meikle (1912), *The French Revolution in English History* by P. A. Brown (1918), *Lord Grey of the Reform Bill* by G. M. Trevelyan (1920), *State Trials*, vol. xxiv, *England and the French Revolution* by W. T. Laprade (1909), and *The History of the English Jacobins* by E. Smith (1881) were consulted for the effect of the French Revolution in England and the nature of the Reform movement, and *The History of the British Army* by Sir John Fortescue, vol. iv (1896) and *William Pitt and the Great War* by J. Holland Rose (1911) as to the French War.

CHAPTER XIII. The extract from Sir Philip Francis's letter is taken from *Memoirs of Sir Philip Francis* by Joseph Parkes (1867), and the extracts from the correspondence with Wakefield from *Correspondence of the late Gilbert Wakefield, B.A., with the late Right Honourable Charles James Fox* (1813).

CHAPTERS XIV AND XV. The *History of the British Army* by Sir John Fortescue, vol. v (1910), was consulted as to the French War, *Memoirs of the Whig Party* by Henry Richard Lord Holland (1811), and Mrs. Fox's diary in *Life and Letters of Lady Sarah Lennox* by the Countess of Ilchester and Lord Stavordale (1901) for Fox's death, and *Character of Charles James Fox* by Philopatris Varvicensis (1809) for the funeral.

INDEX